Key Words for

ASTROLOGY

Key Words for
ASTROLOGY

Hajo Banzhaf & Anna Haebler

WEISERBOOKS

Boston, MA/York Beach, ME

First published in 1996 by
Red Wheel/Weiser, LLC
York Beach, ME
With offices at:
368 Congress Street
Boston, MA 02210
www.redwheelweiser.com

Library of Congress Cataloging-in-Publication Data
Banzhaf, Hajo.
[Schlüsselworte zur astrologie. English]
Key words for astrology / Hajo Banzhaf, Anna Haebler
p. cm.
Includes bibliographical references
ISBN 0-87728-875-5 (pbk. : alk paper)
1. Astrology. 2. Astrology—Terminology.   I. Haebler, Anna. II. Title.
BF1708.1.B3613   1996
133.5—dc20   96-26482
                                    CIP

TCP
Translated by Christine M. Grimm.

Cover art is the title page from
The Astrologer of the Nineteenth Century,
London, 1825.

Typeset in 10 pt Garamond

Printed in Canada

13 12 11 10 09 08 07 06 05
  10 9 8 7 6 5 4 3

Contents

Note to the Reader

In compiling the key words, the description of the planets and signs relates to the gender of the signs (Virgo = feminine, Libra = masculine, for example) and planets (Venus = feminine, Mars = masculine). The reader should understand that both sexes are included when the word "king" is used to describe the qualities of a Leo, for example.

Some words—like "Taurus, the Bull"—cannot be translated into a female equivalent without becoming rather absurd ("the Bulless" or "the Cow"?). Here we must find comfort in astrology, which describes Taurus (along with Cancer) as the most archetypally feminine of all the signs, despite its masculine name. We ask the readers to equally apply all the astrological key words to themselves, despite any inherent gender implications.

Introduction

This book explains all the essential configurations in a horoscope by showing both aspects of its expression—the light and the dark—with vivid key words and concise descriptions.

Readers should avoid the popular error of getting lost in the details and even mistaking a part for the whole: a horoscope consists of an abundance of individual factors which only allow the entire picture to emerge when all the factors are seen in relationship to each other. Correspondingly, if you look up something relating to your horoscope and shake your head in disbelief after reading the description, you should not be too quick to leave it at that. Because of a multitude of reasons, an astrological configuration can be lived in such a concealed manner that the person concerned is quite certain it has nothing to do with him or her. It is certainly easier to admit to the aspects of our personality which flatter the ego or correspond to the spirit of the times. As a result, people had difficulty accepting themselves as mystics during the 50s because the term "mystic" had almost the same meaning as "crackpot" at that time. In contrast, today it is considered an esoteric compliment when a person's mediumistic capabilities are confirmed during astrological consultations.

In a very general sense, it can be said that configurations strongly affected by Saturn or Pluto are permitted access to the conscious mind only with reluctance. Furthermore, in our society we may observe that men prefer to project their feminine planets (Moon and Venus) onto women, and women in response prefer to delegate their masculine planets (Sun and Mars) to men: the more difficult the position of these planets, the greater the tendency toward this type of projection. Even without looking at the horoscope, this kind of projection can be recognized when a man accomplishes overkill with the statement that "all women are . . .," or when a woman generalizes about "men."

As Johannes Kepler very clearly states, the horoscope shows your potential and not your predestination. The situation of astrology is similar to the way researchers can use modern chaos research to perceive the formulas concealed behind a multitude of manifestations (such as weather clouds) without being able to predict in which form this formula will manifest itself. The horoscope is a formula which is the basis for the life of a human being. Yet, what you make of it, how far you let yourself drift along, or to which heights of development you rise, all lie in a realm beyond the possibility of interpretation.

These key words should then be understood as a description of one portion of the whole. Many opportunities for development are concealed in every aspect in the chart. However, how, and to what degree, they are manifested, and what level they attain always depends upon the personality's degree of maturity—and precisely this factor is not revealed in the horoscope. This is why we have also consciously dispensed with stating the commonly made differentiation between good and bad, easy and difficult, harmonious and tension-laden, auspicious and misfortune-bringing configurations. Such definitions are foolish. We have seen horoscopes that were full of so-called harmonious aspects, yet the people affected were caught up in deep crises in life. Life simply ran on without meaning. Nothing had challenged them and/or even forced them to make something of their lives. Everything was simply easy and superficial, and after a certain point in time it became unbearable.

On the other hand, it is widely known that the horoscopes of great personalities are charged with tensions. For this reason, we have described all the horoscope factors in their polar tensions as strengths and problem areas—or—for the aspects—as harmony and discord. We have followed the development from the obstruction to the solution solely in the case of Saturn, the Lord of Time (Cronos). It may certainly be true that a difficult astrological configuration, such as a planet positioned in "detriment" or in "fall," or irritated or impaired by difficult aspects (such as a square or an opposition) initially attracts attention from its critical side. Yet, there is not only the possibility of transformation, but also the responsibility to transform, in each of these configurations. From the astrological perspective, the horoscope describes the starting situation in which we begin our life on Earth. Now our task is polishing ourselves against our various tensions until we succeed in uniting all the original discord into a great harmonious symphony.

Malicious tongues will grumble that this book is a "cookbook" in which astrology has now once and for all been prepared and served like a collection of recipes. These people will have fundamentally misunderstood our intentions. When we describe every detail and give it a pronounced name, the purpose is to make learning and remembering astrological terminology easier and to stimulate thought about the configurations which are infrequently discussed elsewhere, such as the light and shadow sides of the slowly moving planets in the water houses. Above all, however, this book's concentrated form is designed to save the readers from all the superfluous words through which they often must sift to find important concepts, and the tabular form should enable readers to quickly make comparisons, since comparable statements for all the related configurations are always written under the same heading.

Anna Haebler & Hajo Banzhaf

Organization and Levels of Meaning in the Horoscope

The interplay of three different levels of effect are expressed in a horoscope. There are planets in signs, planets in houses, and aspects between planets. A general overview of what that means follows.

1. THE PLANETS IN THE SIGNS OF THE ZODIAC (THE DAILY CONFIGURATION)

This interplay involves the distribution of all ten bodies (eight planets and two luminaries) throughout the entire heavens, no matter whether the "planets" are found below or above the horizon. (Readers should note that the Sun and Moon are not planets, but in order to avoid clumsy language we call them "planets.") You are born under a "sign," and this is where the Sun is located in the heavens at the time of your birth. The zodiac corresponds to the orbit of the Sun, and every year the Sun stands in the same place at the same time, so the position of the Sun (= sign) can be read from the date of birth. The Sun moves through all twelve signs. It does not move into the next sign precisely at midnight. Deviations of up to one day can occur, particularly because of the leap year cycle. The exact position of the Sun on the

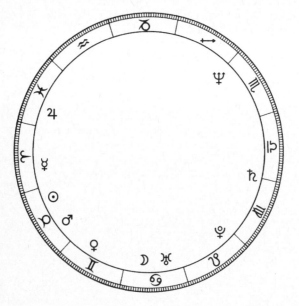

Figure 1. The planets move in different signs based on the date of birth.

day when the signs change must—this applies to all the other planets as well—be read in tables, which we call an ephemeris.

2. THE PLANETS IN THE HOUSES

The decisive factor here is the daily "rotation of the heavens around the Earth" (which means the rotation of the Earth on its own axis). The horizontal axis divides the circle into the visible heavens and the invisible heavens beneath the horizon. This results in the Ascendant (AC), which is the point of sunrise on the eastern horizon, and the Descendant (DC) on the opposite side (figure 2a). This axis from the meridional point (MC = *Medium Coeli*) to the midnight point (IC = *Imum Coeli*) divides the circle into rising and descending signs. The four quarter sections (figure 2b) created in this

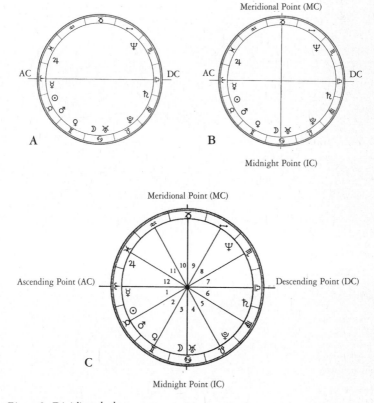

Figure 2. Dividing the horoscope.

manner are then divided again into thirds, whereby a "spoked wheel" with 12 fields (figure 2c) is created. These fields are also called "houses."

3. THE ASPECTS

These are the significant distances of the planets from each other. The aspects can be best illustrated using the example of the Moon, which forms all possible aspects with the Sun during the course of a month.

The so-called harmonious and disharmonious aspects are created (as in music) by dividing the circle with the cardinal numbers, whereby harmonious and disharmonious aspects (tones) result:

$360^o \div 1 = 360 =$ Conjunction $=$ Planets located directly next to each other.

$360^o \div 2 = 180 =$ Opposition $=$ Planets located opposite each other.

$360^o \div 3 = 120 =$ Trine $=$ Distance between planets corresponds to one side of a triangle.

$360^o \div 4 = 90 =$ Square $=$ Distance between planets corresponds to one side of a square.

$360^o \div 5 = 72 =$ Quintile $=$ Distance between planets corresponds to one side of a pentagon.

$360^o \div 6 = 60 =$ Sextile $=$ Distance between planets corresponds to one side of a hexagon.

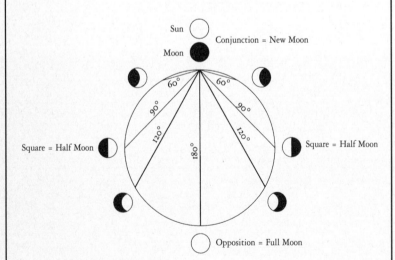

Figure 3. Aspects in the chart.

4. ILLUSTRATION OF THE LEVELS OF MEANING IN A HOROSCOPE

The horoscope portrays the play of life as a comedy or a tragedy, and the planets are the actors in the play. The signs of the zodiac in which they stand illustrate the role. The house in which they are located shows the place on the stage of life where they want to become particularly active, and the aspects describe the way and manner in which the actors interact with each other: they support, impede, or block each other, or they may even be indifferent to each other.

As you can see, a purely harmonious horoscope would be among the most boring of plays. It also illustrates that harmonies and tensions can be expressed not only through aspects, but also through the appropriate or inappropriate roles of the actors and the places where they stand.

How to Use This Book

If you are unaccustomed to reading the horoscope, you need to learn the basic symbols and signs. You will also need to learn the aspects, or you can have an astrologer break these down for you. Many computer-generated charts spell out the details of the chart, and will list the planets (and Sun and Moon) in the signs, the signs that rule the twelve houses in your personal chart, and the aspects between the planets. We have printed a ready reference of the signs and symbols on the inside back cover of this book, so you can quickly look up symbols that are unfamiliar to you. To give you an idea of how signs and symbols work, we have interpreted some of the details of Albert Schweitzer's horoscope.

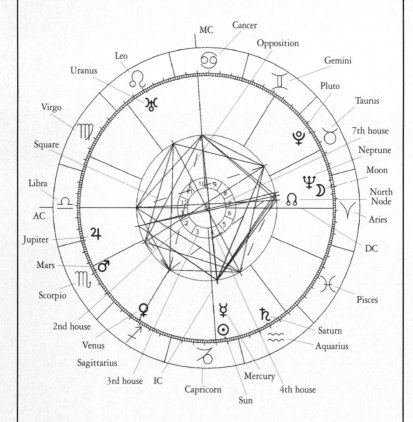

Figure 4. Albert Schweitzer. January 14, 1875, 23:50:00 LMT, Kaysersberg, Alsace. Placidus Houses. Data from brith certificate.

The Sun (☉) is found in the 4th house together with Mercury (☿) in Capricorn (♑), the Moon (☽) together with Neptune (♆) and the Moon's Node (☊) in Aries (♈) in the 7th house. Venus (♀) is located in Sagittarius (♐) in the 3rd house, Mars (♂) in Scorpio (♏) in the 2nd house, etc. The Ascendant (AC) is Libra (♎), the *Medium Coeli* (MC) is Cancer (♋), the Descendant (DC) is Aries (♈), and Capricorn (♑) is located on the *Imum Coeli* (IC).

The aspects can be read from the lines connecting the individual planets. Here Saturn (♄) is located in Aquarius (♒) in the 4th house, which is directly opposite from Uranus (♅) in Leo (♌) in the 11th house and thereby forms an opposition. In contrast, it is one-fourth of a circle away from Mars (♂) in Scorpio (♏) in the 2nd house and forms a square aspect.

When you now look up the meanings of the signs, you should always read both the light and the shadow sides (strengths and problems, or harmonies and dissonances). Two possibilities are always contained in the constellation, and no formula will provide certainty in recognizing whether people live out and fulfill their abilities and tasks on a high level of development, or simply let themselves drift.

There are various ways to discover the meaning of a horoscope. The easiest way is to first look at the main themes. Start with the Sun (☉), symbolizing the intrinsic character of a human being. Then look at the Moon (☽), which embodies the temperament. Next, find the Ascendant for information about your role and behavior. Your ability to assert yourself is shown by Mars (♂), Venus (♀) illustrates your loves, preferences, and tastes. Jupiter (♃) symbolizes the concepts of values and ideals, while Saturn (♄) will show your limitations. Uranus (♅) represents your love of freedom, Neptune (♆) the visions, and Pluto (♇) shows what fascinates you. When doing this, both the sign *and* the position within the house should be taken into consideration, as well as the aspects of the respective planets. If you become confused by the many statements which result, it is helpful to visualize the various levels of meaning (see page 13). This will certainly assist you in finding the red thread once again.

You also have the possibility of summarizing your horoscope into a chain sentence in order to attain the first general survey of your nature. To do this, replace the words in parentheses with the key words you have found under the respective headings in this book:

I am a person with the intrinsic character of (☉ Sun/sign)
and I find my greatest development in (☉ Sun/house).

My role and my feeling for life are	(AC),
supported or impeded by	(planets in the 1st house).

My temperament is that of	(☽ Moon/sign) and it
instinctively draws me in the direction of	(☽ Moon/house).

I think in the manner of	(☿ Mercury/sign)
and prefer to use my mind in	(☿ Mercury/house).

My idea of love, relationships, and beauty is	(♀ Venus/sign).
I mainly express my sense of beauty in	(♀ Venus/house).

I fight like a	(♂ Mars/sign)
and frequently carry out my conflicts in	(♂ Mars/house).

The attitude toward life that I consider valuable and impressive is that of	(♃ Jupiter/sign).
I feel rich in the area of	(♃ Jupiter/house) and
in everything that Jupiter touches	(♃ Jupiter aspects).

I have difficulties with	(♄ Saturn/sign).
My limitations, inhibitions, feelings of guilt, as well as my	
greatest opportunities for growth, lie in	(♄ Saturn/house) and in
everything that Saturn touches	(♄ Saturn aspects).

I live my independence and/or change my standpoint in the area of	(♅ Uranus/house)
and in everything that Uranus touches	(♅ Uranus aspects).

I experience deep longings and desires for liberation in the area of	(♆ Neptune/house) and
in everything that Neptune touches	(♆ Neptune aspects).

I experience power and helplessness, "tunnel experiences," obsession and deepest transformations in the area of	(♇ Pluto/house) and
in everything that Pluto touches	(♇ Pluto aspects).

You can find one further interesting way to approach a horoscope by first looking where your developmental goal lies (☊ **Moon's Node/house**) and how this theme fits in with the area of your main self-development (☉ **Sun/house**), with what is becoming increasingly important in the course of your life (*Medium Coeli*), with your role (Ascendant), your feelings (☽ **Moon**), etc.

You also have the possibility of visualizing the horoscope by using the picture key found at the end of the book (page 263).

The LUMINARIES, *the* PLANETS, *and the* MOON'S NODE

☉
Sun

DIGNITY:	DETRIMENT:	EXALTATION:	FALL:
♌	♒	♈	♎

Orbits through the entire zodiac in one year.
Stays an average of one month in each sign.

ARCHETYPE: The hero, the father, the king.

SHADOW: The overbearing person, the megalomaniac.

PRINCIPLE: The Sun embodies your intrinsic character, your central concerns, the area and manner in which most of your personality development occurs. It symbolizes your path and goal, what is most essential to you. It represents the yang principle, consciousness, the mind, the will, activity, and vital energy, dynamic force, individual creativity and self-realization, radiance, warmth, motivational capability, courage, optimism, and impetus in life. Together with Mars, the Sun embodies the masculine principle in the horoscope. At the same time, the Sun reflects the fatherly masculine element which expresses the attitude toward one's own father, substitute fathers, and people in positions of authority.

STRENGTH: *The self-confident individual.* Powerful development of one's own being. Makes a strong impression and has a striking personality. Healthy self-reliance, very lively, exudes warmth. Is hearty, magnanimous, creative, independent, and self-confident.

PROBLEM AREA: *The overextended person.* Either a self-aggrandizing exaggeration of one's own possibilities and a puffed-up, arrogant personality, or a frail, weak-willed, fawning posture with great difficulties in the development of one's own essence, a late bloomer.

GOAL: The urge to become what one is, *i.e.*, to develop individual character. The search for wholeness, for the inner center, the true identity. The "journey of a hero."

REPRESENTATIVES OF THE SUN PRINCIPLE: All role models and forceful personalities: father, rulers, authority figures, politicians, organizers, aristocracy, but also egotists, tyrants, swindlers, and megalomaniacs.

PHYSICAL CORRELATIONS: Heart, spinal cord, blood circulation, solar plexus, respiratory system.

MYTHOLOGICAL CORRELATIONS: Helios (Greek)/ Sol (Roman), the sun god—above all, Apollo (Greek and Roman), also often called Phoebus (bright), son of Zeus and Leto, god of the bright sunny days, the arts, healing arts, and wisdom.

THE SUN IN THE SIGNS
This has the same meaning as the description of the individual signs of the zodiac on pages 24 to 47.

Since the sun stands for the intrinsic character of a person, all of the essential features, such as the ARCHETYPE, SHADOW, MOTIVATION, and TASK IN LIFE, as well as what he or she STRIVES FOR, and the PITFALLS specific to each sign, EXAMPLES, and the typical GUIDING PRINCIPLE are to be found here. In addition, ACTIONS, THOUGHTS, and FEELINGS are described in their characteristic natures. Without specifically depicting it, the portrait resulting from the features is the picture of a mature man, expressed as part of his self-image in the horoscope of a man, and as part of the searching image in the horoscope of a woman.

The TYPICAL OCCUPATIONAL AREAS are those generally assigned to the respective astrological signs and not limited to the position of the Sun. They can also be addressed by a noticeable grouping of planets within a sign or through Mercury, the MC, or other important configurations.

☽
Moon

DIGNITY:	DETRIMENT:	EXALTATION:	FALL:
♋	♑	♉	♏

Orbits through the entire zodiac in 27 days.
Stays an average of about 2 days in each sign.

ARCHETYPE: The mother, the child.

SHADOW: The monster that devours everything.

PRINCIPLE: The Moon represents the inner nature, the feeling realm, the unconscious, and the instinctive reactions. The position of the Moon shows in what direction you are urged, what you spontaneously react to, and what you instinctively detest and avoid. According to the cyclical character of the Moon, these are delicate and erratic occurrences, which come and go according to their own rhythms. The Moon also stands for the ability to establish contact, the longing for closeness and security, the home, the way of life, attachment to home, memories, and the need for emotional security. Together with Venus, the Moon symbolizes the feminine principle in the horoscope. The Moon embodies the motherly feminine element, through reflecting the mother and childhood experiences as well as substitute mothers, even those of institutions like stock exchanges, universities (alma mater), or the mother church.

STRENGTH: *The soulful individual.* Harmonious configurations support the flourishing of the emotional nature, the willingness to open one's inner self, and trust in the wisdom of unconscious powers which guide people. This represents security, emotional safety, and a healthy relationship to family, background, homeland, and especially to the mother and one's own motherhood.

PROBLEM AREA: *The moody person.* Difficult configurations represent emotional wounds, reticence, mistrust, fear, touchiness, moods, unpredictability, as well as vanity, exaggerated smugness, laziness, and lethargy.

GOAL: Development of feelings and fantasies, encountering the images of the soul. The urge toward emotional security and closeness. The blossoming of female nature. The urge to build a nest, start a family, and be a lively part of the clan. The desire to be well-liked or become popular.

REPRESENTATIVES OF THE MOON PRINCIPLE: Everyone in serving, care-giving, and helping positions: doctors, healers, nurses, spiritual counselors, therapists, and those representing dreams and fantasies in art, in writing, and in the circus and theater.

PHYSICAL CORRELATIONS: Stomach, uterus, lymph system, female breasts, circulation of fluids, autonomous nervous system.

MYTHOLOGICAL CORRELATIONS: The triple Goddess as expression of the cycles of life: 1. Artemis (Greek)/Diana (Roman), the virgin = growth. 2. Selene (Greek)/Luna (Roman), the woman = maturity. 3. Hecate (Greek and Roman), the old one = decline.

THE MOON IN THE SIGNS
See pages 50 to 61.

The description initially reflects the typical mother-child relationship for the sign which can be read from the position of the Moon: the CHILD in the person, the DIFFICULT LESSONS TO LEARN, and INNER MOTHER IMAGE or the way in which the respective person is prepared to see the mother.

Furthermore, a description is given of how the Moon is expressed as MOTHER in the mature adult and its meaning as light and shadow aspects in the IMAGE OF THE WOMAN. For a feminine horoscope, an essential aspect of the self-image for the mature woman is expressed. In contrast, in a man's horoscope this signifies a part of his inner femininity and his searching image in a partnership.

The additional meaning of the respective Moon position for each person, independent of age and sex, can be found in the two sections STRENGTH and PROBLEM AREA .

Since the Moon also stands for home, homeland, and the type of home, the corresponding image is described under STYLE OF LIVING.

☿
Mercury

DIGNITY: ♊ and ♍	DETRIMENT: ♐ and ♓	EXALTATION: ♍	FALL: ♓

Orbits through the entire zodiac in about 87 days.
Stays an average of 7 days in each sign.

ARCHETYPE: The trader, the naviga-
tor, the scout.

SHADOW: The crook, the liar.

PRINCIPLE: Mercury stands for mind and intellect, for the theory of combinations, speech, communication, mediation, tactics, knowledge, mental
flexibility, orientation facility, analytical and logical thought, and the manner of judging and deciding. Mercury is also the negotiator between the
conscious and the unconscious mind because its powers of thought support
the recognition and understanding of the images of the unconscious, such as
dreams. Mercury also represents expression in speech, curiosity, the thirst for
knowledge, and a certain readiness, ambition, and ability to learn.

STRENGTH: *The clever person.* Quick, clear ascertaining of thoughts and ideas.
Ingenious capacity for following a train of thought; combining, analyzing,
and differentiating. Talent for observing and having a "good grasp."
Excellent capacity to adapt or orient oneself. Collects information with great
curiosity. Pursues knowledge and enjoys the pleasure of recognition.
Nimbleness of language, quick-wittedness, and rhetorical knowledge.
Smooth sales person and negotiator. Methodical doubt which leads to steadily increasing insight. Carefully thinks through and weighs ideas and exam-
ines for accuracy and usefulness.

PROBLEM AREA: *The trickster.* Interest in everything is only superficial and
passing. Cunning, sly bluffer. Calculating, corruptible, crafty, audacious,
false, and wily. Cannot see the whole picture. Feels no obligation to honor
values. Profanes the holy, is ice-cold in business, and would "sell his grand-
mother."

GOAL: Collecting, mediating, and distributing knowledge and information. Search for new perceptions and new paths. Critical examination and fine differentiation of thoughts, ideas, and theories, as well as logical points of view, including their usefulness. But, also bluffing, deceiving, and tricking.

REPRESENTATIVES OF THE MERCURY PRINCIPLE: Teachers, school children, university students, poets, salespeople, analysts, doctors, critics, scientists, researchers, journalists, linguists, orators, translators, attorneys, but also forgers, counterfeiters, cheaters, thieves, liars, and swindlers.

PHYSICAL CORRELATIONS: Respiratory system, nervous system, speech center.

MYTHOLOGICAL CORRELATIONS: Hermes (Greek)/Mercury (Roman)—messenger of the gods with winged shoes, mediator between heaven and earth. God of paths and journeys, business people and artisans, shepherds, thieves, and highwaymen. God of speech and guide for souls into the underworld. Messenger of dreams.

MERCURY IN THE SIGNS
See pages 62 to 67.

In addition to the STRENGTH and PROBLEM AREA specific to this sign, the NARRATIVE STYLE and the manner in which the respective Mercury MAKES DECISIONS, along with the criteria BETWEEN which Mercury prefers to differentiate is presented here. (How the decision is implemented is decided by the position of Mars.)

♀
Venus

DIGNITY:	DETRIMENT:	EXALTATION:	FALL:
♉ and ♎	♈ and ♏	♓	♍

Orbits through the entire zodiac in 225 days.
Stays an average of about 19 days in each sign.

ARCHETYPE: The muse, the lover, the beautiful one.

SHADOW: Persephone, the femme fatale, the whore.

PRINCIPLE: Venus is the symbol for love, feeling, harmony, the ability to give and take, relationships, and partnership. As the embodiment of the erotic, Venus also means temptation, the capability to devote oneself completely, longing, and the desire for union, connection, and merging. Venus represents esthetic perception and therefore, on one hand, artistic interests and talents; on the other hand, good taste and sensory pleasures that grant us the enjoyment of hearing, smelling, touching, tasting, and seeing. Both the Moon and Venus represent the female principle. However, Venus represents the aspect of the young woman, the beloved, and the independent woman.

STRENGTHS: *The temptress.* Aspires toward vivacious relationships, harmony, balance, reconciliation, and warm-hearted empathy. Would like to be sought after, loved, pampered, and flattered. Loves luxury, elegance, and good manners. Patient, can be very devoted, understanding, benevolent, sincere, sociable, affectionate, graceful, and unselfish. Certain of taste and artistically talented. Sensuous, esthetic, with a cultivated enjoyment of life. Enjoyment of everything that is beautiful.

PROBLEM AREA: *The phony.* Separates from others easily and often. Overemphasizes external factors. Vain, superficial, tasteless, tricky, perverse, addicted to amusement, easily seduced, greedy to possess, compulsive, lazy, unscrupulous, infantile and unrestrained, uncouth, jealous, cruel, snobbish, argumentative, and depraved.

♀

GOAL: To be sought after and to search for, enter into and create relationships. To cultivate love and eroticism in their highest forms. To express and nurture beauty, art, and harmony in this world. To develop and maintain good style, cultivated manners, and fine taste.

REPRESENTATIVES OF THE VENUS PRINCIPLE: All people who bring beauty or love into the world: painters, sculptors, actors, authors, musicians, designers, cosmeticians, architects, and loving people, including those who work in the area of the fine or dubious entertainments.

PHYSICAL CORRELATIONS: Sense of equilibrium, mucous membranes, veins, kidneys, inner sex organs, sweat glands, and erogenous zones.

MYTHOLOGICAL CORRELATIONS: Aphrodite (Greek) or Venus (Roman)—the goddess of love, beauty and peace, also of art and harmony.

VENUS IN THE SIGNS
See pages 68 to 73.

In addition to the STRENGTH and the PROBLEM AREA is the IMAGE OF THE YOUNG WOMAN, which Venus embodies. In a feminine horoscope, this describes an essential part of the self-image, whereas Venus in the masculine horoscope symbolizes the anima and thereby the central aspect of his inner femininity and his searching image in partnerships. Venus' typical sensitivity for taste and style are expressed in the related section of STYLE OF ART and the coloration of its erotic tension is found in the section EROTICISM.

♂
Mars

DIGNITY:	DETRIMENT:	EXALTATION:	FALL:
♈ and ♏	♉ and ♎	♑	♋

Orbits through the entire zodiac in 687 days.
Stays an average of about 2 months in each sign.

ARCHETYPE: The hero and conqueror.

SHADOW: The violent person, the destroyer.

PRINCIPLE: Mars represents strength of will and the desire of an individual to conquer. It stands for stamina, the perseverance and energy that you need to fight the obstacles in life and penetrate the world. Mars shows straightforwardness of approach, a high degree of determination, readiness to take on conflict, and enjoyment of risk. In every conflict Mars embodies the energy you fight with and how you fight. It represents aggression, problems of aggression, as well as drive, urge, and passion. Together with the Sun, Mars symbolizes the masculine principle in the horoscope, with Mars embodying the youthful aspect, the lover, and the hothead.

STRENGTHS: *The resolute individual.* Strong, goal-oriented action with great staying power. Imposing willpower, great commitment, and considerable willingness to take risks (while keeping a level head!). The force of aggression finds an appropriate goal which it can conquer, simultaneously discharging itself and spontaneously developing in committed, courageous, decisive, passionate, or persevering ways. Powerful, but controllable drives. Lusty, satisfying sexuality.

PROBLEM AREA: *The brute.* Spontaneous, completely uncontrollable discharge of energy or pent-up aggressions with unpredictable outbursts. Impatient, hot-headed, brutal, unrestrained, sadistic, distracted by vague drives. The force of aggression spreads out destructively, and not infrequently, self-destructively. Frustrated, extreme, violent, and totally dissatisfying sexuality.

GOAL: The goal of Mars' power is the actualization of your essential nature, to further your development and accomplishments, and also to protect and safeguard you from the attacks of others. Mars is the fighting strength with which you stand up for yourself, which helps you win, to get what is yours by right and to keep it, or to be the first. The goal of Mars is also sexual satisfaction. Problematic goals, which Mars can also lead to, concern violent wrongs, such as robbery and murder, revenge campaigns, wars and war crimes, and all situations in which the bare "might" of those who are stronger triumphs.

REPRESENTATIVES OF THE MARS PRINCIPLE: All pioneers, conquerors, warriors, daring entrepreneurs, leaders, adventurers, soldiers, athletes, and other competitors. Everyone who uses knives, from butchers to knife-throwers to surgeons. But, also those who destroy blindly, fanatics, egotists, and tyrants along with their torturers.

PHYSICAL CORRELATIONS: Muscles, gallbladder, blood, red blood cells, the body's heat regulation system, male sexual organs.

MYTHOLOGICAL CORRELATIONS: Aries (Greek)/Mars (Roman)—the god of war, whom the Greeks considered a brute and was therefore unloved and disfavored, but raised to the status of a god of state by the Romans.

MARS IN THE SIGNS
See pages 74 to 86.

In addition to the STRENGTH and PROBLEM AREA specific to the sign, the IMAGE OF THE YOUNG MAN is to be found here.

In a man's horoscope, this describes an essential part of his self-image, whereas in the feminine horoscope it symbolizes the central aspect of the animus, the inner masculinity, and the woman's searching image.

The energy with which Mars carries out its decisions and plans is found under RESOLUTION. Its combative attitude is shown by the sections AGGRESSION, OUTLETS FOR AGGRESSION, and WAY OF FIGHTING, whereby the strength and form of expression of the respective Mars energy is listed under SEXUALITY.

♃
Jupiter

DIGNITY:	DETRIMENT:	EXALTATION:	FALL:
♐ and ♓	♊ and ♍	♋	♑

Orbits through the entire zodiac in around 12 years.
Stays an average of about one year in each sign.

ARCHETYPE: The high priest, the missionary, the just person.

SHADOW: The Pharisee, complacent person, the self-righteous individual.

PRINCIPLE: Jupiter represents trust in life, the belief in life's meaning, the ideals and values of a person, and the search and discovery of personal meaning in life. It also stands for the forces of growth which give life its impetus, promotes thriving, good fortune, and prosperity, and especially benefits the development of the personality and broadening of individual horizons. A person experiences everything Jupiter touches as being rich. Jupiter also means dignity, wisdom, belief, hope, morals, grace, convictions, confidence, trust, affluence, wealth, and growth, success, future, optimism, generosity, expansion, justice, reverence, goodness, goodwill, and abundance.

STRENGTH: *The dignified person.* Highly developed sense of morality and ethics, as well as strong inner belief and great trust in yourself and in life. Generosity, sense of responsibility, justice, goodness, compassion, reverence, and willingness to forgive. The talent to understand meaning and connection in a global or higher sense. Jupiter also stands for individual luck, in that everything it touches in a person's horoscope is experienced full of trust and certainty of success.

PROBLEM AREA: *The degenerate.* Overestimates his or her own personality. Unscrupulous, high-handed, vain, power-hungry, addicted to pleasure, lazy, and self-satisfied. The otherwise benevolent Jupiter becomes unpleasantly exaggerated or purely superficial in an attitude of hypocrisy, fanaticism, self-aggrandizement, degenerating in terms of body, emotions, and character.

4

The tendency to smugly overstep laws, have both extravagant expectations and standards in life, as well as feigned generosity and intolerance is manifested.

GOAL: Aspires to truth, higher understanding and global, commonly binding principles and values. The search for the personal God. The fulfillment of meaning and experience of being carried through life by meaning. Fortune and fulfillment.

REPRESENTATIVES OF THE JUPITER PRINCIPLE: Exemplary and/or cultivated personalities. Teachers, educators, priests, prophets, philosophers, poets, scholars, legal experts, judges, athletes, doctors, alternative health practitioners, healers, adventurers, world travelers, and patrons of arts and other worthy causes.

PHYSICAL CORRELATIONS: Liver, growth of cells, fat reserves.

MYTHOLOGICAL CORRELATIONS: Zeus (Greek)/Jupiter (Roman)—father of the gods and lightening-hurling ruler of Olympus. Protector of the people, bringer of victory, preserver of justice, freedom, tradition, and order.

JUPITER IN THE SIGNS
See pages 86 to 91.

In addition to the STRENGTH and PROBLEM AREA specific to this sign, there is the IDEAL toward which Jupiter aspires, as well as the RELIGION or PHILOSOPHY to which Jupiter's position most often corresponds. The explanations given emphasize the characteristic feature of religion or philosophy as classified by Jupiter.

♄
Saturn

DIGNITY:	DETRIMENT:	EXALTATION:	FALL:
♑ and ♒	♋ and ♌	♎	♈

Orbits through the entire zodiac in 29 years.
Stays an average of about two years in each sign.

ARCHETYPE: The old, wise man, the hermit.

SHADOW: The embittered person, the adversary.

PRINCIPLE: Saturn represents structure, steadfastness, and limitation. It therefore means security, stability, stamina, and consistency. Saturn also represents the ability of a person to set boundaries, but also the boundaries you experience as unpleasant, those which do not let you reach what you desire. Saturn is the ruler of time, who sees to it that everything comes to an end at some point. As a result, Saturn symbolizes separations and farewells. As ruler of "the great silence," it also represents seclusion, which can be experienced as being painfully abandoned or as inner composure in stillness. Furthermore, Saturn means conscience, form, structure, compression, concentration, crystallization, obligation, deceleration, justice, law and order.

STRENGTH: *The humble individual.* Authentic humility, genuine modesty. The power to be true to oneself and the willingness to face the most difficult jobs. Greatly developed ambition combined with immense endurance. Takes duties unusually seriously. Extremely disciplined, achievement-oriented, and dependable. Mature contentment. Aspires toward material security and public recognition. Sets rules and boundaries, creates clear structures, imposes and monitors laws, takes care of order and safety. Willing to take on responsibility. Conscientiousness, patience, wisdom, dependability, consistency, and content modesty.

PROBLEM AREA: *The hard-hearted person.* Afraid to live, most of all afraid to fail, to not be good enough or lovable enough. Conflicts with authority. Determined hardness, obstinate inflexibility, dark ambition, and a cold need for admiration. Strangles all living impulses with the danger of losing one-self in depression, melancholy, bitter negation of life, or self-destructive drudgery. Compulsiveness to achieve, rigidity, inferiority complex, ingrati-ating subservience, shabbiness, lack of success, embitterment, and loneli-ness. Wasted, suppressed emotional life, and rigid behavior. Complete deficit of human warmth and sincerity as well as the playful elements in life. Inhibited, constrained, awkward, cruel, evil, cold, narrow-minded, stub-born, reticent, irreconcilable, and relentless.

GOAL: Development of the autonomous personality and a steadfast character through the actualization of existing capabilities and your true calling. Increase of experience and wisdom in life. Clarity, self-control, and self-restraint. Recognition of the unvarnished truth, naked reality, and concen-tration on what is most essential.

REPRESENTATIVES OF THE SATURN PRINCIPLE: Philosophers, wise men and wise women, hermits, monks and nuns, elderly people, ancestors. Lawmakers and keepers of the law, judges, critics, bosses, gray eminences, mentors, sculptors, architects, and builders.

PHYSICAL CORRELATIONS: Skeleton, bone marrow, calcium balance, teeth, structural and connective tissue, spleen, ears.

MYTHOLOGICAL CORRELATIONS: Cronus (Greek)/Saturn (Roman)—the god who rebelled against his father Uranus, but also ate his own children. Ruler of time and keeper of threshold between life and death, between time and eternity. Also the ruler of Elysium, the island of the blessed, and the ruler of the Golden Age.

SATURN IN THE SIGNS
See pages 92 to 97.

In its most difficult form, Saturn means a block opposing the typical qual-ities of the prevailing sign, which are listed under PROHIBITION OR DISDAIN OF. The corresponding fear is under the heading of THRESHOLD. Experience shows that Saturn, on its way toward freedom, turns to compulsive behav-ior, somewhat in opposition to its original bans, and more or less lives as if it were a compulsion. This phase is described in the section COMPULSION, while the behavior of a liberated and transformed Saturn is portrayed in the section on LIBERATION.

⛢

Uranus

DIGNITY:	DETRIMENT:	EXALTATION:	FALL:
♒	♌	♏	♉

Discovered on March 13, 1781 by Friedrich Wilhelm Herschel.
Orbits through the entire zodiac in around 84 years.
Stays an average of about 7 years in each sign.

ARCHETYPE: The (wise) fool, the hero of freedom.

SHADOW: The revolutionary, the traitor.

PRINCIPLE: Uranus represents the ideals of the French Revolution—freedom, equality, and brotherhood. It embodies what is ingenious in human beings, their striving for independence and individual freedom. Uranus is also considered to be the great liberator. It stands for surprising changes, flashes of inspiration, and sudden upheavals.

STRENGTH: *The individualist.* Striving for independence and freedom on all levels (mental, emotional, and material). Split-second perceptions, spontaneous solutions, and the spirit of discovery. Intuitive perceptions at the right moment. Urge toward cosmic consciousness and expansion of consciousness. Original, unconventional, enjoyment of experimentation. The gift of the "seventh sense."

PROBLEM AREA: *The person who changes viewpoints.* Restless and constantly "charged up." Unsettled and always searching for something new, for change, revolution, and subversion. Arbitrary, unpredictable, inconsiderate, destructive, and extremely willful. Compulsive aversion to everything obligatory. Freedom at any cost, which frequently causes a breach of contract to be committed so that others feel betrayed. Unwilling or incapable of being concerned with the "banal" problems of everyday life.

GOAL: Realization of democracy, freedom, and human rights. Overcoming old structures, attitudes, ideas, and opinions on an individual and collective level. Liberation from old ties. Disintegration of all bonds.

REPRESENTATIVES OF THE URANUS PRINCIPLE: Inventors, technicians, pilots, artists, revolutionaries, anarchists, astrologers, futurists, mental acrobats, yogis with double consciousness (for this world and other worlds), eccentrics, philosophers, and recluses.

PHYSICAL CORRELATIONS: Nervous system, tension and discharging of tension, rhythm.

MYTHOLOGICAL CORRELATIONS: Ouranous (Greek)/Uranus (Roman)—lord of the heavens, son of chaos, husband of Gaea (Earth), and father of Cronus. Original ruler. Symbol of mental fertility, creative ideas, and the lofty standpoint.

URANUS IN THE SIGNS
See pages 98 to 99.

Uranus orbits through the zodiac in 84 years, which means an average of seven years in each sign. Its position in the sign of the horoscope therefore primarily makes a statement about the generation born within this time period. The individual coloration that Uranus gives a horoscope can only be read from its position by house and from its aspects to the personal planets. Since Uranus is always a fervent advocate of individual freedoms, the values relating to freedom that arise for a generation under the respective position of Uranus, together with their problematic opposite pole, are listed in the table as both STRENGTH and PROBLEM AREA .

♆
Neptune

DIGNITY:	DETRIMENT:	EXALTATION:	FALL:
♓	♍	♋	♑

Discovered on September 23, 1846 by Johann Gottfried Galle.
Orbits through the entire zodiac in 156 years.
Stays an average of about 14 years in each sign.

ARCHETYPE: The mystic, the visionary, the martyr.

SHADOW: The crackpot, the addict, the alcoholic.

PRINCIPLE: Neptune represents the principle of dissolving boundaries. It corresponds to a person's "cosmic antennas" which permit one to feel the transcendental and the subtle. It allows one to sense concealed correlations, future trends, and other developments. At the same time, Neptune stands for the individual's longing to overcome everyday consciousness and see the highest things. In the process, Neptune's striving is actually directed toward the spiritual realm, but is frequently confused with spirits and other intoxicants. The permeability to which Neptune gives rise frequently results in one of the highest levels of sensitivity and a weakening of the body.

STRENGTH: *The medium.* Strong spiritual aspirations. Deep inner conviction, often based on personal experience, that a divine power is at work in everything and should be recognized as such. Great receptivity and sensibility. Compassionate behavior, characterized by almost boundless sympathy. Idealistic, soft, able to be devoted, and mediumistic. Strong desire for mystic experience. Full of faith in being protected and guided by a higher power. Strong visionary abilities, excellent intuitive understanding, and an unusual wealth of emotional images and imagination.

PROBLEM AREA: *The drunk or drug addict.* Drawn in a dangerous direction by a strong—frequently unrecognized or underestimated—inner force. Easily seducible and endangered by addiction, particularly to intoxicants. Also in danger of being overcome and swept away by collective currents, ranging from less harmful trends of the period to the violent excesses of mass hysteria. Falls easily into the role of the victim and the person who suffers, as well as that of the seducer, charlatan, schemer, or liar. Unstable, intangible, unpredictable, destructive, and slimy. Great difficulties in setting limits, up to the point of total identification with other people. Incapable of assuming responsibility for one's own life. Letting oneself drift without any solid ground to stand on. Desperation, melancholy, confusion, self-deception, and lack of orientation.

GOAL: The striving to go beyond the limits of the self and merge into a "we" feeling. The longing to be found, touched, and redeemed in trance and ecstasy by the divine. To find true spirituality and be a living witness of the divine effect in the world.

REPRESENTATIVES OF THE NEPTUNE PRINCIPLE: Inspired artists, talented actors and actresses, musicians, poets, priests and priestesses, preachers, mystics, occultists, chemists, nurses, doctors (particularly homeopaths), psychologists, trend researchers, forecasters, as well as addicts, the down-at-the-heels, the unstable, swindlers, and criminals.

PHYSICAL CORRELATIONS: The pineal gland.

MYTHOLOGICAL CORRELATIONS: Poseidon (Greek)/Neptune (Roman)—god of the seas, earthquakes, and fertility.

NEPTUNE IN THE SIGNS
See pages 100 to 101.

Neptune orbits through the zodiac in 165 years and therefore stays an average of about 14 years in each sign. Its position in the sign of the horoscope therefore primarily makes a statement about the generation born within this time period. The individual coloration that Neptune gives a horoscope can only be read from its position in a house and from its aspects to the personal planets. Since Neptune always represents DISSOLUTION, dream, vision, and IDEALIZATION for a generation under the respective position of Neptune, this is listed together with its problematic side of LACK OF DISCIPLINE and WEAKENING in the table under Neptune.

Pluto

DIGNITY:	DETRIMENT:	EXALTATION:	FALL:
♏	♉	♌	♒

Discovered by Percival Lowell on February 18, 1930.
Orbits through the entire zodiac in about 248 years.
Stays an average of around 21 years in each sign.
Because of its very unusual orbit, the length of its stay in a sign
fluctuates between 11 and 30 years.

ARCHETYPE: The magician, the shaman.

SHADOW: The black magician.

PRINCIPLE: The power of deepest transformation. Pluto represents the black gold of the alchemist, the dark wealth of the depths, the archaic original source, and the archetypal forces beyond all moral valuation. Pluto embodies the archaic feminine element that can be both fruitful, creative, and healing, as well as dark, cruel, brutal, sadistic, destructive, devouring, and lethal. The solar consciousness fears it as an abyss of Hell. Experiences with Pluto are always related to power and helplessness, dependency, subjection, and emotional entanglement. They sometimes also include an aspect of obsession. Pluto, the smallest and most distant planet, has its effect according to the principle of homeopathy: the smaller and less comprehensible the dosage, the stronger its effect.

STRENGTH: *The powerful person.* Mighty forces of the soul such as the powers of suggestion, hypnotic capabilities, and strong healing forces. Tremendously creative potency, intensive strength, and an almost insuperable will. Drive for far-reaching changes in oneself and others. Does not shy away from the deepest abysses. Overcoming and fundamental transforming of old values and structures.

PROBLEM AREA: *The obsessed individual.* Misuse of power. Inclination toward sadism and tyranny. Unconscious forces (autonomous complexes) that possess the conscious mind. Compulsive and obsessive character, destructive, uninhibited, dominated by instincts, fanatic, destructive for oneself and others. Pathological addiction to control. The inability to simply let things be, let go of people and things, and gain distance to the situation.

GOAL: Radical transformation in favor of a deep truth. The perception that nothing in life can stay as it is, that every beginning, every birth already bears its own end and rebirth within itself.

REPRESENTATIVES OF THE PLUTO PRINCIPLE: Analysts, doctors, researchers, dictators, scientists, speculators, violent criminals, charismatic leaders, demagogues, leaders of mass movements, hypnotists, and occultists.

PHYSICAL CORRELATIONS: Sexual organs, ability to regenerate.

MYTHOLOGICAL CORRELATIONS: Hades (Greek = the invisible)/Pluto or Dis-Pater (Roman = the rich man)—god of the underworld. Son of Cronus and Rhea, brother of Zeus and Poseidon, and husband of the (abducted) Persephone. Symbol for the realm of the shadow, the knowledge from the depths, and the experience of death and rebirth.

PLUTO IN THE SIGNS
See pages 102 to 103.

Pluto orbits through the zodiac in 248 years and thereby stays an average of 21 years in each sign. Its position in the sign of the horoscope therefore primarily makes a statement about the generation born within this time period. The true individual coloration that Pluto gives a horoscope can only be read from its position by house and from its aspects to the personal planets. Since PLUTO always stands for TRANSFORMATION, which means extensive changes in favor of a deeper truth, as well as EXPERIENCES OF POWER AND HELPLESSNESS (for culprit and victim), the themes specific to a sign that are significant to a generation under the respective position of Pluto, are listed in the table.

☊ ☋
Moon's Nodes

The Moon is located in part to the south and in part to the north of the Sun's orbit. Moon's Nodes is the name given to the interface of its orbit with that of the Sun. If the Moon comes from the south, it is called the Ascending Moon's Node, North Node, or Dragon's Head ☊. If it comes from the north, it is called a Descending Moon's Node, South Node, or Dragon's Tail ☋. Both points are opposite each other: an aspect to one of the Moon's Nodes automatically means an aspect to the other.

The astrological meaning of this Moon's Node axis is the crucial point in a person's life. It shows the tasks to be mastered and the purpose of existence. The South Node symbolizes the past—old patterns and ways of behaving that the soul of an individual has already brought along with it. Karmic astrology speaks of past lives here. In contrast, the North Node points to the future. It shows the direction to be pursued and symbolizes the tasks waiting to be resolved.

It is essential to meaningfully connect both themes of the Moon's Nodes, for the Descending Node tends to obstruct development and functions as a brake; in contrast, the Ascending Node indicates the challenging new direction. Aspects between the Moon's Nodes and the planets provide further information about supportive or inhibitive powers.

This means that nodal axis provides an initial, direct insight into the tasks presented in the horoscope, even though these themes are usually expressed elsewhere in the chart. However, the information given in the Moon's nodal position reduces the horoscope to a common denominator, reflecting the issue at hand—the quintessence.

MOON'S NODE IN THE SIGNS

The meaning of the Nodes is expressed primarily by house position rather than the sign involved. The individual meaning of the Moon's Node axis must therefore be looked up under the corresponding house. An impression of the themes addressed by the position in the sign will be provided by checking the significance of the house as it relates to the sign (Aries = 1st house, Taurus = 2nd house, Pisces = 12th house, etc.).

The TWELVE SIGNS
of the ZODIAC,
or the SUN IN THE SIGNS

♈ Aries (the Ram)   *The Fighter*

From March 21st to April 20th

RULER: ♂	EXALTATION: ☉	DETRIMENT: ♀
FALL: ♄	ELEMENT: Fire	QUALITY: Cardinal
CHARACTERISTIC: Warm and dry	SEX: Masculine	TEMPERAMENT: Choleric (quick-tempered)

SYMBOL: Man rune ♈ = the outstretched hands as a symbol of the adult human being. Furthermore, it symbolizes new life and striving for light. Later, it was also interpreted to mean the horns of the ram.

PHYSICAL CORRELATIONS: Head, face, blood.	CORRELATION TO SEASONS: The awakening of the forces in Spring.
ARCHETYPE: The warrior.	SHADOW: The destroyer.
MOTIVATION: Spontaneous enthusiasm.	STRIVES FOR: Development of will and achievement of conquests.
TASK IN LIFE: Attack, struggle, and assertion.	PITFALL: Too much activity, always taking the bull by the horns.
EXAMPLES: Heroes, great generals, and leaders.[1]	GUIDING PRINCIPLE: I want!

MYTHOLOGICAL MOTIFS: Helle and Phrixus. The quest for the Golden Fleece.

CENTRAL THOUGHT: Aries is the awakening of the forces. The central concern of this sign is the development of the ego, asserting one's own will, and conquering the world. Aries represents the archetypal masculine force which acts in an impetuous, strong-willed, and impulsive manner. It is characterized by activity, initiative, impatience, and rushing forward without becoming weary. Aries quickly recovers from low blows. The Aries person is considered indefatigable and daring. The Aries type is a pioneer with a warm, carefree openness which often has something sympathetically boyish (or girlish) about it, even when he or she is older. A contagious, untroubled optimism and vigorous joy of living can also give other people the momentum and courage to face life.

Actions

STRENGTH: *The energetic individual.* Spontaneous, impulsive, and sometimes quite the go-getter. Uncomplicated, direct, spirited, and lighthearted. Very dynamic, but never long-winded. Spontaneously switches from one goal to another. Never has the feeling of disgracing himself or herself.

PROBLEM AREA: *The impatient person.* Wants everything right away. Thoughtlessly rushes into plans without any sign of patience or stamina. Hurts others through inconsideration, often because of thoughtlessness. Primitive daredevil.

Thoughts

STRENGTH: *The pioneer.* Unburdened by other people's experiences, Aries goes his or her own way and finds surprising and unusual perceptions, methods, and solutions in the process. Open for new insights, even at a ripe old age.

PROBLEM AREA: *The headstrong individual* Explains the world to himself or herself in the way that he or she would like to have it. Is not concerned about objective viewpoints or an explanation of his or her standpoint. Irresponsible because of immaturity. Stubborn and arbitrary.

Feelings

STRENGTH: *The never-say-die person.* Recovers in a flash from every defeat, stands up and storms on. Inexhaustible optimism, a great deal of initiative, boldness, enthusiasm, and carefree confidence.

PROBLEM AREA: *The inconsiderate person.* Reckless egotism. Extremely shortsighted attitude toward life. Lack of understanding and self-control. Brutal.

TYPICAL OCCUPATIONAL AREAS: Medicine—above all surgery. Sports, police, and military. Technical occupations and crafts that work with fire, as well as processing of metal. Risk professions like race driver or pilot. Tasks that demand a pioneer spirit.

♉ Taurus (the Bull)

The Connoisseur

From April 21st to May 20th

RULER: ♀	EXALTATION: ☽	DETRIMENT: ♂ and ♇
FALL: ♅	ELEMENT: Earth	QUALITY: Fixed
CHARACTERISTIC: Cold and dry	SEX: Feminine	TEMPERAMENT: Melancholic

SYMBOL: ♉ a circle with the semi-circle above it = the horned cow or bull's head. The image of the nurturing mother cow, as well as the symbol of the life-giving Mother Earth.

PHYSICAL CORRELATIONS: Neck, nape, shoulders, mouth, throat, esophagus.

CORRELATION TO SEASONS: The time in which plants take root and become strong.

ARCHETYPE: The farmer.

SHADOW: The bullheaded person.

MOTIVATION: Routine and the joy of familiar things.

STRIVES FOR: Security and enjoyment.

TASK IN LIFE: Preserving what has been tested by time, developing enjoyment of the pleasures of life.

PITFALL: Immoderation as a form of stupor or addiction to an ultraconservative approach.

EXAMPLES: Shepherds, protectors, and preservers.

GUIDING PRINCIPLE: I possess. I maintain! Or also: I wait.

MYTHOLOGICAL MOTIFS: The Minotaur. The abduction of Europa.

CENTRAL THOUGHT: Taurus is the sign of rootedness and the greatest degree of inertia. It is characterized by love and loyalty to what is familiar, taking care of what has grown and been tested by time, as well as the patience with which the Taurus can integrate himself or herself into the natural growth cycles. Taurus can wait—longer than any of the other signs. Solely because of this ability, Taurus is able to achieve certain things. Taurus loves to stand on solid ground and defends self against surprising innovations and incalculable risks (particularly those which are financial). The enjoyment of the pleasures of life achieves its highest level of development in this sign and makes the Taurus into a thankful connoisseur.

Actions

STRENGTH: *The person of action.* Practical, down-to-earth, decisive, and persevering. Taurus is slow to warm up to things, but then emphatically stays with them and accomplishes something. Likes to work with other people.

PROBLEM AREA: *The loafer.* Lethargic, lazy, recklessly self-indulgent, gluttonous, a slave to the instincts, unreliable. Patient and sullen tolerance can lead to apathy. One-sided material striving.

Thoughts

STRENGTH: *The pragmatic person.* Thinking is concrete and practice-oriented. Is not fond of theoretic flights of fancy or a confusing variety of ideas. When considering a situation, always asks the question: What can you do with it?

PROBLEM AREA: *The slow-witted individual.* One-sided, unteachably stubborn, and sometimes very slow as well. Sticks to reality and has difficulty with abstractions.

Feelings

STRENGTH: *The faithful and social person.* Loves the stimulation of what is familiar and time-tested. Has a natural manner, is cheerful, tender, affectionate, and sociable. Capable of deep friendship and partnership (likes to form a "pack"). Faithful and reliable.

PROBLEM AREA: *The jealous heart.* Uncontrollably monopolizing and possessive. Extremely jealous and greedy. So stubborn that he or she can't be talked into changing his or her mind. Dangerously hot-tempered once he or she sees "red."

TYPICAL OCCUPATIONAL AREAS: The maintenance of values in relation to property and soil: agriculture, gardening, real estate, architecture. In the figurative sense: banks, stock market, applied and political economy. Fields in which enjoyment and taste are in the foreground: food, gastronomy, hotel trade, fashion, jewelry, cosmetics, music, painting, sculpture, and the art trade. Professions related to the past: historians, archaeologists, ethnologists. Crafts and natural sciences.

♊ Gemini (the Twins)   *The Curious Person*

From May 21st to June 21st

RULER: ☿	EXALTATION: —	DETRIMENT: ♃
FALL: —	ELEMENT: Air	QUALITY: Mutable
CHARACTERISTIC: Warm and moist	SEX: Masculine	TEMPERAMENT: Sanguine (optimistic)

SYMBOL: ♊ = the two temple columns as symbol of the day and night side, as the division of unity, as the differentiation into subject and object, masculine and feminine, the conscious and unconscious, light and dark, heaven and earth, etc.

PHYSICAL CORRELATIONS: Lungs, bronchial tubes, collarbone, arms and hands.	CORRELATION TO SEASONS: The time when sprouts divide themselves into stem, leaf, and bud, differentiating themselves from other shoots.
ARCHETYPE: Trader or intellectual.	SHADOW: The cynic.
MOTIVATION: Curiosity and the joy of acting as a mediator.	STRIVES FOR: Knowledge and diversity.
TASK IN LIFE: Differentiating lies from truth through constant doubt.	PITFALL: Ice-cold rationality.
EXAMPLE: Great thinkers and universal scholars.	GUIDING PRINCIPLE: I think. I doubt.

MYTHOLOGICAL MOTIFS: All of the dissimilar brothers or sisters: Castor and Polydeuces, Hercules and Iphicles, Prometheus and Epimetheus, Cain and Abel, Gilgamesh and Enkidu, Parsifal and Feirefiz, Osiris and Seth, Isis and Nephtys, Inanna and Ereshkigal.

CENTRAL THOUGHT: Gemini is the sign of versatility. Gemini people love to perceive what is only apparently homogeneous in all of its facets. As intellectually-oriented people, it is a great joy for them to see things in a very differentiated manner, particularly on the mental level. This makes them masters in the revelation of differences, but also relativists and doubters who must even question the sublime and the holy without restraint. They are characterized by the desire to take up new thoughts and ideas and pass them on, making them good traders and agents. This primarily applies to news, but naturally also for goods with a quick turnover.

Actions
STRENGTH: *The clever mind.* Deliberate, well-planned, methodical actions subject to rational approaches on the basis of clear perceptions and critically examined concepts without significant emotional participation. Smart, quick, and clever.
PROBLEM AREA: *The fickle person.* Begins much and finishes nothing. Must be constantly occupied, but continually dissipates strength. Lacks in depth.

Thoughts
STRENGTH: *The philosopher.* Resourceful, practical, logical, and emphatically intellectual. Great imaginative faculty. Able to analyze precisely. Quick ability to combine and think independently. Agile, quick-witted, ingenious, and sophisticated.
PROBLEM AREA: *The superficial individual.* Appallingly superficial, ingratiating and crafty, phony, and cynical. Pure "head knowledge" without inner participation. Perpetually doubts everything.

Feelings
STRENGTH: *The butterfly.* Lively, carefree, happy, curious, dazzling and cheerful, slightly ironic, charming, sociable, and entertaining. Always tries to be fair.
PROBLEM AREA: *The fugitive.* Superficial, flighty feelings, fleeting love play and flirtations. Restless, always looking for something new. Tends to intellectualize, rationalize, or "explain away." Fears emotional depth and flees to intellectual realm or seeks dissipation and distraction.

TYPICAL OCCUPATIONAL AREAS: Agent: particularly stockbrokers, real estate agents, or sales representatives. Commercial professions, above all in connection with communication: publisher and book dealer, writer, positions in trade and commerce, correspondent, interpreter, journalist, reporter, teacher. Intellectually-oriented occupational areas like mathematics, philology, and study of literature.

♋ Cancer (the Crab)   *The Romantic*

From June 21st to July 22nd

RULER: ☽	EXALTATION: ♃ and ♆	DETRIMENT: ♄
FALL: ♂	ELEMENT: Water	QUALITY: Cardinal
CHARACTERISTIC: Cold and moist	SEX: Feminine	TEMPERAMENT: Phlegmatic (lethargic)

SYMBOL: ♋ = the claws of the crab are two spirals moving in opposite directions as symbols of the ascending and descending course of the Sun. At the time of the summer solstice, the Sun reaches the Tropic of Cancer and begins to travel "backward."

PHYSICAL CORRELATIONS: Stomach, female breasts, glands.	CORRELATION TO SEASONS: The time when the fruit is formed.
ARCHETYPE: The poet, the mother.	SHADOW: The mother-hen, the eternal child.
MOTIVATION: Solicitude, helpfulness, but also ambition.	STRIVES FOR: Emotional safety and security.
TASK IN LIFE: Forming emotional bonds and expressing deep feelings.	PITFALL: Flight into wishful thinking, refusal to become an adult.
EXAMPLES: Great poets; romantics.	GUIDING PRINCIPLE: I feel.

MYTHOLOGICAL MOTIFS: The crab which bit Hercules in the heel as he fought against the Hydra, and all the stories related to the Great Mother.

CENTRAL THOUGHT: Cancers are the romantics of the zodiac. They have access to the images of the soul, which they experience in dreams and express in new forms time and again. Cancers protect themselves against their own fearfulness by gathering people around like a protective shield, binding people closely through help and solicitude. The domain of Cancer is the family, which offers true safety and security. If it were not for their enormous ambitions, they would never leave this protective area. Enduring attachment to homeland, family, and childhood, intensive yearnings, and a capacity for deep emotions allow truly loving people to develop from this sign.

Actions

STRENGTH: *The indirect person; one willing to help.* Instinctive reactions based on unconscious impulses, feeling (sympathy), and ambition. Develops great tenacity. Never takes a straight path, but reaches goals indirectly. Social-minded, tender, and prepared to help or protect another person at any time.

PROBLEM AREA: *The childlike individual.* Apparently selfless actions based on the fear of otherwise being abandoned. Shy, faint-hearted, fearful, and hardly willing to change things. Fears conflicts. Flight into a dream world, depression, or exaggerated ambition. Regression into childlike behavior.

Thoughts

STRENGTH: *The dreamer, the psychologist.* Vivid, imaginative thinking strongly influenced by the unconscious mind. Great capability for feeling other people's desires and thoughts and reacting to them. Deep understanding of the concerns of the soul.

PROBLEM AREA: *The wishful thinker.* Caught up in wishful thinking far removed from logic and objectivity. Also clings to absurd ideas just because they feel more pleasant than hard reality. Narrow point of view which is meant to be the standard for other people as well. Lack of independence. Mechanically repeats what other people say.

Feelings

STRENGTH: *The romantic.* Capable of very deep feelings. Sensitive, impressionable, devoted. Emotional connection to homeland and family are just as essential as the confirmation from other people. Is enthusiastic, naive, trusting, and affectionate in relationships. Great need for safety and security.

PROBLEM AREA: *The overly devoted person, the blackmailer.* Possessive. Clings to the beloved, whom he or she stifles with solicitude and misuses as a personal support. Superimposes moods on the surroundings. "Guilt-feeling politics." Tears as means to an end. "Tyranny of the weak." Emotional egotism.

TYPICAL OCCUPATIONAL AREAS: All helping, caring, and socially committed occupations, particularly doctors, medical and geriatric nurses, kindergarten teachers, psychologists, occupations in the artistic area such as acting, poetry, music, writing, literature, and art history. Positions in area of family, groups, and homeland, such as the preservation of regional traditions, local politics, gastronomy, society and club work.

♌ Leo (the Lion)   *The Supremely Confident Person*

From July 23rd to August 22nd

RULER: ☉	EXALTATION: ♇	DETRIMENT: ♄
FALL: —	ELEMENT: Fire	QUALITY: Fixed
CHARACTERISTIC: Warm and dry	SEX: Masculine	TEMPERAMENT: Choleric (quick-tempered)

SYMBOL: ♌ = the snake, an ancient sign of the sun and its course, symbol of life as it constantly renews itself and of eternity.

PHYSICAL CORRELATIONS: Heart, circulatory system, spinal column.	CORRELATION TO SEASONS: The splendor of completely ripened fruit.
ARCHETYPE: The king.	SHADOW: The lord and master, the braggart.
MOTIVATION: Joy in creativity and generosity.	STRIVES FOR: Greatest possible degree of self-expression and admiration.
TASK IN LIFE: Becoming a dignified focus of attention.	PITFALL: Superficiality and self-aggrandizement.
EXAMPLES: The truly great rulers and leaders.	GUIDING PRINCIPLE: I create. I came, I saw, I conquered.

MYTHOLOGICAL MOTIFS: Hercules and the Nemean Lion. All the sagas of Sun heros and Sun gods.

CENTRAL THOUGHT: Life stands in its fullest blossom and finds its most magnificent development in the sign of Leo. This is expressed in the Leo person's distinct self-confidence and rousing joy of life. The true kings, for whom the Earth has produced gold, diamonds, purple robes, and silk, are at home here. Luxury has been created for them, and they know how to enjoy it with the proper attitude. Leos are masters of the generous gesture and expressive design. They know how to create the best effects. They have an extraordinary understanding of how to plan and organize on a large scale. They love to sun themselves in the light of their own generosity.

Actions

STRENGTH: *The organizer.* Calm, self-reliant, optimistic, and decisive actions. Constantly plans and risks the "great success" because they are uncomfortable with small steps. Life is considered to be a stage for showmanship. The distinct self-confidence also encourages and motivates other people. Leos are frequently self-made people and masters of organization.

PROBLEM AREA: *The high and mighty.* Complacent, ego-related behavior, narcissistic, vain, and megalomaniac. Others are reduced to the role of admirers. Too good for trivial everyday affairs.

Thoughts

STRENGTH: *The careerist.* Intuitively comprehends and evaluates things with an overall perspective. Creative intelligence. Strong convictions, self-confidence, and a vital optimism color his or her way of thinking.

PROBLEM AREA: *The condescending person.* Completely undifferentiated thinking in the form of clichés. No interest in objective perceptions. Superficial and overbearing, without a sense of subtlety. Hates criticism and has no idea what self-criticism is.

Feelings

STRENGTH: *The zestful individual.* Hearty, benevolent, humorous, and always generous. Passionate and cheerful. Loves feeling self-important.

PROBLEM AREA: *The boaster.* Dependent on constant admiration and confirmation from others. Embarrassing "lord and master" behavior. Only short-lived passions. Feelings are vulgarized, and emotional sympathy reduced to a minimum. Love is only possible as a narcissistic reflection.

TYPICAL OCCUPATIONAL AREAS: Leadership tasks that emphasize prestige and demand self-confidence and initiative: the manager, organizer, representative, politician, senior physician, wholesale merchant, officer, director, and actor. Careers devoted to luxury: gold, jewelry, and art trades, interior decoration, textile branch, and cosmetics.

♍ Virgo (the Virgin)   *The Thorough Person*
From August 23rd to September 22nd

RULER: ☿	EXALTATION: ☿	DETRIMENT: ♃
FALL: ♀	ELEMENT: Earth	QUALITY: Mutable
CHARACTERISTIC: Cold and dry	SEX: Feminine	TEMPERAMENT: Melancholic

SYMBOL: ♍ = the *m* is interpreted as the analogy to a death rune (corresponds to harvest time).

PHYSICAL CORRELATIONS: Intestinal tract, metabolism, solar plexus.	CORRELATION TO SEASONS: The time of harvest.
ARCHETYPE: The person who harvests, the craftsman.	SHADOW: The Philistine, the pedant, the misanthropist.
MOTIVATION: Joy in details.	STRIVES FOR: Purity and health.
TASK IN LIFE: Critically examining everything for its suitability.	PITFALL: Perfectionism.
EXAMPLES: The master; the sober-minded, critical scientist.	GUIDING PRINCIPLE: I take it literally. Or: I examine.

MYTHOLOGICAL MOTIFS: Astraeus, the goddess of justice who left the Earth and became the constellation Virgo. The myth of Demeter.

CENTRAL THOUGHT: The sign Virgo corresponds to the harvest in which the chaff is separated from the wheat. No other sign has such strong instincts when it comes to differentiating between what is healthy and unhealthy, useful and pointless, valuable and damaging. Since Virgo people like to place this ability at the service of humanity, they prefer to take on tasks in which they can care for and protect an organism. They do this for the human organism in the role of doctor, for the business world as business economists, and for the nation as political economists. The love of detail contrasts to timidity when it comes to "great success." Virgos are cut out to be the "second man or woman" leaving entrepreneurial risks to others, while putting more effort into looking after the computations, detail planning, and practical matters.

Actions

STRENGTH: *The economist.* Always concerned with what is optimum: achieving the greatest possible use with the minimum amount of (work) effort. Orderly, diligent, thorough, and reliable. The Virgo person is considered extremely orderly, but this is not always true. Seen in more precise terms, he or she fights against chaos. One individual may be more successful at this, the other less.

PROBLEM AREA: *The fussy person.* Mistrustful, pedantic, and one-sided in an orientation toward practicality. Cleaning mania, exaggerated striving for security, and fearful thriftiness. Nerve-racking perfectionism.

Thoughts

STRENGTH: *The scientist.* Clever, critical approach that looks toward the future and is oriented toward sober, measurable, and verifiable results. Objective, pragmatic, down-to-earth, shrewd, but also flexible attitude.

PROBLEM AREA: *The narrow-minded thinker.* Fanatic for security. Narrow-minded and obsessed with details. A compulsive slave to rationality and dogged faith in science because of fear of what cannot be explained. Only believes in what can be "proved."

Feelings

STRENGTH: *The cautious person.* Careful, reserved, almost demure, chaste, and pure. Slowly warms up to things only after a detailed critical examination. Then is reliable, faithfully caring, and very willing to help.

PROBLEM AREA: *The inhibited individual.* Critical, cool, and inhibited. Love and the ability to be devoted are subject to considerations of practicality. Only falls in love when everything is "just right." Tends to find faults, be resigned, envious, and bitter.

TYPICAL OCCUPATIONAL AREAS: Areas in which the chaff is critically separated from the wheat: as a critic or economist. Also, jobs in which the love of detail has a primary position such as bookkeeping, editing, data processing, but also the medical profession—particularly dentists. Occupations in which a practical mind (technology, crafts) or manual skills are required (from precision mechanic to massage therapist). Also, teachers, specialists, and sober-minded (natural) scientists. Prefers to work as a salaried employee.

♎ Libra (the Scales)   *The Artist*

From September 23rd to October 22nd

RULER: ♀	EXALTATION: ♄	DETRIMENT: ♂
FALL: ☉	ELEMENT: Air	QUALITY: Cardinal
CHARACTERISTIC: Warm and moist	SEX: Masculine	TEMPERAMENT: Sanguine (optimistic)

SYMBOL: ♎ = symbol of a scale, or the evening Sun above the horizon, both symbols of equilibrium and peace in the sign of the autumnal equinox

PHYSICAL CORRELATIONS: Kidneys, renal pelvis, bladder, skin.	CORRELATION TO SEASONS: Autumnal equinox, the time of balance in nature.
ARCHETYPE: The artist, the wise judge.	SHADOW: The eternally indecisive person, the snob.
MOTIVATION: Love of beauty.	STRIVES FOR: Beauty and harmony.
TASK IN LIFE: Bringing beauty into the world.	PITFALL: Beautiful hollowness, esthetic superficiality.
EXAMPLES: The great artists, esthetics, and people who have attained their perfect form.	GUIDING PRINCIPLE: I weigh. Or: I balance.

MYTHOLOGICAL MOTIFS: Cupid and Psyche. The Judgment of Paris.

CENTRAL THOUGHT: Libra is the sign of harmony. Its main concern is creating harmony, maintaining it, and enjoying it. This applies to the harmony of forms in architecture, art, and design, as well as to forms of social manners, particularly the harmony in close interpersonal relationships like friendship, marriage, and partnership. This makes it the sign of the artist, the aesthetic, as well as the mediator and peacemaker. It is a pleasure for Librans to let life become graceful beyond all the dry necessities to bring joy to the senses through beauty, harmony, and good taste. Despite all the relating to other people, Libra people still do not want to be monopolized. Instead, they love the feeling of freedom. In the search for decisions that least disturb harmony (which means not hurting or doing injustice to anyone, if possible), Librans need considerably more time than other signs, which explains their famous weakness in making decisions.

Actions
STRENGTH: *The person who balances.* A creative and impulse-giving way of functioning, always with style and concern not to rub anyone the wrong way. Tactful, enterprising, good-natured, tolerant, and sociable.

PROBLEM AREA: *The half-hearted individual.* Notorious difficulties in making decisions, unable to engage in conflict, and therefore dependent on the surrounding world and people's sympathy. Puts on act of pseudo-superiority. Starry-eyed and unrealistic.

Thoughts
STRENGTH: *The highbrow.* Graphic way of thinking, influenced by form and harmony. Clever strategist in questions of an equilibrium of energies. Very good style in manner of expressing thoughts. Open for innovations. Enjoys communication.

PROBLEM AREA: *The fickle person.* Indecisive, susceptible, superficial, suppresses unpleasant insights. Sometimes calculating and very cunning.

Feelings
STRENGTH: *The peacemaker.* Enjoys contacts, easily willing to compromise, compensatory. Always oriented toward the other person, but at the same time concerned about freedom and inner independence.

PROBLEM AREA: *The uncommitted individual.* Because of fearing the highs and lows of life, piteously fixated on the uncommitted happy medium. Greedily demands sympathy from others, is moody and capricious. Suppresses feelings. Telltale craving for compromise because of pathological need to avoid conflict.

TYPICAL OCCUPATIONAL AREAS: All professions that bring beauty into the world such as art—especially music, dance, acting, fashion, photography, advertising, interior design, work with flowers, colors, luxury articles, cosmetics. Tasks in which cultivated style and sociability can be expressed: representatives, solicitors, diplomats, entertainers, and mediators. The entire legal field is represented here with the task of mediating peace, producing compromises, and representing the just cause.

♏ Scorpio (the Scorpion)   *The Gray Eminence*

From October 23rd to November 21st

RULER: ♂ and ♇	EXALTATION: ⛢	DETRIMENT: ♀
FALL: ☽	ELEMENT: Water	QUALITY: Fixed
CHARACTERISTIC: Cold and moist	SEX: Feminine	TEMPERAMENT: Phlegmatic (lethargic)

SYMBOL: ♏ = the *m* is attributed to a death rune completed by the death sting of the scorpion.

PHYSICAL CORRELATIONS: Genitals.	CORRELATION TO SEASONS: When the outer nature dies to form humus beneath the Earth for the new year.
ARCHETYPE: Magician, shaman.	SHADOW: The vampire.
MOTIVATION: Impulse into the depths.	STRIVES FOR: Security and power.
TASK IN LIFE: Being a true, completely irritating healer.	PITFALL: Intoxication with power.
EXAMPLES: All the gray eminences, alchemists (Faust).	GUIDING PRINCIPLE: I probe. Or: I desire.

MYTHOLOGICAL MOTIFS: Orion's death. Gilgamesh and the scorpion people.

CENTRAL THOUGHT: Scorpio is the sign of depth and the extremes. Nothing interests the Scorpio less than what is superficial and mediocre. Scorpio's world is cryptic. Scorpio is the Faustian human being, irresistibly drawn by the urge to explore everything that is concealed, secretive, suppressed, to the taboos that a society produces. The spectrum of feelings contains only extremes, like love and hate. Scorpio is a stranger to medium tones. Scorpio possesses immense powers of the soul that can be used for the benefit of others. Scorpio can be a healer and a helper, but can also use this ability to make other people dependent, or can even destroy others. This makes a responsible manner of dealing with power the explosive theme of this sign.

Actions

STRENGTH: *The uncompromising person, the breaker of taboos.* Scorpio does not enter into lazy compromises, and can be an example and leading figure for others. Places a finger mercilessly and with a sure instinct on the sore spots of others and can thereby initiate a healing process. Tough, tenacious, strong-willed, provocative, and often uncomfortable for others.

PROBLEM AREA: *The destroyer.* All actions serve the intensification of personal power. Tyrannical, destructive, and self-destructive.

Thoughts

STRENGTH: *The detective.* The urge to reveal secrets and courage to also venture into dangerous areas in the process. Profound and analytic. Sharp-witted and unyielding in the quest for the last truth. Is certain to talk about what everyone else would like to keep silent about.

PROBLEM AREA: *The pigheaded person.* Cynical, fanatic, dogmatic, and stubborn. Strongest powers of wishful thinking, which easily become fixated on one idea.

Feelings

STRENGTH: *The powerful individual.* Enormous emotional strengths and wishful powers that can be compelling for others. Intensive, inscrutable, passionate, and lustful feelings. Strong sexuality. Access to dark, archaic powers of the soul.

PROBLEM AREA: *The vampire.* Giving in to the temptations of one's own power. Sucking other people dry emotionally and keeping them in subjection and dependence. Pathologically jealous and envious, vindictive, sadistic, and blindly destructive. Desperately at the mercy of the extremes of one's own emotions.

TYPICAL OCCUPATIONAL AREAS: Wherever the penetration and exploration of the unknown, the mysterious, and the concealed is concerned: explorers, investigators, detectives, cave-explorers; in espionage as well as psychoanalysis; x-ray technology, but also esoterics and secret teachings. The entire field of healing and therapy; professions treated as outcasts by society, such as garbage collection; tasks associated with death: companion to the dying, director of funeral home, executor of wills, and trustees in bankruptcy.

♐ Sagittarius (the Archer)   *The Citizen of the World*

From November 22nd to December 21st

RULER: ♃	EXALTATION: —	DETRIMENT: ☿
FALL: —	ELEMENT: Fire	QUALITY: Mutable
CHARACTERISTIC: Warm and dry	SEX: Masculine	TEMPERAMENT: Choleric (quick-tempered)

SYMBOL: ♐ = the arrow aims into the heavens and symbolizes striving for higher things. The winged centaur reminds us that Sagittarius also has an instinctual nature, which should not be forgotten, despite lofty striving.

PHYSICAL CORRELATIONS: Hips, thighs, liver and gallbladder.	CORRELATION TO SEASONS: The Advent season, leading to the new birth of the light on the shortest day of the year.
ARCHETYPE: The high priest, the missionary.	SHADOW: The pharisee, the hypocrite.
MOTIVATION: The search for meaning.	STRIVES FOR: Ideals, religous convictions, and justice.
TASK IN LIFE: Proclaiming the meaning and guiding.	PITFALL: Self-righteousness and hypocrisy.
EXAMPLES: The great preachers and evangelists.	GUIDING PRINCIPLE: I believe. It is clear to me.

MYTHOLOGICAL MOTIFS: The wise centaur Chiron who taught Hercules.

CENTRAL THOUGHT: In the sign of Sagittarius, the issue is expanding the horizons of both the inner and outer worlds. This can be seen in the distinct fondness of travel, leading to encounters with distant cultures, as well as the endeavor to expand inner horizons thanks to these trips and continual improvement of one's knowledge. Above all, Sagittarius is driven to seek meaning. Deeply religious on the inside, aware that a higher purpose is concealed within all of Creation, it is the concern of this sign to find this meaning and proclaim it. Since the feeling for justice is strongly developed, Sagittarians strive for justice, guided by truly high values or by extreme prejudices and embarrassing slips into self-righteous priestly smugness.

Actions

STRENGTH: *The self-motivated person.* Great joy in achievement and movement, associated with an ability to be inspired and motivated. Aspires to leave narrow surroundings and strives for higher goals. Dignified, supremely confident, sophisticated. Acts on the basis of noble convictions, guided by respect, love, and reverence for humanity and Creation.

PROBLEM AREA: *The arrogant individual.* Big-mouthed dazzler and show-off. Incapable of setting limits or developing modesty and humbleness. Fearfully concerned with outward appearances. Can admit no weakness.

Thoughts

STRENGTH: *The educated mind.* Strives for higher education and broad horizons. Liberal mind. Inner convictions and acquired worldview subjectively color thinking. Tends to have magnificent plans and far-reaching goals.

PROBLEM AREA: *The conceited thinker* Moral arrogance, fanatic convictions, know-it-all, presumptuous infallibility, insincerity, hypocrisy, lies, sensitivity to criticism. Condescending talkativeness (the small-time philosopher).

Feelings

STRENGTH: *The enthusiast.* Flooded with and spurred on by high to holy feelings. Great ability to become enthusiastic. Doesn't want to disappoint anyone in any way, shape, or form. Need for freedom which also demands considerable elbow room in partnerships. Loves to work together with the partner on the realization of mutual goals and ideals.

PROBLEM AREA: *The masked person.* Fear of disgrace, particularly of being unmasked and exposed as simply a normal human being with all one's faults and weaknesses.

TYPICAL OCCUPATIONAL AREAS: Everything that deals with foreign countries, travel, and foreign trade, particularly in connection with representative assignments: diplomats, politicians, foreign correspondents, interpreters, exporters, tour operators and managers. People searching for meaning and guides in life like philosophers, theologians, spiritual advisors, and counselors. Judicial professions and the world of sports.

♑ Capricorn (the Goat)   *The Patriarch*

From December 22nd to January 20th

RULER: ♄	EXALTATION: ♂	DETRIMENT: ☽
FALL: ♃ and ♆	ELEMENT: Earth	QUALITY: Cardinal
CHARACTERISTIC: Cold and dry	SEX: Feminine	TEMPERAMENT: Melancholic

SYMBOL: ♑ = symbol of the sun which slowly rises upward from the depths (winter solstice).

PHYSICAL CORRELATIONS: Bone system, knees, nails.	CORRELATION TO SEASONS: Clear, cold, harsh winter.
ARCHETYPE: The patriarch, the hermit.	SHADOW: The grumbler.
MOTIVATION: Feeling of responsibility.	STRIVES FOR: Completion of the work that has been started.
TASK IN LIFE: Resolutely representing law and order, principles and standards.	PITFALL: The joyless drudge.
EXAMPLES: Old Testament father figures or the king as the first servant of his state.	GUIDING PRINCIPLE: I complete. I am responsible.

MYTHOLOGICAL MOTIFS: The goatfish, as well as Atlas, Christopher, and other great bearers of burdens.

CENTRAL THOUGHT: The true prime movers are at home in the sign of Capricorn. Here they work with patience and resilient persistence to dutifully fulfill the tasks that they have assumed and bring them to completion. This is less meant to enhance their own fame than to complete the work, behind which they then step into the background. Faithfulness, discipline, resolution, and a sense of duty are the essential characteristics of this sign, as well as supporting the inclination toward law and order, standards and structures.

Actions
STRENGTH: *The individual who bears responsibility.* Naturally assumes responsibility and does not let go until plans that have been set in motion are put into effect. Only tangible results count. Diligent, precise, persevering, dependable, sober, down-to-earth, indefatigable, energetic, and persistent.

PROBLEM AREA: *The person who has no mercy on himself or herself.* Listless fulfillment of responsibilities, joyless drudgery, addicted to work and responsibility, permanent pressure to perform, dread of innovation, and fears of competition. Rigid clinging to old time-tested patterns and structures. Unsociable, restless, gruff, unfair, and stingy.

Thoughts
STRENGTH: *The clear mind.* Clear, precise evaluation of effort, expenditure, and yield. Immediately recognizes what is feasible and what is not. Practical and healthy common sense. Sensible, profound, and extremely concentrated.

PROBLEM AREA: *The uncomprehending person.* Headstrong, ponderous, inflexible, ruled by "time-tested" patterns of thought and persistently closed to innovations.

Feelings
STRENGTH: *The serious soul.* Only opens up very slowly and hesitantly, but then is loyal, reliable, dependable, dutiful, and very responsible. Can clearly set boundaries. Sensuality is well-controlled but strong. Takes feelings seriously. Is careful and tends to be mistrustful.

PROBLEM AREA: *The withdrawn person.* Sharp separation between feeling and actions. Reserved, closed, ice-cold, ruthlessly cool, and inconsiderate. At times sentimental, depressive, and melancholy. Denies the childlike, playful, tender side that needs devotion.

TYPICAL OCCUPATIONAL AREAS: Positions that bear responsibility in public life: politicians, state officials, managers in all areas. Wherever a good sense of lasting values is required: in the field of banking and real estate, in the insurance business, or as a trustee. Where clear structures are created and solid material (above all, stone) is processed, from the construction industry to sculpture. Professions that require a sober attitude, prudence, seriousness, and much endurance.

≈ Aquarius (the Water Bearer) *The Individualist*

From January 21st to February 19th

RULER: ♄ and ♅	EXALTATION: —	DETRIMENT: ☉
FALL: ♇	ELEMENT: Air	QUALITY: Fixed
CHARACTERISTIC: Warm and moist	SEX: Masculine	TEMPERAMENT: Sanguine (optimistic)

SYMBOL: ≈ = wave lines as the symbol of constant movement that disappears into infinity.

PHYSICAL CORRELATIONS: Lower leg, pancreas.	CORRELATION TO SEASONS: Cool, clear, still winter, and Carnival time.
ARCHETYPE: The wise fool.	SHADOW: The lunatic, the lonely person, the eccentric.
MOTIVATION: Originality and hunger for knowledge.	STRIVES FOR: Utopia or stoic tranquillity.
TASK IN LIFE: Overcoming old to bring innovation into the world.	PITFALL: Always needing to be special.
EXAMPLES: Great humanists, philosophers, reformers, and rationalists.	GUIDING PRINCIPLE: I know (that I don't know anything).

MYTHOLOGICAL MOTIFS: Ganymede, the cup-bearer of the gods.

CENTRAL THOUGHT: Aquarius topples old values in order to replace them with new ones. It clears away class distinctions in order to produce equality between employer and workers, the sexes, the races, varying cultures, etc. Concerned with the realization of utopia, with the freedom of the individual, and with bursting encrusted structures. At the medieval court, this principle was demonstrated in the role of the court jester, the only one who had the jester's license to speak the truth. Since the French Revolution, which resulted shortly after the discovery of the planet Uranus (ruler of this sign), its principles of "freedom, equality, brotherhood" have been on everyone's lips. Aquarius possesses extraordinary powers of abstraction, tends to view things from above, and is very imaginative and inventive.

Actions
STRENGTH: *The considerate person.* Strives for independence. Wants to be free from all limitations and inhibitions. Always wants to set self apart from the masses and emphasize personal qualities. After careful consideration, he or she works conscientiously, cleverly, and with endurance.

PROBLEM AREA: *The withdrawn individual.* Ego weakness and unmastered feelings of inferiority can lead to dangerous overcompensation. Unpredictable and slightly crazy. Has a difficult time being resolute, integrating or even subordinating himself or herself.

Thoughts
STRENGTH: *The observer with a perspective.* Likes to get a clear, objective picture of things, properly evaluate situations, develop far-reaching prospects, and contribute ingenious ideas from a "bird's-eye view." Original, witty, imaginative, quick-witted, bizarre, and objective; a rational, aloof mind.

PROBLEM AREA: *The armchair philosopher* Detached from the "heaviness of the earth," lost in intellectual edifices. Has the entire world in his or her head, but no drive to translate the ideas into action or examine them for feasibility.

Feelings
STRENGTH: *The buddy.* Charming and noncommittal, lively, sympathetic, fair, companionable. Feeling or showing feelings is complicated. Prefers to conceal feelings behind a friendly and cool, reserved attitude. Shies away from committed relationships, preferring to be alone. May also avoid relationships because of a love of variety.

PROBLEM AREA: *The eccentric, the isolated individual.* The unusual and eternally misunderstood person with claim to all special rights. Anarchistic tendencies. An anti-attitude at all costs. Fear of deep feelings in which one could get lost. Impersonal, distanced, controlled, and ice-cold, which explains being lonely and isolated.

TYPICAL OCCUPATIONAL AREAS: Professions that demand creativity and allow great freedom of movement: above all marketing, advertising, and public relations. Tasks in which the latest technology is applied, new developments take place, and inventions are made. Foresighted occupations such as futurist, and astrologer. Scientists who take unusual paths or employ the newest methods that are difficult to explain (alternative medicine and homeopathy).

♓ Pisces (the Fishes)   *The Medium*
From February 20th to March 20th

RULER: ♃ and ♆	EXALTATION: ♀	DETRIMENT: ☿
FALL: ☿	ELEMENT: Water	QUALITY: Mutable
CHARACTERISTIC: Cold and moist	SEX: Feminine	TEMPERAMENT: Phlegmatic (lethargic)

SYMBOL: ♓ = two fish are attached to each other, both trying to swim in a different direction.

PHYSICAL CORRELATIONS: Feet and ankles.	CORRELATION TO SEASONS: Fasting period when the saved seeds are offered to Mother Earth as a sacrifice.
ARCHETYPE: The prophet, the Samaritan.	SHADOW: The addict, the unstable person.
MOTIVATION: Longing to leave the prison of the body.	STRIVES FOR: Being one with the Holy Spirit.
TASK IN LIFE: Living witness to the work of God in this world.	PITFALL: Mistaking the spirit of wine for the Holy Spirit.
EXAMPLES: Great peacemakers, spiritual advisers, and artists.	GUIDING PRINCIPLE: I sense. Or: I love.

MYTHOLOGICAL MOTIFS: Fish that save the heroes (Jonah) by swallowing them and spitting them out after a phase of purification (rebirth).

CENTRAL THOUGHT: Pisces has great longing for spiritual experiences, transcendent worlds, or simply release from the confines of the body, which can be experienced as a prison. Pisces places little value on the values of this world and is therefore willing to make sacrifices to help others. Boundless sympathy often moves Pisces. This is the sign of great spiritual advisers who listen and understand without evaluating. Their problem is developing a distinct feeling of self-identity, which is why Pisces tends to experience the Ascendant as the ego instead of the Sun.

Actions

STRENGTH: *The guided individual, the altruist.* Seismographic sensing of outer impressions and inner knowing about the right point in time. Is inclined more toward strongly instinctive, passive reactions than active, resolute actions. Understands the art of "being able to let things happen." Willing to help, self-sacrificing, selfless.

PROBLEM AREA: *The eternal victim.* Constantly makes oneself into the pitiable victim. Flight into illness and depression. Manipulates others with helplessness. Charming facade which can conceal a contradictory personality that behaves in a vicious and cruel manner. Chameleon-like feigned accommodation, instability, and vulnerability to seduction that borders on being controlled by others. In danger of becoming addicted.

Thoughts

STRENGTH: *The intuitive person.* Good antenna and unerring sense of correlations are the qualities of a great creative fantasy, the insights of which often cannot be substantiated. Strives for insight and wisdom.

PROBLEM AREA: *The vague thinker.* Airy-fairy, mysterious, inconstant, and insincere. Incapable of assuming a clear, objective standpoint for more than a moment. Delusions and vague opinions.

Feelings

STRENGTH: *The sensitive person.* Selfless love, willing to make sacrifices. Boundless empathy, enormous ability for devotion, and deep understanding. Longing to become one and merge. Enchanting and bewitching, seductive, emotional, sense of delicacy, and all-encompassing love.

PROBLEM AREA: *Someone who is easy to seduce.* Can't set limits. Oversensitive, highly vulnerable, slightly depressive, but also capable of developing extreme harshness and coldness. Masochistic tendencies. Longing for death.

TYPICAL OCCUPATIONAL AREAS: Professions that demand sympathy, spirituality, and willingness to help or to sacrifice, such as spiritual advising or charitable tasks. The world of fantasy and imaginary reality, like the circus, theater, and film business. Art, and above all, music, poetry, and painting. Occupations that demand a strong instinct, tasks in subtle areas, such as the work of a medium, naturopath, or homeopath. Activities with or in water: shipping, fishing, and diving. The pharmaceutical industry.

The MOON *and the* PLANETS
in the SIGNS

☽♈   Moon in Aries   *The Amazon*

AS A CHILD: *The little berserker.* Lively, demanding, willful, loud, courageous, impetuous. The state of being small is felt to be an offense. Early development of motor skills; needs sufficient freedom of movement. Low threshold of frustration. Seeks lively confrontation with the mother. Feelings are expressed spontaneously, directly, without disguise. Attempts to break the childish obstinacy results in catastrophes. Easy detachment from the parents.

INNER MOTHER IMAGE: The strong, proud, unbending, courageous woman.	DIFFICULT LESSONS TO LEARN: Patience and consideration for others.

AS A MOTHER: *The vigorous individual.* Brings up her child to be self-reliant and independent. Teaches her child to assert itself. Resists emotional ties. A dependent, cuddly child will not receive just rewards from her.

IMAGE OF THE WOMAN: *The wild woman.* Impulsive, direct, and impatient. Loves everything uncomplicated and direct. Emotionally approachable and irritable. Fiery, hefty, passionate requirements. Great need for independence and self-responsibility. Always feels exactly what she wants. In partnership: chummy, tom-boyish, autonomous, always ready to argue. Incapable of devotion. Likes to conquer, but not let herself be conquered. Always out to satisfy her own needs.
SHADOW: *The virago.*

STRENGTH: *The adventuress.* Strong feelings and spontaneous reactions. Open, direct, inwardly restless, likes to be on the road. Lifelong youthful feeling, open-minded, always ready for the new, the inspiring, and the exciting. Loves thrills and suspense. Does not put up with nonsense. Ready to take risks and engage in conflict.

PROBLEM AREA: *The quarrelsome soul.* Highly sensitive to (perceived) discrimination. Constant inner irritability mixed with anger and frustration. Inconsiderate and nervous when it comes to one's own advantage. Has difficulty tuning in to others, listening, or just being there. Highly impatient, sensitive to criticism, and arrogant. Little sense of self-criticism. Might misunderstand gentleness to be weakness.

KEY PRINCIPLE: Don't put up with anything.	STYLE OF LIVING: A nomad's tent.

| ☽♉ | **Moon in Taurus** | *The Sociable Soul* | Exaltation |

AS A CHILD: *Little Miss or Mister Sunshine.* Very sensual, calm, soulful, contented, and quite oral. Fully contented, or contented when full. Needs an especially intense and constant physical relationship with the mother, especially in the first years. Tends to be a late bloomer, needs leisure and time to mature. Leaving mother and home is difficult.

INNER MOTHER IMAGE: The warm, nourishing, protecting woman.

DIFFICULT LESSONS TO LEARN: Departures, courage to change.

AS A MOTHER: *The good-natured woman.* The practical, down-to-earth, protective, and caring mother. Devotes herself to her child with patience and care, gives a deep feeling of security and safety, shows her child how to easily manage daily routines. Has difficulty letting go of her child.

IMAGE OF THE WOMAN: *The sensuous one.* Very feminine. Erotic, sensuous, physical, heartfelt, charming, seductive, steady, domestic, and faithful. Seeks emotional security and stability. She can be lover, whore, wife, and mother to her partner all in one.
SHADOW: *The ponderous person.*

STRENGTH: *The faithful heart.* Pronounced need to be physically close to the partner: to sense, taste, and enjoy the other person. In spite of the sense of stability, a slight hesitance when it comes to binding and making a commitment because once the decision is made, it's forever. Separation, change, and new starts feel like uprooting and are therefore feared. Loves security in a circle of trusted people. Good-natured, content, inner serenity, patience, and love of peace. A collector, sedentary, and very fertile.

PROBLEM AREA: *The hedonist.* A tendency toward being thick-skinned and ponderous. Lazy, stubborn, immovable, stuck in old habits, coarse, boring, and gluttonous.

KEY PRINCIPLE: I have what I have.

STYLE OF LIVING: The farmhouse.

| ☽♊ | **Moon in Gemini** | *The Inquisitive Individual* |

AS A CHILD: *The bookworm.* Restless, spirited, smart, curious, interested in everything. Learns to speak and read early. Reads a lot (at the same time). Experiences an over-caring, physical mother as a bother. Critically distant on the emotional level, therefore emotionally independent at an early age. Easy detachment from the parents.

INNER MOTHER IMAGE: The smart mother or the cool, busy, restless mother.

DIFFICULT LESSONS TO LEARN: Making decisions and sticking to them; emotional commitments.

AS A MOTHER: *The clever woman.* The carefree mother, without any unnecessary worries. Light and sunny disposition. Finds clever and handy solutions, is interested in her child and always ready to listen. Has an answer for every question. Darkness and unpleasantness get shaken off. On the cool side.

IMAGE OF THE WOMAN: *The intellectual.* Clever, curious, emotionally on the superficial side, carefree, playful, extroverted, charming, social, sunny, a coquette, creative, and unreliable. Ignores nagging personal problems. Other people's problems can be discussed. Emotionally aloof and hard to reach. Dislikes getting into deep relationships.
SHADOW: *The fickle person.*

STRENGTH: *The intellectually curious individual.* A very active intellect, interested in everything and communicative. Loves exchanging ideas, arguing, discussing, is curious and vicarious. Skeptical rather than gullible. The mind is the path to the heart: feelings are analyzed, questioned, explored, and straightened out, if possible.

PROBLEM AREA: *The doubting Thomas.* Constantly changing feelings. Sooner or later everything is torn apart by doubt. Nothing can be really trusted. The mind always finds a way out, sometimes to its own disadvantage. Egregious hair-splitting. Shallow feelings, mocking, cynical, superficial, and skeptical. A tedious know-it-all. Avoids confronting the darker sides of feelings.

KEY PRINCIPLE: What's new?

STYLE OF LIVING: The airy, light apartment, editorial office, book store.

| ☽♋ | Moon in Cancer | *The Helpful Person* | Dignity |

AS A CHILD: *The nestling.* Sensitive, rather shy, childlike, imaginative, dreamy. Needs a warm nest, a great deal of protection and security against the harsh realities of life. Likes to retreat into a world of dreams and fantasies. Pronounced sense of family. Childhood is often thought of as a paradise. Often a great wish to be allowed to always remain a child. Difficult detachment from the parents.

INNER MOTHER IMAGE: The good, caring, nourishing mother.

DIFFICULT LESSONS TO LEARN: To become independent and grown-up.

AS A MOTHER: *The mama.* The ideal mother: loving, devoted, protective, considerate, and warm-hearted. Loves children. A mother-hen who protects, takes care of, and tends her brood, who might not like it when her children become independent and adult. Has trouble letting go emotionally.

IMAGE OF THE WOMAN: *The dreamy individual.* The romantic woman. Gentle, tender, affectionate, adaptable, very motherly, loving, careful, hesitant, and very devoted in safe circumstances. Entertaining, but also sensitive. Subject to strong emotional fluctuations and moody.
SHADOW: *The mother-hen.*

STRENGTH: *The teller of fairy tales.* Imaginative, dreamy, romantic, and entertaining. A vibrant spiritual life that is expressed in dreams or other images. Deep spiritual sensitivity and empathy. Feelings change like the phases of the Moon. Strong need for love, attention, and the sense of being supported. Very good with children. Family-oriented and faithful.

PROBLEM AREA: *The moody woman.* Extreme mood fluctuations. A great demand for constant security makes her dependent or lacking in self-reliance, and prevents her from growing up. Affection and attention are often extorted with moodiness as a threat. Childish and easily insulted, with long periods of sulking. Kitschy.

KEY PRINCIPLE: I love being close to you.

STYLE OF LIVING: The nest, the fairy-tale castle.

☽♌	**Moon in Leo**	*The Classy Woman*

AS A CHILD: *The little queen.* The sunny, cheerful, beaming child, full of high spirits, carefree, and natural. Expresses feelings in a direct and clear manner. Needs much attention and admiration, always wants to be the first, and has difficulty accepting defeats. Easily hurt when she isn't "the biggest." The detachment from the parents causes no particular difficulties.

INNER MOTHER IMAGE: The magnificent, supremely confident mother.

DIFFICULT LESSONS TO LEARN: Tolerating justified criticism, modesty.

AS A MOTHER: *The generous individual.* Benevolent, hearty, natural, and very proud of her child. Likes to sun herself in the mirror of her own generosity. Supports her child through praise and encouragement. Conveys great self-reliance. Can let her child "go out into the world."

IMAGE OF THE WOMAN: *The elegant woman, the queen of drama.* Proud, demanding, and hungry for life. Is naturally at the center of attention. Spreads a warm atmosphere, optimism, joy of living, and brings momentum into everyday life. Enjoys being pampered. Can dramatically put herself into the limelight.
SHADOW: *The luxury-craving individual.*

STRENGTH: *The woman who loves life.* Catchy, life-affirming, optimistic basic attitude. Sunny disposition. Enjoys feeling like someone special. Loves luxury, pleasure, and grand gestures. Very proud. Considerable leaning toward showmanship with a great need of recognition.

PROBLEM AREA: *The prima donna.* Jealous, sensitive to criticism, overbearing, and a delicate sense of self-worth. Always high-strung in order not to miss anything in life. Tendency toward irate, impulsive, exaggerated reactions and overestimation of her own capabilities. Finds even her own weakness to be worth admiration.

KEY PRINCIPLE: Life is worth living.

STYLE OF LIVING: The villa or luxury apartment.

☽ ♍	**Moon in Virgo**	*The Sensible Person*

AS A CHILD: *The conscientious one.* Careful, critically observant, somewhat reserved, and smart. Would like to do everything right, be useful and helpful. Seeks recognition by helping others and conscientiously fulfilling assigned tasks. Tends to be reserved and self-denying. Clean.

INNER MOTHER IMAGE: The reliable, competent, diligent mother.

DIFFICULT LESSONS TO LEARN: Spontaneity, tolerance, magnanimity.

AS A MOTHER: *The competent mom.* Skillful, quick, conscientious, reasonable, in control, and clean. Very concerned with healthy food and healthy lifestyle. Teaches her child to be fit and master everyday tasks effortlessly. Sometimes too anxious.

IMAGE OF THE WOMAN: *The clever, diligent lady of the house.* Reliable, practical, understanding, sometimes a little aloof, severe, and reserved. Fear of chaos and chaotic feelings. Therefore has the tendency to put everything in order, carefully organize or analyze so that she can at least think everything is under control.
SHADOW: *The stickler.*

STRENGTH: *The orderly person.* Inner compulsion to live reasonably, healthfully, and rather modestly. Accepts what is necessary and willing to adapt. Tends to criticize others and self. Loves order, cleanliness, and hygiene. Great need for security. Exceptionally reliable.

PROBLEM AREA: *The hyper-perfectionist.* Exaggerated striving for order, perfection, health, combined with an addiction to criticism. Very intolerant. Blocked, withered feelings, sexual hang-ups, and a pigeonholing mentality.

KEY PRINCIPLE: Foresight is better than hindsight.

STYLE OF LIVING: The house built on ecological principles.

| ☽♎ | **Moon in Libra** | *The Esthete* |

AS A CHILD: *The ballerina.* The nice, sweet, smart, and charming child. The coquette. Starts flirting at an early age. Needs much attention and admiration. Very adaptable out of fear of discord and dread of being deserted. In extreme cases, there are difficulties in developing opinions and a consciousness of personal identity.

| INNER MOTHER IMAGE: The carefree, peaceable mother. | DIFFICULT LESSONS TO LEARN: Willingness to engage in conflict, decisiveness. |

AS A MOTHER: *The conciliatory person.* Mediating, always concerned with fairness. Strives for harmony and peace as the uppermost commandment in the family. Promotes the artistic capabilities in her child.

IMAGE OF THE WOMAN: *The graceful one.* Charming, friendly, sensitive, stylish, and diplomatic. Tends to have thin skin and is easily insulted. Enchanting, enticing, and great at flirting. Orients toward whoever he or she is involved with, but without opening up on a deep emotional level. Good companion.
SHADOW: *The noncommittal individual.*

STRENGTH: *The diplomat* Understands how to assert wishes with charm. Highly tasteful and esthetic sensibilities. Esthetic, artistic, and cultural interests. Needs to have a peaceful, refined, and stylish environment. Very partner-oriented. Seeks love, attention, sympathy, harmony, high spirits, and variety. Always ready to make a compromise. Has a talent for presenting himself or herself in the right light (fishing for compliments).

PROBLEM AREA: *The eternally indecisive person.* Emotionally unstable. Great fluctuations in the realm of the emotions. Unrealistic, addicted to relationships and harmony, and often incapable of making decisions for this reason. Too much concerned with the external form, style, or a good reputation.

| KEY PRINCIPLE: Always be quite friendly. | STYLE OF LIVING: The high-style apartment, the social meeting place. |

| ☽ ♏ | Moon in Scorpio | *The Sorceress* | Fall |

AS A CHILD: *The mysterious one.* Need for an intensive relationship with the mother. Seeks conflicts with, provokes, and wants to feel the mother with intensity. Sharp sense of the moods within the family and for the relationship between the parents. Early and strong attraction to anything forbidden, mysterious, all taboos, the subconscious world, and sexuality. That is often the challenge for the mother. There is an urge to explore. May deal with a state of rage that leads to destructiveness. Cutting the umbilical cord is a life-long task.

| INNER MOTHER IMAGE: Strong, fascinating, powerful mother, and/or the horrible, evil witch. | DIFFICULT LESSONS TO LEARN: Not to destroy every toy right away. |

AS A MOTHER: *The dark fairy.* Emotionally very bound and committed to her child. Wants to know everything about her child, and therefore leaves it no secrets. Can be challenging, but also annihilating. Tends to keep her child in a state of emotional dependency. When it comes to principles, she is ruthless and uncompromising.

IMAGE OF THE WOMAN: *The black Madonna.* The serpent woman, the spider woman, and the uncanny seductress. Emphasis on feelings. Fascinating, mysterious, thorough, and passionate. Able to totally charm others. Possessive, devouring, infamous, and irresistible.
SHADOW: *The wicked witch.*

STRENGTH: *The healer.* Strong instinctive nature combined with an almost eerie power to makes wishes come true. Can resist the temptation of power and use spiritual strength to heal. Overcoming of the self. Unflagging mobilization of new powers. Irresistibly attracted to all taboos.

PROBLEM AREA: *The power maniac.* Wants to conquer other souls and create dependencies. Extremely jealous, unforgiving, vengeful, reckless, and obsessed by power. Demands unconditional devotion from her partner. Often caught up in a depressive, melancholic mood. Overly secretive. Addicted to the feeling of control. Strong destructive powers that can even destroy what she actually loves. A shot of poison.

| KEY PRINCIPLE: I would love to know what's in or at the bottom of that. Or: Just don't let up. | STYLE OF LIVING: A bewitched magic castle or the home of Dracula. |

☽♐   Moon in Sagittarius   *The Noble-Minded Person*

AS A CHILD: *The good (pious) child.* Pronounced feeling of being special. Inner urge to be good: morally, spiritually, or in terms of achievements. Dislikes disappointing others. Longs to be loved, admired, and recognized. The mother cannot be narrow-minded. She must allow her child a great deal of space, support the child, provide new impulses, and show the way. Injustice is unbearable and difficult to overcome.

INNER MOTHER IMAGE: The ideal and/or the pious mother.

DIFFICULT LESSONS TO LEARN: Learning to lose and emotional sincerity.

AS A MOTHER: *The jovial woman.* Supportive, well-meaning, optimistic, and idealistic attitude toward the child. Can always arouse new optimism. Wants to be the ideal mother. However, major domestic responsibilities put a great strain on joy and enthusiasm.

IMAGE OF THE WOMAN: *The cosmopolite, the globe-trotter.* Humorous, impulsive, easy enthusiasm, an open mind,restless, and independent. Enjoys international contacts. Loves to be praised. Often concerned with religious questions or the meaning of life, sometimes a bit sanctimoniously. Sacrifices sensuality to dogmatic moral ideas.
SHADOW: *The arrogant individual.*

STRENGTH: *The enthusiast.* Bubbling, idealistic, enthusiastic feelings, grand gestures, high goals, and easily motivated. Freedom-loving. A traveler at home anywhere on the globe. Well-developed feeling for justice. High opinion of herself, but less prepared to hear criticism. Positive attitude toward life. Great need to make sense of things.

PROBLEM AREA: *The self-righteous person.* Exaggerated cultivation of the self, overbearing, arrogant, conceited, extremely sensitive to criticism. An unpleasant know-it-all. Condescending, unreliable, and inconsistent. Too good for almost everything.

KEY PRINCIPLE: The human being is noble, refined, and good.

STYLE OF LIVING: High ceilings, the top-floor apartment, the shrine.

| ☽ ♑ | Moon in Capricorn | *The Reliable Person* | Detriment |

AS A CHILD: *The little adult (or the serious child).* Zealous, well-behaved, serious, reserved, and able at an early age to take on tasks with a sense of responsibility. Draws self-security from this and the feeling of being valuable, loved, and needed. Rarely demands what he or she wants or needs. Can also be unbelievably willful, stubborn, and develop obstinate sides, especially when put on the spot. Not as childlike as other children. Affectionate, causing problems with detachment.

INNER MOTHER IMAGE: The conscientious, reliable, but also austere mother.

DIFFICULT LESSONS TO LEARN: Showing one's feelings and expressing one's own needs.

AS A MOTHER: *The strict mom.* The conscientious, down-to-earth, caring, rather conventional mother, who offers her child a solid framework and clear structures. Hard-working, reliable, responsible. Tends to forget the childish, playful element.

IMAGE OF THE WOMAN: *The reserved individual.* Affection, feelings, and emotions are dosed, held back, and controlled. They cannot flow spontaneously. The fear of injury means this person is slow in warming up to others. Deep inside he or she remains closed to self and others for a long time, even forever. The reliable, strong woman who offers support and security. Very hard-working.
SHADOW: *The embittered person.*

STRENGTH: *The uncomplicated woman.* Serious basic feelings. Inner urge to take on responsibilities, to be there for someone else, to support and offer a safe space and security. Eager, conscientious, ready to achieve, self-controlled, and modest. Basically happy with self. Finds refuge in work in times of crisis. Dignified modesty and independence even at an advanced age. Likes clear, severe, and simple forms. Holds back on emotional issues.

PROBLEM AREA: *The responsibility addict.* Takes on far too many tasks and responsibilities, causing frequent pressure. Tends to be envious and have guilt feelings. Constant fear of being rejected and unloved. Distrusting, pessimistic, and lacking in feelings.

KEY PRINCIPLE: Every individual is alone.

STYLE OF LIVING: Zen style.

☽ ≈   Moon in Aquarius   *The Individualist*

AS A CHILD: *The little prince or princess.* Flees the nest and makes his or her own way in the world at an early age. Feels a stranger in the world, but also as something very special. Cannot stand being compared to someone else. Often feels he or she does not belong to the family (or to the world). No problem with detachment.

INNER MOTHER IMAGE: The (overly) independent, unreliable mother.

DIFFICULT LESSONS TO LEARN: To be normal, to adapt, to get emotionally involved.

AS A MOTHER: *The freedom-lover.* Constant conflict between the duties of a mother and the claim to freedom and self-development. Gives the child (too) much space. Sees her child as a good conversation or discussion partner. Brings her child up to be independent at an early age.

IMAGE OF THE WOMAN: *The cool lady.* Always needs contact, inspiration, and activity. Loves freedom in a big way, always out for independence. More a companion than a lover. Ultimately aloof and spiritually inaccessible. Separates easily.
SHADOW: *The loner.*

STRENGTH: *The independent person.* Original, creative, and self-sufficient. Gives the feeling he or she doesn't really need anyone. Too much closeness seems oppressive. Can only be in a place where all doors and windows are wide open. Only acts on own free will. When put on the spot, or under pressure, this person rebels. Likes floating on higher planes and basically disdains getting involved with this world. Loves to experiment.

PROBLEM AREA: *The contract-breaker.* Restless, fickle, and explosive temperament. Always takes the liberty to unilaterally revoke an agreement. Superficial, lonely, without any warm, protective, and emotional contacts. Feels at home nowhere, is constantly on the road. A victim of own compulsive idea of freedom.

KEY PRINCIPLE: Gotta go!

STYLE OF LIVING: A loft, utopia, cloudland.

| ☽♓ | **Moon in Pisces** | *The Medium* |

AS A CHILD: *The anxious or shy child.* Dreamy, full of fantasy, creative, and affectionate. Very sensitive, therefore inclined to poor health. Would like to get rid of the border separating mother and child. Senses clearly what is going on in others. Has trouble finding own standpoint. Learns late how to say "I."

INNER MOTHER IMAGE: The highly sensitive, self-sacrificing mother.

DIFFICULT LESSONS TO LEARN: Establishing limits, cutting the umbilical cord, standing on one's own two feet.

AS A MOTHER: *The self-sacrificer.* Gentle, protective, and tolerant. Senses very clearly what her child needs and makes sacrifices to fulfill those needs. Cannot establish limits and easily becomes a martyr who accepts everything with patience. Subtly maintains a grip on her child. Conveys guilt feelings.

IMAGE OF THE WOMAN: *The nymph.* Particularly empathetic. Unfathomable, thin-skinned, and sensitive. Senses the hidden wishes and abilities in others. Is sometimes a little ephemeral. Easily seduced. Tends to become a victim or fall into dependency.
SHADOW: *The shaky individual.*

STRENGTH: *The mysterious person.* Very devoted, with a longing to merge with the partner. Instinctive urge for transcendental experiences. Limitless empathy. Longs for redemption. Medial, profound, sensitive, intuitive, imaginative, adaptable, subjective, and forgiving.

PROBLEM AREA: *The helpless one.* Inclined to play the victim's role, become involved in tragic entanglements, and be helplessly open. Cannot establish limits. Tendency to flee from reality and to go to seed. Moody, unstable, melancholic, unsteady, and easily seduced. Problems with addiction.

KEY PRINCIPLE: Only those who are familiar with longing know what I suffer.

STYLE OF LIVING: An old house by the sea.

☿♈   Mercury in Aries   *The Argumentative Type*

STRENGTH: *Snappy thinking.* Subjective and combative thinking, loves discussions. Gives an opinion spontaneously, articulately, openly, honestly, directly, in a committed fashion, and with sarcasm. Willful thinking process.

PROBLEM AREA: *Arbitrary thinking.* Impatient thinker, quarrelsome, inclined to being opinionated. Exaggerates and delivers verbal knock-out punches. Quick but often rash judgments. Loud argumentation. Always thinks of self first.

NARRATIVE STYLE:	MAKES DECISIONS:	BETWEEN: I want this
Exciting, adventurous.	Spontaneously.	and I don't want that.

☿♉   Mercury in Taurus   *The Patient Listener*

STRENGTH: *Down-to-earth thinking.* Healthy common sense. Deliberate, sometimes slow, but thorough, logical, and persevering perceptive faculty. Realistically, materialistically, and sensually oriented. Practical rather than abstract intelligence. Thinks in tried and true lines and concepts. Avoids versatility, preferring to build on a single foundation.

PROBLEM AREA: *Simplistic thinking.* Narrow-minded, dogmatic, stubborn, immovable, inflexible, incorrigibly rigid, and conservative. Suspicious of all theories and new ideas.

NARRATIVE STYLE:	MAKES DECISIONS:	BETWEEN:
Relaxed, sensual.	Deliberately, but irrevocably.	Valuable and worthless (financially).

☿♊   **Mercury in Gemini**   *The Quick Thinker*   Dignity

STRENGTH: *Discriminating thinking.* A master of argument and counterattack. Loves punch lines and puns, discriminating thinking, and deliberation. Developed talent as a negotiator and mediator. Enjoys discussions with self. Multifaceted, curious, and nimble. Intellectually and rhetorically versatile, humorous, sharp, articulate, and brilliant. Often intellectual.

PROBLEM AREA: *Superficial thinking.* Inclined toward hasty, rash conclusions. Pseudo-intellectual. Phony, underhanded, cheating, distracted, and talkative.

NARRATIVE STYLE: Humorous, ironic, brilliant.	MAKES DECISIONS: Quickly.	BETWEEN: Clever and stupid.

☿♋   **Mercury in Cancer**   *The Poet*

STRENGTH: *Imaginative thinking.* Expressiveness that is full of feeling, flowery, and rich in images. A good storyteller and poet. Empathetic, and with a talent to sense correlations and the thoughts of others. Good memory. Thinks for the benefit of others.

PROBLEM AREA: *Wishful thinking.* Desires and longings transform perception and memory into a "comfortable" truth. Easily influenced, sensitive, moody, and inconsistent thinking. Arbitrary use of words.

NARRATIVE STYLE: Fairytale-like, imaginative.	MAKES DECISIONS: Carefully, emotionally.	BETWEEN: Pleasant and unpleasant.

☿

☿♌   Mercury in Leo   *The Official Speaker*

STRENGTH: *Self-confident thinking.* Likes to think and plan on a large scale, prefers to leave the details to others (which is a good idea). Vivid and graphic in terms of expression. Knows how to motivate others for ideas. Creative, strongly expressive, convincing, optimistic, and circumspect. Good organizational talent.

PROBLEM AREA: *Self-complacent thinking.* Overbearing, without an eye for the details. Allergic to any type of criticism. Uncomprehending, presumptuous attitude of infallibility, and false sense of intellectual superiority. All thoughts are too self-centered. Theatrical, sometimes vociferous and terribly complicated manner. Speculative, highly subjective thinking.

NARRATIVE STYLE:	MAKES DECISIONS:	BETWEEN:
Strongly expressive, graphic, dramatic.	With supreme confidence (infallible).	Wonderful and dull.

☿♍ Mercury in Virgo   *The Precise Person*   Dignity & Exaltation

STRENGTH: *Methodic thinking.* Analytical understanding that realistically, instinctively, and incorruptibly decides between what is practical and impractical, useful and useless, purposeful and a waste of time. Clear, concise, sober, methodical, and smart. Loves dealing fastidiously with details. Very precise written and oral expression. Businesslike and scientific thinking.

PROBLEM AREA: *Categorical thinking.* Attention to detail causes loss of oversight. Parochial, timorous, narrow-mindedness wrapped in prejudice. Opportunistic, nagging, envious, dissatisfied, and inclined to constant criticism.

NARRATIVE STYLE:	MAKES DECISIONS:	BETWEEN:
From spicy to dry.	With a sober attitude.	Useful and useless.

☿♎   Mercury in Libra   *The Diplomat*

STRENGTH: *Esthetic thinking.* Balanced thinking aimed at harmony. Loves complex, but developed and balanced thought constructions and strategies. Elegant rhetorical style. Plays with words. Friendly, charming, and diplomatic means of expression. Even criticism never sounds insulting.

PROBLEM AREA: *Fickle thinking* Hesitant, difficult decision-making. Fear of conflict leads to opportunistic accommodation to others' opinions. Holier-than-thou, unrealistic theorizing.

NARRATIVE STYLE:	MAKES DECISIONS:	BETWEEN:
Elegant, charming, conversational, with a sense of style.	Hesitantly.	Balanced and imbalanced.

☿♏   Mercury in Scorpio   *The Revealer*

STRENGTH: *Thorough thinking.* Sharp mind, decisive, persistent, and ambitious. Questions everything down to the last detail, likes to reveal mysteries, and is always curious to get to the bottom of taboos and prohibitions. Mercilessly open, passionate, and—if need be—injurious language. But can also be very quiet.

PROBLEM AREA: *Obsessive thinking.* Pessimistic, distrusting, and fanatically caught up in fixed ideas. Sharp, cynical, cutting, insulting expression, and provocative pinpricks. Underhanded and poisonous. Likes intrigues and exaggerated mystification. Sniffs around in the private life of others. Overwhelms listeners with long-windedness.

NARRATIVE STYLE:	MAKES DECISIONS:	BETWEEN:
Suspenseful, mysterious, in whispers.	Reliably and absolutely.	Extremes (everything or nothing).

☿♐   Mercury in Sagittarius   *The Convincer*   Detriment

STRENGTH: *Candid thinking.* Cosmopolitan, open, and with a wide range of interests. Seeks ideals, strong (religious) convictions, and further education. Great power to believe and convince. Strong optimism that can build up others and restore their faith. Articulate.

PROBLEM AREA: *Arrogant thinking.* Gullible, arrogantly conceited, and with a missionary know-it-all attitude. Superficial, uncritical, self-complacent, and dogmatic. Sentimental, condescending style of expression. Hypocritical moralist.

NARRATIVE STYLE: Epic, rousing, sermonizing.	MAKES DECISIONS: In a self-assured fashion.	BETWEEN: Valuable and worthless (ideals), fair and unfair.

☿♑   Mercury in Capricorn   *The Straightforward Individual*

STRENGTH: *Logical thinking.* Persistent, sober, strictly methodical thinking, with a great deal of concentration and perseverance. Incorruptibly sharp, always keeps the essentials in mind, even with the most complex thought processes. Very realistic, serious, and without delusions. Precise in written and spoken word. Fine rhetorician.

PROBLEM AREA: *Narrow-minded thinking.* Unimaginative, bone-dry, inflexible, humorless, hard, cold, and monosyllabic. Thinks in norms and empty forms. A pessimist who always says no. Monotonous.

NARRATIVE STYLE: Dry and vigorous.	MAKES DECISIONS: In a no-nonsense way.	BETWEEN: Correct and wrong.

☿≈   **Mercury in Aquarius**   *The Imaginative Person*

STRENGTH: *Creative thinking.* Thirsty for knowledge, progressive, open to whatever is new and original, open-minded and objective. An excellent abstract thinker, with the ability to synthesize intellectually. Bursting with ideas, and very inventive. Excellent spontaneous thoughts and flashes of brilliance. Tolerant thinker, with a liberal and humanitarian attitude. Pronounced intuition.

PROBLEM AREA: *Smart-alecky thinking.* Overly intellectual, lost in an abstract labyrinth of thought, erratic, distracted, arrogant, and illusory. An obnoxious know-it-all.

NARRATIVE STYLE: Light and original.	MAKES DECISIONS: On the basis of theory.	BETWEEN: New and old-fashioned.

☿♓   **Mercury in Pisces**   *The Emotional Thinker*   Detriment & Fall

STRENGTH: *Intuitive thinking.* Lively fantasy and accurate, intuitive ideas. First-class ability to empathize. Can guess very well. Expresses in images. Good sense of correlations and meaning. Telepathic disposition.

PROBLEM AREAS: *Illusory thinking.* The mind is flooded with fantasies. Easily influenced, uncritical, over-sensitive, dishonest, and quirky.

NARRATIVE STYLE: Imaginative, "tells yarns."	MAKES DECISIONS: Intuitively.	BETWEEN: What feels right and what's fishy.

☿

♀♈	**Venus in Aries**	*Love at First Sight*	Detriment

STRENGTH: *The love affair.* Strong projection of the self, great ability for enthusiasm, and hefty—sometimes short-lived—passion. Attraction is expressed spontaneously, directly, and impulsively.

PROBLEM AREA: *Egotistic love.* Incapable of developing bonds, extremely self-centered, and cannot give of self. Demanding love.

IMAGE OF THE YOUNG WOMAN: *The direct individual, the tough girl.*
Courageous, strong, impulsive, self-assured, and honest. A lively, adventurous woman who would rather (or more quickly) seduce than be seduced, and with whom one can go through hell and high water.
SHADOW: *The radical feminist.*

EROTICISM: Demanding, loves touch and go situations,	STYLE OF ART: Action painting, happenings.

♀♉	**Venus in Taurus**	*Intimate Love*	Dignity

STRENGTH: *Sensual love.* Natural sensuality, strong capacity for devotion, capable of enjoyment, content, attractive, and faithful. Loves sensual, physical closeness. Artistic potential. Likes to work with natural materials, art, and restoration.

PROBLEM AREA: *Monopolizing love.* Possessive and jealous. Seeks pleasure and enjoyment. Exaggerated need for security in love.

IMAGE OF THE YOUNG WOMAN: *The milkmaid.* The feminine, very erotic woman who is close to nature and shows strongly physical emphasis. She seeks a solid bond in a relationship.
SHADOW: *The indolent woman.*

EROTICISM: Sensual and warm.	STYLE OF ART: Baroque.

| ♀♊ | **Venus in Gemini** | *Playful Sensuality* |

STRENGTH: *Happy-go-lucky love.* Charming, entertaining, sociable, but with no claim to durability. Multifaceted contacts and friendships. Loves flirting. Reflects carefully on matters of the heart.

PROBLEM AREA: *Fickle love.* A dazzling butterfly, capricious, unreliable, calculating, dislikes making a commitment, and suppresses feelings.

IMAGE OF THE YOUNG WOMAN: *The cool lady, the talkative one.* A modern, intelligent woman, smart, well-read, and capable. Multifaceted. Enjoys being in love now and again, but ultimately aloof and inaccessible in the depths of her heart.
SHADOW: *The icicle.*

EROTICISM: Slightly animated, yet always on the cool side. Likes change.

STYLE OF ART: Art Nouveau.

♀

| ♀♋ | **Venus in Cancer** | *Complete Love* |

STRENGTH: *Romantic love.* Dreamy, full of longing, very impressionable. Profound desire for harmony, unification, and spiritual and physical exchange.

PROBLEM AREA: *Delusional love.* Forever in love with Prince Charming or the Dream Woman. Therefore always the victim of own delusions. Illusory, indiscriminate, unpredictable, and depressed as a result of countless disappointments.

IMAGE OF THE YOUNG WOMAN: *The cuddly kitten.* The empathetic, tender, romantic woman, looking for and capable of providing a warm nest, with strong feelings and devotion.
SHADOW: *The eternal daughter.*

EROTICISM: Gentle and cuddly, very passionate in a safe place.

STYLE OF ART: Romanticism.

♀♌	**Venus in Leo**	*Lively Desire and Passion*

STRENGTH: *Magnificent love.* Loves the kind of love one can be proud of. Intense love of life. Warmhearted, generous, self-confident, and very erotic. The endless game of love. Artistic talent.

PROBLEM AREA: *Superficial love.* Artificial, fake feelings, demonstrated for the sake of effect. Can be very costly.

IMAGE OF THE YOUNG WOMAN: *The star, the lady of luxury.* The zestful, self-confident, proud, extravagant woman who likes to be put on display, pampered, and admired. Also, the superb artist.
SHADOW: *The playgirl.*

EROTICISM: A combination of pride, passion, and feline agility.

STYLE OF ART: High Renaissance.

♀♍	**Venus in Virgo**	*Shy Sensuality*	Fall

STRENGTH: *Practical love.* Expresses her love best with practical gestures, such as cooking or a massage. Reliable, faithful, modest, and very helpful.

PROBLEM AREA: *Love for a purpose.* Calculating feelings, fake adaptability, prim, standoffish, dull, overly critical, and austere. Inhibited feelings of shame; prudish and dry.

IMAGE OF THE YOUNG WOMAN: *The pure woman.* The decent, responsible, disciplined, reliable, and competent woman who likes to do her part.
SHADOW: *The prude.*

EROTICISM: On the considerate and reserved side. Thaws rather slowly.

STYLE OF ART: Biedermeier.

♀︎♎︎	Venus in Libra	*Harmonious Love*	Dignity

STRENGTH: *Egalitarian love.* Loves loving and flirting. Seeks contact with an equal partner. Very intent upon harmony, proper style, and good manners. Great love of art.

PROBLEM AREA: *Non-committal love.* Always undecided and generally superficial. Emotionally remote and inaccessible.

IMAGE OF THE YOUNG WOMAN: *The angel.* The charming, feminine, elegant, cultivated woman, sociable, well groomed, and very interested in art and culture. A classic beauty, alluring, but always a bit cool and distant.
SHADOW: *The doll.*

EROTICISM: Charming attraction. Playful, graceful eroticism.

STYLE OF ART: Classicism.

♀︎♏︎ Venus in Scorpio	*The Uncanny Powers of Seduction*	Detriment

STRENGTH: *Deep passion.* Pronounced power of fascination, highly emotional, passionate, very intense, sensual, free of taboos, and unforgettable. Loves the thrill of the morbid and uncanny beauty. Love spell.

PROBLEM AREA: *Passionate entanglements.* Mentally cruel and sadistic. Creates emotional or sexual addiction. Likes to manipulate. Obsessed with sex, perverted.

IMAGE OF THE YOUNG WOMAN: *Circe.* The dark, irresistible, sexually attractive woman, intense, passionate, and seductive. Sin incarnate.
SHADOW: *The poisonous snake.*

EROTICISM: Irresistible temptation, unfathomable passion.

STYLE OF ART:
Surrealism.

♀

♀♐   Venus in Sagittarius   *Flaming Love*

STRENGTH: *Holy love.* A particularly honorable and idealistic concept of love. Upright and direct. Inclined toward international or exotic relationships.

PROBLEM AREA: *Phony love.* Inconstant in her feelings and fickle in relationships. Tendency to flee. Illusionary affairs. Uninhibited and foolhardy.

IMAGE OF THE YOUNG WOMAN: *The noblewoman.* The optimistic, independent, and proud woman, who knows in the depths of her heart that she will always remain single. Elegant, sincere, and educated.
SHADOW: *The hypocrite.*

EROTICISM: Easily kindled. Exotic.

STYLE OF ART: International Gothic.

♀♑   Venus in Capricorn   *Profound, Serious Love*

STRENGTH: *Enduring love.* Love is never a game but always and immediately serious. Hardly flirts, is reserved, careful, and warms up rather slowly but then lastingly. Reliable, responsible, and faithful.

PROBLEM AREA: *Hardened love.* Loaded with complexes, inhibited, morose, and cold. Considerable age differences in relationships. Love grown cold and relationships that continue in form only. Will even dispense with love.

IMAGE OF THE YOUNG WOMAN: *The dutiful woman, the controlled individual.* The responsible, consistent, and reliable individual, offering support and security. Always keeps a cool head and never loses control. Serious, tends to be uncomplicated, and sometimes austere.
SHADOW: *The reserved person.*

EROTICISM: Strong sexual energies, which can nevertheless be controlled without difficulty during long periods of ascetic abstention.

STYLE OF ART: Romanesque, Zen art.

♀≈	Venus in Aquarius	*Companionable Love*

STRENGTH: *Unconventional love.* Free, original, and independent love. Is faithful of her own free will but cannot be forced into anything. Needs the liberty to leave or stay whenever she wants. Values fairness and equal rights in a relationship.

PROBLEM AREA: *Love without passion.* Changes superficial relationships quickly and often. Indifferent and lacking in feelings. Eccentric and totally unreliable.

IMAGE OF THE YOUNG WOMAN: *The companion.* The interesting, unconventional, and independent woman. Can be faithful to the "right" partner. A better friend, companion, and comrade than lover.
SHADOW: *The cold woman.*

EROTICISM: Aloof, little charisma, but enjoys experimenting.

STYLE OF ART: Constructivism, as well as everything modern and abstract.

♀

♀♓	Venus in Pisces	*Boundless, Divine Love* Exaltation

STRENGTH: *All-embracing love.* Endless devotion, selfless, helpful, tender, affectionate, sensitive, and self-sacrificing. Longing for what is fathomless.

PROBLEM AREA: *Disappointed love.* Loses herself in wishful thinking and illusions. Has difficulty setting borders, Easily exploited, always a victim. Melancholic and plaintive.

IMAGE OF THE YOUNG WOMAN: *The nymph.* Seducible, devoted, loving, mysterious woman and muse who senses the hidden talents of her partner and loves them out into the open.
SHADOW: *The woman lost in dreams.*

EROTICISM: Mysterious, seductive, and unifying.

STYLE OF ART: Early Gothic.

♂♈	Mars in Aries	*The Fighter*	Dignity

STRENGTH: *Impulsivity.* Spontaneous energy, courage, and well-developed spirit of enterprise. Heads straight for the goal. Can ram his head through the wall. Pronounced sense of competition. Subjective standpoint influences the process of negotiation.

PROBLEM AREA: *Belligerence.* Takes either/or stance. Compelled to demonstrate his (sexual) potency. Arbitrary, arrogant, egotistical, and reckless. Easily excitable. Acts on the basis of excessive impatience.

IMAGE OF THE YOUNG MAN: *The hothead.* The energetic, wild, hot-blooded lover. Active, self-confident, and roguish. A hunter, hero, and conqueror. An adventurer, macho, or ruffian. Direct, spontaneous, hefty, and quickly aroused. Ready for an affair in even the most impossible situations.
SHADOW: *The brute.*

RESOLUTION: Spontaneous, pronounced willpower when it comes to following a momentary impulse, but not necessarily enduring. Many flashes in the pan.

AGGRESSION: Always unreflecting, spontaneous, self-evident.

OUTLETS FOR AGGRESSION: Boxing, soccer (offense), rifle practice, fast driving.

WAY OF FIGHTING: The daredevil—direct, aggressive, barbaric, impulsive, but short-lived.

SEXUALITY: Spontaneous, conquering, hot-blooded, quick, intense, egotistic, sometimes like a competition.

| ♂♉︎ | **Mars in Taurus** | *The Defender* | Detriment |

STRENGTH: *The diesel engine.* Warms up slowly. Once this person gets going, he or she runs a long time. Sufficient (financial) incentive keeps this individual persevering at work with great diligence. Is in top form when it comes to resisting or defending something.

PROBLEM AREA: *The time-bomb.* Considerable pent-up aggression that builds up over a long period and can become increased by sexual frustration. An explosion (caused by a red cloth) can result in devastation.

IMAGE OF THE YOUNG MAN: *The lord of the manor.* The solid, strong, and sensual person who offers material security. The epicure and provider, gentle lover and protector.
SHADOW: *The bottomless barrel.*

RESOLUTION: Slow, deliberate, and irreversible. Endless stamina. Stubborn.

AGGRESSION: Slow build-up of aggression, the discharge is then violent, frequently emotional.

OUTLETS FOR AGGRESSION: Wherever something gets soundly hit: tennis, squash, drumming, chopping wood, or beating carpets. Playing soccer as a goalkeeper or in defensive position.

WAY OF FIGHTING: Defensive but emphatic, stubborn and with full weight. Staunch defiance. Increases pressure a little each day. Cannot be subdued. Tough as nails.

SEXUALITY: Strong sexual energy, very sensual, and possessive. Relaxed at the start, very passionate thereafter. Very unforgiving if frustrated.

♂♊   **Mars in Gemini**   *The Critic*

STRENGTH: *Smartness.* Sharp-tongued, articulate, clever, facile, quick, and agile. Can pursue many aims simultaneously. A keen tactician.

PROBLEM AREA: *Distraction.* Tendency to go off on too many tangents. Cynical, sarcastic, with no resilience. Ice-cold. Much ado about nothing.

IMAGE OF THE YOUNG MAN: *The eloquent speaker.* The charming but often flighty lover. The rogue and the flatterer. Bright, entertaining, lively, smart, creative, but emotionally unreliable. The eternal adolescent.
SHADOW: *The windbag.*

RESOLUTION: Quick, smart, and skillful. All aims are made relative and adjusted to suit new ideas. Intentions are often left hanging in mid-air.

AGGRESSION: Easily aroused, but with no staying power. Generally expressed verbally.

OUTLETS FOR AGGRESSION: Quick and lively types of sports such as sprinting, squash, but also fencing and chess.

WAY OF FIGHTING: Talks the other person to death. Skillful tactician, very agile, articulate, cynical, and ice cold. Biting ridicule and profoundly injurious malice. First confuses with a hail of words, and then delivers the KO punch.

SEXUALITY: Not very impulsive, interest is more theoretical. Verbal eroticism. Likes diversity and experimentation. Seeks "refined" eroticism.

| ♂♋ | **Mars in Cancer** | *The Emotional Individual.* | Fall |

STRENGTH: *Indirect action.* Imaginative and creative. Pursues interests independently and ambitiously, but not directly. Vacillating, changing moods and goals.

PROBLEM AREA: *Sulking.* Highly sensitive, moody, and easily insulted. Tortures himself or herself. Wishes rather than acts. Is capable of dragging others into his or her guilt or pain.

IMAGE OF THE YOUNG MAN: *The admirer, the poet.* The sensitive, imaginative, and dreamy lover. Ideal image of the gentle, romantic, caring, emotional, and devoted man.
SHADOW: *The moody man.*

♂

RESOLUTION: Emotional, yet generally stemming from an inclination or a mood. Uses lots of inconsequential detours.

AGGRESSION: Indirect. Little ability to express aggression outright. At first pretends to adapt but with subliminal reproaches that lead to extremely agitated feelings.

OUTLETS FOR AGGRESSION: Dancing, enjoying and making music. Doing handicrafts or working at a hobby.

WAY OF FIGHTING: Accuses. Gives others a bad conscience. Emotional pressure through bad mood, sulking, and acting insulted.

SEXUALITY: Shy at first. Develops great devotion, emotion, and fantasy in a familiar situation.

♂♌	**Mars in Leo**	*The Optimist*

STRENGTH: *Superior style.* Optimistic, self-confident, and imperial manner with grand gestures. Life-affirming and spirited when carrying out plans.

PROBLEM AREA: *The lord and master.* Egoistic, presumptuous, and arrogant behavior. Choleric and theatrical. Extremely sensitive to criticism.

IMAGE OF THE YOUNG MAN: *The victor, the star.* The carefree, self-confident, and magnificent lover. Vital, generous, optimistic, and full of a lust for life. Sunnyboy or playboy.
SHADOW: *The domineering stag.*

RESOLUTION: Self-confident and self-assured. Would like to achieve plans in the least complicated and most lasting manner possible, with a direct approach in the long run and showing a great deal of style.

AGGRESSION: Can become irritated, particularly through criticism. Tensions are reduced quickly and easily.

OUTLETS FOR AGGRESSION: Driving a car, elite types of sports.

WAY OF FIGHTING: Direct and certain of victory. Loud, dramatic scenes. Barking at the other person and "beating" him through dignity and might.

SEXUALITY: Self-confident, with a strong sex drive and desire. Sometimes also performance-oriented.

| ♂♍ | **Mars in Virgo** | *The Energy-Saver* |

STRENGTH: *The right dosage.* Methodical, critically careful, and above all precise approach. Optimal expenditure of energy and means to reach a goal. Loves details and fastidious precision. Avoids everything that's damaging, above all the useless expenditure of energy.

PROBLEM AREA: *The fussy fool.* Pedantic, overscrupulous, too critical, dull, and apathetic. Slave of a fearful routine.

IMAGE OF THE YOUNG MAN: *The skilled worker.* The reliable, clean lover. Diligent, caring, faithful, dependable, and controlled. Has a practical disposition.
SHADOW: *The perfect bore.*

RESOLUTION: After critical examination, skillful, steadfast, precise, very economical, and enduring.

AGGRESSION: Very controlled, rarely "blows a fuse."

OUTLETS FOR AGGRESSION: Jogging, handicrafts, cleaning, fitness training.

WAY OF FIGHTING: Sharp or incisive criticism, obstinate nagging, and blatant catechizing. Nerve-wracking pedantry (the bureaucrat's approach to nastiness).

SEXUALITY: Medium-strong sensuality, but well-controlled. More clean than passionate. Sometimes on the prudish side.

♂♎	**Mars in Libra**	*The Diplomat*	Detriment

STRENGTH: *The chess-player.* Uses charm and friendliness to achieve goals. A clever strategist who always considers the other person's move. Perfect on the theoretical end, but somewhat wanting in practice.

PROBLEM AREA: *The appeaser.* Lack of willingness to engage in conflict leads to indecision and compromise. Problems with aggression. Plans often do not progress beyond that stage.

IMAGE OF THE YOUNG MAN: The charming, elegant, and stylish lover. The respectable, considerate, neat, gallant seducer with class.
SHADOW: *The halfhearted individual.*

RESOLUTION: Makes decisions for others rather than self. Decides very hesitantly, and usually in theory only. In addition, it's easy to change his or her mind.

AGGRESSION: Avoids aggressive discussions. On the other hand, is always ready to compromise.

OUTLETS FOR AGGRESSION: Dancing, fencing.

WAY OF FIGHTING: With style. Never direct or unbuttoned. Makes the effort to remain fair and avoid hurting his or her opposite. When the "fuse blows," ice-cold and rejecting.

SEXUALITY: Partner-oriented, sensitive, not very impulsive, but cultivated, elegant, refined, and with style.

♂♏︎	Mars in Scorpio	*The Passionate Man*	Dignity

STRENGTH: *The effective person.* Can mobilize great amounts of spiritual power to achieve envisioned goals. Ambitious, persevering, consistent, and extremely single-minded. Very tough stamina.

PROBLEM AREA: *The destroyer.* Strives to develop personal power by skillful, and sometimes reckless, exploitation of others. Inclined toward manipulation and blackmail. Can become completely obsessed with a specific plan. Destructive drive that is sometimes self-destructive.

IMAGE OF THE YOUNG MAN: *The irresistible individual, the black knight.* The passionate, dark and mysterious, unfathomable, erotic lover and hunter—charismatic, intense, fascinating, but also dangerous. The man one falls for hook, line, and sinker, who takes possession of the soul and creates an addiction.
SHADOW: *The sadist, the hangman.*

RESOLUTION: Spiritually important decisions are made emotionally. They are reliable and lasting, sometimes extreme.

AGGRESSION: Subtle, accurate, unforgiving, profoundly injurious. Explosive in an emotional situation. Throws poisoned darts.

OUTLETS FOR AGGRESSION: Knife-throwing, archery, deep-sea diving, fishing with a harpoon, sex.

WAY OF FIGHTING: Dangerous, very effective, but mean, nasty, and underhanded. The poisoned needle that constantly pricks and spreads bad blood.

SEXUALITY: Strong sexual impulse. Very passionate and without taboos.

♂♐   **Mars in Sagittarius**   *The Noble-Minded Person*

STRENGTH: *Enthusiasm.* Great enthusiasm and a buoyant manner when it comes to achieving goals. Can motivate and sweep others along as well. Impulse to travel.

PROBLEM AREA: *The crusader.* Militant and missionary tendencies. Inclined toward exaggeration and overestimating self.

IMAGE OF THE YOUNG MAN: *The noble knight.* The grand, full-fledged lover. The cultivated man of the world. The respectable man you can "be seen with," for whom love and sexuality are something special, perhaps even sacred.
SHADOW: *The arrogant jackass.*

RESOLUTION: Decisions are made spontaneously. If they deal with superior convictions, sacred feelings, or a righteous issue, they cannot be changed.

AGGRESSION: Grows out of a sacred anger or hurt sense of justice.

OUTLETS FOR AGGRESSION: Hunting, riding, golf.

WAY OF FIGHTING: Holy anger. Disarms, makes derogatory judgments about, or morally annihilates the opposition.

SEXUALITY: Spontaneously aroused desire. With noble, virtuous, or sometimes immoderate tendencies.

| ♂ ♑ | **Mars in Capricorn** | *The Marathon Runner* Exaltation |

STRENGTH: *Perseverance.* Concentrated energy that grows when resisted. Uncompromising, reliable, patient, disciplined, and persistent. Obstinate and unbending when pursuing a set goal. Life force that resiliently renews itself.

PROBLEM AREA: *Hardening.* Merciless, reckless use of strength. Can also be rigid, inhibited, or hung-up. Cannot be persuaded.

IMAGE OF THE YOUNG MAN: *The unbending person.* The reliable (sexually) powerful lover. The responsible, persistent, faithful, and fatherly man, who provides a strong shoulder.
SHADOW: *The grump.*

RESOLUTION: Decisions are made carefully and thoughtfully. Then they are irrevocable and carried out even in the face of massive opposition.

AGGRESSION: Under control, sometimes in forced manner, difficult to arouse, but can then be very strong, cold, unforgiving, and irreconcilable.

OUTLETS FOR AGGRESSION: Trekking, mountain climbing, marathon running, cross-country skiing, ice hockey, survival training.

WAY OF FIGHTING: Always has more breath to spare and greater stamina. Cold anger can be mercilessly annihilating.

SEXUALITY: The long-distance runner. Very strong sexuality, which can nevertheless be easily controlled in periods of abstinence. Here, too, inclined to engage in "marathons" and performance thinking.

♂

♂ ≈   **Mars in Aquarius**   *The Willful Individual*

STRENGTH: *The urge to discover.* Unusual, eccentric approach to pursuing a goal. Sometimes purely theoretical and abstract, without any thought on practical matters. Willful, independent, and unconventional.

PROBLEM AREA: *The shadowboxer.* Crazy, revolutionary, unpredictable, with an ice-cold approach. Uncompromising. Forces opinions onto others.

IMAGE OF THE YOUNG MAN: *The individualist.* The ingenious, creative, independent man, more comrade than lover. Intellectual, imaginative, crazy, and hardly able to commit to relationships.
SHADOW: *The lone wolf.*

RESOLUTION: Makes binding decisions in theory, but sometimes not related to practice. Little urge to turn decisions into actions.

AGGRESSION: Is not easily provoked. Tensions that do arise disappear quickly.

OUTLETS FOR AGGRESSION: Parasailing, kite-flying, parachuting.

WAY OF FIGHTING: Well-considered, unusual, strategically clever, and cold. Looks down on opponents.

SEXUALITY: Little impulse, more theoretical interest. Likes to experiment. Loves sex outside the norm.

♂︎♓︎ **Mars in Pisces**	*Fights for Peace*

STRENGTH: *The spiritual warrior (Samurai).* Unusual, intuitive accuracy. Powerful spiritual forces lead—unpredictable when seen from the outside—to the achievement of higher, greater goals. Wins through apparent yielding.

PROBLEM AREA: *Misfire.* Very fluctuating, unpredictable energies that often burn out with no effect. Extremely sensitive to pain. Very dependent on moods.

IMAGE OF THE YOUNG MAN: *The dreamer.* The sensitive, mysterious, devoted lover who gives wings to fantasies. The charming man with a thousand faces, capable of slipping into any desired role.
SHADOW: *The bamboozler.*

RESOLUTION: Dependent on mood. Decides intuitively. Acts on instinct without pressure based on deep inclination.

AGGRESSION: Frequently only seen indirectly—but vehemently when under the influence of alcohol.

OUTLETS FOR AGGRESSION: Swimming, deep-sea diving, listening to music, enjoyment of art.

WAY OF FIGHTING: Creates chaos, confuses. Uses helplessness as a weapon, giving his opposite a bad conscience: How can you do this to me?—the eternal victim.

SEXUALITY: The love trip. Strong impulse, particularly in conjunction with an altered state (Tantra, trances, and drugs). Very sensitive and easily seduced.

♂︎

♃♈   Jupiter in Aries

IDEAL: Personal freedom and self-assertion

STRENGTH: *The advocate of the faith.* Values those who won't put up with anything and stand up for themselves. Is courageous and committed in championing values and ideals of freedom. Distinct feeling for personal dignity. Natural leader.

PROBLEM AREA: *The intolerant individual.* Inclines toward hubris and high-handedness. Is intolerant and endures no contradictions. Asserts will and convictions, with violence, if necessary. Wastes energy.

RELIGION/PHILOSOPHY: *Islam.* A religion without mysticism, which challenges a person to fight for holy convictions.

♃♉   Jupiter in Taurus

IDEAL: Growth, abundance, enjoyment of life.

STRENGTH: *The guardian.* Sense for care and defense of everything that grows and has been tested by time. Knows how to value outer happiness, prosperity, sociability, and sensuality. Satisfied with what he or she has. Proud modesty.

PROBLEM AREA: *The braggart.* Extravagant, pleasure-seeking, and conceited. Looks down on other people's possessions and flaunts what he or she has. Insolent attitude of expectation.

RELIGION/PHILOSOPHY: *Epicureans of ancient Greece.* Sensual happiness in life within a circle of good friends is the highest goal in life.

♃♊	Jupiter in Gemini	Detriment

IDEAL: Critical common sense.

STRENGTH: *The priest of doubt.* Values common sense and praises skepticism as a virtue which, through constant questioning and doubting, can lead to ultimate, true perception beyond all contradiction. Interested in philosophy, resourceful, and an enemy of any type of gullibility.

PROBLEM AREA: *The cynic.* Superficial, contradictory, and in conflict regarding concepts of values and convictions. Gets involved in other people's affairs without being asked to do so, posing as the judge of the situation. Bitter cynicism disturbs others in their beliefs and satisfaction with life.

RELIGION/PHILOSOPHY: *Encyclopedist and the philosophy of Descartes.* Question everything that you can question, and only believe in what remains afterward.

♃

♃♋	Jupiter in Cancer	Exaltation

IDEAL: Helpfulness and loving care.

STRENGTH: *The protector.* Places great value on deep feelings, indulgence, love, and forgiveness. Always endeavors to repay evil with good and protect the weak and helpless. Vast sympathy and a good antenna for the emotional needs of human beings. Sense of domesticity, family, and rootedness in one's own homeland.

PROBLEM AREA: *Moral indifference.* Goes to such extremes of indulgence, sympathy, and forgiveness that everything is ultimately forgiven without any differentiation. Very inconsequential and irresponsible in this respect, above all when this bighearted sense of forgiveness is directed at self.

RELIGION/PHILOSOPHY: *The Romantic (Novalis, Clemens von Brentano).* Nostalgia and the worship of the feminine—particularly as the Great Mother in nature and as Mary in Catholicism.

♃♌   Jupiter in Leo

IDEAL: Grandeur and kindness.

STRENGTH: *The patron.* Values whatever shines, is dignified and magnificent, as well as luxury and the sense of comfort. Has a feeling of benevolent superiority. Warmhearted, kind, indulgent, and optimistic. Lets others participate in his or her happiness. Supports and promotes other people.

PROBLEM AREA: *The superficial person.* Constantly avoids the shadow sides and problems of life. Replaces the lack of depth and seriousness with superficial pathos and dramatic exaggerations.

RELIGION/PHILOSOPHY: *Sun religions of the Incas or of Akhenaton. Life philosophy.* Nietzsche's teaching of the superman.

♃♍   Jupiter in Virgo   Detriment

IDEAL: Virtue and reliability.

STRENGTH: *A sense of order.* Values what is exact, perfect, and visible at a glance. Needs an explicable image of the world that holds up to critical attacks. Takes action for the general good. Practices orderliness, modesty, and dependability. Has a sense for everything that is methodical, useful, and practical.

PROBLEM AREA: *The embittered teacher.* Dogged, fainthearted ambition, intellectual narrow-mindedness, and vehement feelings of envy lead to embittered fault-finding, a nasal know-it-all attitude, obtrusive patronage, and a misanthropic basic attitude.

RELIGION/PHILOSOPHY: *Confucianism.*
The teaching of ordered circumstances.

♃ ♎   Jupiter in Libra

IDEAL: Peace and justice.

STRENGTH: *The peace-loving person.* Sense of balance, fairness, and equality. Very much knows how to value harmony, beauty, and esthetics. Companion of equality, justice, and peace. Interested in philosophy and art.

PROBLEM AREA: *The noncommittal individual.* Never wants to commit in decisions, relationships, or in moral, ethical matters. Unwarranted claims to happiness and high expectations without even wanting to do anything to achieve them. Envious and morose because other people (supposedly) have it better.

RELIGION/PHILOSOPHY: *Greek classicism.* The completely harmoniously balanced conception of life as viewed by the ancient philosophers.

♃

♃ ♏   Jupiter in Scorpio

IDEAL: Magic and power.

STRENGTH: *The occultist.* Sense of the enigmatic, the concealed, far-reaching changes, and the development of the emotional powers. High degree of self-confidence in connection with the powers of suggestion can have a beneficial effect on others. Also is aware of the transforming powers of sexuality.

PROBLEM AREA: *The power-driven person.* Misuses the powers of his soul to dominate and use others, make them dependent on him, or enslave them. Irresponsible and inconsiderate. Inclined toward mental cruelty.

RELIGION/PHILOSOPHY: *Machiavellianism—esotericism—shamanism.*
Exploration and application of the archaic powers of the unconscious mind.

| ♃♐ | Jupiter in Sagittarius | Dignity |

IDEAL: Justice, noble-mindedness, and exalted virtues.

STRENGTH: *The sublime.* Sense of exalted ethical and moral values, for a religious view of the world, for a high level of education, and a noble-minded, virtuous lifestyle. Trust in a higher guidance gives the feeling of always being protected. Optimism in life also inspires other people and creates a positive mood. Sense of justice.

PROBLEM AREA: *The overly-emotional person.* Complacent, pompous, passionate dogmatist and know-it-all with guru mannerisms. Obtrusive fanatic right-winger. Likes to speak—or only speaks—"ex cathedra." Inexorable attainment of personal—supposedly more lofty—ideals.

RELIGION/PHILOSOPHY: *All high religions.*

| ♃♑ | Jupiter in Capricorn | Fall |

IDEAL: Sense of duty, law and order.

STRENGTH: *The conservative.* Sense of responsibility, reliability, performance of one's duties, and clear rules and limitations. Keeper of law, order, and tradition. Very much values straightforwardness, sincerity, seriousness, simplicity, discipline, and inner strength. Willing to assume a great deal of responsibility (governmental assignments).

PROBLEM AREA: *The dark cloud.* Extremely strict with self and others. Lack of trust in the flow of life. Loss of spontaneity, cautious, fearful, rigid, depressive. Terrible glorification of normality and the ultraconservative. Miserly, petty, and pedantic.

RELIGION/PHILOSOPHY: *Zen Buddhism.* Strict, austere, resolute, and impressively simple.

♃ ≈   Jupiter in Aquarius

IDEAL: Equality, liberty, brotherhood.

STRENGTH: *The free spirit.* Values what is modern and trend-setting. Strives for utopia, for overcoming old barriers and class distinctions. Glorifies individual freedom and the right of self-determination for every person. Champions human rights. Enlightened mind in search of wisdom and the ability to judge everything from a higher, more-than-personal standpoint. Sense of solitude and detached contemplativeness.

PROBLEM AREA: *The eccentric.* Lost in abstract intellectual edifices and models meant to explain the world. One-sided glorification of the intellect and know-it-all demystification (= cheaply explaining away everything) related to transcendental or numinous experiences. Embarrassing superficiality and complacent refusal to examine the advocated theories for their suitability in the practice.

RELIGION/PHILOSOPHY: *Enlightenment/atheism.* The glorification of the mind.

♃ ♓   Jupiter in Pisces   Dignity

IDEAL: Selflessness and brotherly love.

STRENGTH: *The spiritual advisor.* Sense of helpfulness, kindness, indulgence, and forgiveness. Great willingness to make sacrifices. Deep understanding for all who are in need and suffer from emotional oppression. Can give comfort and hope as a spiritual advisor and confessor. Able to help the stricken get back on their feet. Feels drawn to mysticism, trances, and spiritual teachings of redemption.

PROBLEM AREA: *The daydreamer.* Uncritical absorption of trashy pseudo-esoteric foolishness. Gullible, false, and vacillates between self-pity and self-admiration.

RELIGION/PHILOSOPHY: *Early Christianity.* The teaching of true brotherly love. Or Taoism: the paradoxical face of the truth.

♄♈   Saturn in Aries   Fall

PROHIBITION OR DISDAIN OF: Aggression, strife, egotism, spontaneity.

THRESHOLD: Fear of defeat, difficulties in assertion.

COMPULSION: Self-assertion at any cost, exaggerated demands. Merciless, cruel, violent.

LIBERATION: Self-confidence, inner strength, personal initiative, dynamics, healthy aggression.

♄♉   Saturn in Taurus

PROHIBITION OR DISDAIN OF: Enjoyment in life, laziness, sensuality, faithfulness.

THRESHOLD: Fear of losing security, fear of ruin, fear of privations, and other fears of loss.

COMPULSION: Striving for security or enjoyment at any cost. Compulsive about faithfulness.

LIBERATION: Satisfied modesty, healthy consciousness of reality, appropriate striving for security, balanced ability to enjoy. Clear sense of self-worth.

♄⚹   Saturn in Gemini

PROHIBITION OR DISDAIN OF: Versatility, intellectual doubt, curiosity.

THRESHOLD: Fear of losing intellectual freedom, being dense or at a loss for words.

COMPULSION: Cynical thinking, embittered and sarcastic, entangled in extremes and contradictions.

LIBERATION: Concentrated, serious, consequential thinking. Always prepared to consider the other side and letting it have its say.

♄♋   Saturn in Cancer   Detriment

PROHIBITION OR DISDAIN OF: Deep feelings, sentimentality, motherliness, family, romanticism, a feeling of being rooted in the homeland.

THRESHOLD: Fear of the depths of feelings, of emotional attachments, of the confines of the family. Fear of being "eaten up" by the feminine element.

COMPULSION: Sentimental emotional exhibitionism instead of expressing deep, true feelings. Feeling oneself at the mercy of heavy, negative feelings and depressive moods. Starting a family for compulsive reasons.

LIBERATION: Taking one's own feelings seriously, healthy self-control without frustrating suppression. Inner peace, feeling of emotional safety and security without fear of dependency.

♄

♄♌ **Saturn in Leo**	Detriment

PROHIBITION OR DISDAIN OF: Luxury, showmanship, pompousness.

THRESHOLD: The fear of not being respected, admired, and loved. The fear of being insignificant, but also the fear of having to be at the focus of attention. Fear of authorities.	COMPULSION: Having to be generous and magnificent at any cost. The oppressive duty of having to find life exciting and wonderful every day.

LIBERATION: Dignified modesty, humble superior style, mature self-confidence, willingness to take responsibility, and healthy self-criticism. Free expression of personal uniqueness.

♄♍   **Saturn in Virgo**

PROHIBITION OR DISDAIN OF: Domesticity, precision, flexibility.

THRESHOLD: Fear of tests. Fear of being useless, awkward, maladjusted, or inappropriate. Fear of illness.	COMPULSION: Obtrusive perfectionism, exaggerated organization, pedanticism, and fault-finding that criticizes everything. Fanaticism for what is utilitarian. Fitness addiction. Extreme modesty.

LIBERATION: Awareness of social responsibility, sensible love of order, stable health. Synthesis of mind and body.

♄♎ Saturn in Libra	Exaltation

PROHIBITION OR DISDAIN OF: Grace, charm, aesthetic, willingness to compromise, peacemaking, art, playfulness.

THRESHOLD: The fear of having to be considerate or becoming dependent on another person.	COMPULSION: Forcing oneself into a partnership or entering into too many social obligations.

LIBERATION: Seriousness and maturing in relationships with other people. Commitment and responsibility in one's partnership. Clear discernment and distinct sense of justice.

♄♏ Saturn in Scorpio	

PROHIBITION OR DISDAIN OF: Taboos, borderline areas, minorities, sexuality, power, esoteric study.

THRESHOLD: The fear of destructive forces, of emotional commitment, sexual devotion, the depth and passion of one's own feelings. Fear of emotional entanglements and dependencies. Fear of death.	COMPULSION: Feeling oneself attracted to what is dark and forbidden. Dogged striving for power. Sexual collecting mania. Being obsessed by occult or sexual topics. Compulsively overstepping taboos.

LIBERATION: Mature, chastened treatment of power. Overcoming the fantasies of dependency and helplessness. Growing trust and willingness to be devoted in the partnership. Deep sexual satisfaction.

♄♐   Saturn in Sagittarius

PROHIBITION OR DISDAIN OF: Religiousness, faith, search for meaning, moral values, everything foreign and strange, distant journeys.

THRESHOLD: The fear of being thwarted by questions of faith, by hopelessness, or the absurdities of life. Fear of infiltration with foreign elements and fear of one's own lack of significance. Fear of distant journeys.

COMPULSION: Hard, rigid, dogmatic ideas about faith or dogged atheism. Prudish moral strictness. Moral self-righteousness. Overly organized trips where nothing happens.

LIBERATION: Tolerance, wise perception and discovery of meaning. Extended and lively inner and outer journeys.

♄♑   Saturn in Capricorn   Dignity

PROHIBITION OR DISDAIN OF: Ambition, awareness of one's duty, reliability, willingness to take responsibility.

THRESHOLD: Fear of failing. Fear of being controlled, limited, or repressed by others. Fear of being bound to do something.

COMPULSION: Dogged career planning. Rigid strictness with oneself and others. Enslaving oneself.

LIBERATION: Healthy self-discipline and willingness to take responsibility. Far-sighted and prudent determination. Matured authority. Sober clarity and down-to-earth view of the world.

♄ ≈   Saturn in Aquarius   Dignity

PROHIBITION OR DISDAIN OF: Freedom, extravagance, individuality, progress, utopia.

THRESHOLD: The fear of loneliness, of being deserted, of being inferior to someone else, or of developing individual peculiarities and becoming an outsider who doesn't belong anywhere as a result. Fear of innovations.

COMPULSION: Pathological obstinacy and constant, stubborn insistence on always having special treatment. Doing crazy things in order to be something special. Obsessed by ideas of reform.

LIBERATION: Mature and relaxed manner of living out independence and peculiar characteristics. Sober attitude toward all experiments and innovations. Inventor and developer of truly useful innovations.

♄

♄ ♓   Saturn in Pisces

PROHIBITION OR DISDAIN OF: Devotion, selflessness, chaos, mystic tendencies, and mediumistic abilities.

THRESHOLD: The fear of losing oneself in chaos, in the inexplicable, or in what cannot be seen at a glance. Fear of deep emotions and sympathy. Fear of becoming helpless and a slave to others or of being used by other people.

COMPULSION: Self-sacrifice at any cost. Deep feelings of guilt and experiences of pain. Extreme interest in mystic or mediumistic topics to the point of craziness.

LIBERATION: True brotherly love, deep sensitivity, selfless love, mature trust in the Higher Self, and the honest willingness to pardon and forgive.

Uranus, Neptune, and Pluto

The three outer planets move extremely slowly. This means that Uranus spends an average of seven years in each sign of the zodiac. Neptune takes fourteen years and Pluto twenty-one years. As a result, aspects from these planets to each other often remain in orb for years. The respective position of the sign the slow moving planet is in therefore makes a statement about the generation coming into the world during this period of time. The individual significance of such an aspect can only be read from the house position in the personal horoscope and by cross-linking it with the aspects to the personal planets.

For this reason, the following tables only show the themes typical for the sign that are characteristic for the respective generation.

Uranus in	Strengths/Advocacy for	Problems
♈ Aries	Freedom of the will, freedom to conquer new territory.	Inconsiderate individualism.
♉ Taurus FALL	Freedom to enjoy life according to your own tastes; freedom of possessions.	Becoming a burden for others instead of securing the foundation of your own life.
♊ Gemini	Freedom of opinion, thought, and speech.	Heartless intellectualism.
♋ Cancer	Freedom of the homeland, the free development of children and the soul.	Fleeing the nest; the rigorous bursting of family ties and structures.

Uranus in	Strengths/Advocacy for	Problems
♌ Leo DETRIMENT	Free development of personality; for the individual happiness in life.	Development of own happiness in life at the cost of others.
♍ Virgo	Freedom of science and teaching; freedom in education.	Feeling superior to necessities of everyday life, obsessively non-conformist.
♎ Libra	Free choice of partner and freedom within the partnership; freedom of the arts.	Inability to commit to a relationship.
♏ Scorpio EXALTATION	Freedom to research, break taboos, undertake occult studies; sexual freedom.	Massive suppressed desires, uncontrolled overstepping of all prohibitions.
♐ Sagittarius	Religious freedom, freedom of opinion, freedom of movement.	Idolatrous glorification of individuality.
♑ Capricorn	Freedom to choose your own duties and responsibilities.	Freedom from laws, norms, and any type of responsibility.
♒ Aquarius DIGNITY	Freedom for everyone, freedom of opinion, and freedom of development.	The isolated loner, solipsist.
♓ Pisces	Freedom to take your own path of redemption; freedom to follow your own vision.	Chaotic tendencies; "self-redemption" through intoxicants.

Neptune in	Dissolution of	Idealization of
♈ Aries 1861/62-1872/75	Old images of the enemy.	The fighting spirit, freedom of will.
♉ Taurus 1874/75-1887/88	Encrusted property structures, traditional values.	Tradition, spiritual security, sensuality.
♊ Gemini 1888/89-1901/02	Old thought patterns and habits of thought.	Inspired perceptions, harmonious connection of fantasy and intellect.
♋ Cancer 1901/02-1914/15 EXALTATION	Family structures and rootedness in the homeland.	Motherhood, family warmth, romanticism.
♌ Leo 1914/15-1928/29	Superficial splendor.	Examples, luxury, snobbishness, or the superman.
♍ Virgo 1928/29-1942/43 EXILE	Old methods of working and teaching; social differences between the classes.	Order, striving for practicality, utilitarian thinking, health consciousness.
♎ Libra 1942/43-1956/57	Old forms of relationships; the previous understanding of art.	Peacefulness, love, and art.
♏ Scorpio 1956/57-1970/71	Old fixations and power structures.	Archaic powers, magic, and sexuality.
♐ Sagittarius 1970/71-1984/85	Dogmas and old concepts of faith.	Noble-mindedness, religious striving, ethical consciousness of values.
♑ Capricorn 1984/85-1998/99 FALL	Hierarchies and laws.	Law, order, duty, awareness of responsibility.
♒ Aquarius 1998/99-2011/12	Individualism and striving for independence.	Equality, freedom, brotherhood of all human beings.
♓ Pisces 2011/12-2024/25 DIGNITY	Old dream images and concepts of redemption.	Willingness to sacrifice; brotherly love, mysticism.

Lack of Self-Discipline	Weakening
Boundless inconsideration.	Weak ego, lack of assertiveness.
Getting off the track in area of sensuality.	Weak ability to set limits, weak feeling of security.
Dishonesty, boundless doubt, or transfiguration of the intellect.	Limited intellectual abilities; nebulous, unrealistic thinking.
Fantasies that get out of hand; blurring of boundary between fiction and reality.	Weak feeling of being safe and secure; weak trust in one's own emotional world.
Narcissism, self-glorification that gets out of hand, megalomania.	Weakness of ego; lack of self-worth.
Spineless, exaggerated conformity, narrow-mindedness, and uncritical belief in science.	Diminished sense of order; weak ability to differentiate.
Boundless emotional freedom, independence, and unfaithfulness.	Limited ability to commit to a relationship; lack of good taste.
Outgrowths of perverse striving for power; extreme sexual excesses.	Shallow expression of passion; weakening of power.
Outgrowths of arrogant sectarianism, fundamentalist excesses.	Reduced ability to have faith and nebulous search for meaning.
Uncontrolled authoritarian and reactionary tendencies.	Irresponsibility.
Untenable utopias, unrealistic egalitarianism, and eccentricity.	Clouding of individual consciousness.
Consumption of intoxicants, vulnerability to seduction; airy-fairy concept of the world.	Blurred sense of reality.

Pluto in	Themes of Transformation	Experiences Power & Helplessness Through
♈ Aries 1823-1852 and 2068-2096	The power and courage to take truly new, unfamiliar, as well as revolutionary paths, and overcome the past.	Arbitrariness.
♉ Taurus 1852-1884 and 2096-2128 DETRIMENT	Experiences of radical change in connection with possessions and money; fundamental transformation of traditional concepts of values.	Money and possessions.
♊ Gemini 1640-1669 and 1884-1914	Breakthrough and new perceptions in research and science, uncompromising translation of new insights, ideas, and thoughts.	Intellectual superiority.
♋ Cancer 1669-1694 and 1914-1939	Complete destruction and transformation of current attitude toward family, keeping family, homeland, the people of one's nation, and one's own origins together.	Emotional ties and solidarity of the clan.
♌ Leo 1694-1711 and 1939-1957 EXALTATION	Deep-reaching transformation in the self-image of human beings and their possibilities of self-development.	Development of self.
♍ Virgo 1711-1726 and 1957-1972	Deep-reaching changes and radical challenges in the scope of working conditions, through questions regarding health, and as a result of ecological problems.	Necessity of integration and conformity to society.

Pluto in	Themes of Transformation	Experiences Power & Helplessness Through
♎ Libra 1726-1737 and 1972-1984	Deep-reaching transformation of previous forms and concepts of relationships, as well as changes in the area of art.	Marriage and other forms of partnership.
♏ Scorpio 1737-1749 and 1984-1995 DIGNITY	Things that have been blocked, believed to be lost, and concealed come to light; knowledge that has been kept secret, rituals that have been passed down, and original healing powers experience new valuation.	Outward and inward striving for power.
♐ Sagittarius 1749-1762 and 1995-2008	Fundamental radical changes and transformation regarding religious and moral values, as well as in the area of search for meaning and discovery of meaning.	Religious concepts and questions of finding meaning.
♑ Capricorn 1762-1777 and 2008-2023	Deep-reaching transformation of the social order, hierarchies, and laws, as well as in the area of personal responsibility, fulfillment of duties, and general understanding of destiny.	Laws and norms.
♒ Aquarius 1777-1799 and 2023-2044 FALL	Deep-reaching transformation in the valuation of freedom and independence, as well as in the individual possibilities of development for each human being.	Intellectual superiority.
♓ Pisces 1799-1823 and 2044-2068	Understanding of the world of the unconscious and the inexplicable, above all in the areas of mediumism, mysticism, and trance.	Power of the unconscious mind.

The

CARDINAL AXIS

The Rising Sign or Ascendant

The Ascendant (AC) is the sign of the zodiac that was rising on the eastern horizon at the time of birth. The time and place of birth determine which sign this is. Because of the apparent rotation of the ecliptic around the Earth in a period of 24 hours, a new sign of the zodiac rises on the eastern horizon on an average of every two hours, which means that the Ascendant changes every two hours in purely mathematical terms. However, based on the slanted position of the ecliptic, the signs rise at various speeds when seen from Earth. Pisces is the quickest sign in the northern hemisphere, rising in about 30 minutes, while Virgo is the slowest to rise, with a time of more than three hours. In accordance with this, the Pisces Ascendant is relatively rare in the northern hemisphere, while the Virgo Ascendant is quite widespread. This ratio is reversed in the southern hemisphere.

The sign of the Ascendant represents the way in which you spontaneously approach your surrounding world, and the basic mood and manner with which you start something new. It also describes the experience that you had with your birth. This can be a fighting nature (Aries-Mars) or reserved and hesitant (Capricorn-Saturn). In the truest sense of the word, this could be a matter of life and death (Scorpio-Pluto) or a liberating experience (Aquarius-Uranus). This first impression of life, embodied by the Ascendant, is taken on the path through life and re-experienced in every new beginning. In the following portrayal, the attitude that results from it will be described under IMAGE, FEELING TOWARD LIFE, and APHORISM.

As the basic mood of life and the feeling of self, the Ascendant also shows the ATTITUDE TOWARD MARRIAGE AND PARTNERSHIP, the individual themes expressed by the Descendant.

The Ascendant stands for the image of the personality that the surrounding world often experiences as the initial impression of the individual. Of all the horoscope factors, the Ascendant has the greatest significance for the appearance of an individual. This is why the typical characteristics of a sign are listed under the heading of EXTERNAL APPEARANCE in the following chapter. Appearance is not just dependent on one individual factor, but is also influenced by other important configurations, such as planets in the 1st house, the Sun, or—in the female horoscope—by the Moon. In this respect, the signature listed here is only typical of the sign and should not be understood as compulsory of the Ascendant. The entire horoscope is ultimately expressed through the various aspects of the body.

When considering the Ascendant, it is important to analyze the corresponding ruling planets, their signs and house positions, as well as the aspects of the Ascendant and the ruling planets. The position of the Ascendant ruler shows where and in which manner the original energy of the Ascendant can best be expressed. One example of this, depicted in a simplified manner, is that someone with a Gemini Ascendant and Mercury in Virgo in the 3rd house encounters life with curiosity and interest (Gemini Ascendant), is capable of analytical, critical thinking (Virgo), and desires to establish contact with her surrounding world using talents relating to the spoken and written word, and enjoys presenting herself or himself (3rd house).

Planets close to the Ascendant—in the 1st or 12th house—complement and highlight the qualities of the Ascendant. But they can also mean conflicts when their themes are in contradiction to those of the Ascendant.

Because many horoscope factors are reflected in a person's appearance, the characteristics listed on the following pages for the various signs are not to be found in every person with that particular Ascendant. However, the signature specific to each sign does permit the conclusion that people with the appearance described by the sign will have a strong emphasis on that sign's energy in the horoscope.

AC

| ♈ | **Aries Ascendant** | *The Fighter* |

| ELEMENT: Fire | TEMPERAMENT: Choleric (quick-tempered) | RULER: ♂ |

THEME: Leadership, initiative, activity.

STRENGTH: *The go-getter.* Doesn't give up and doesn't resign ("never-say-die"). Very lively, active, direct, and creative. Goes his or her own way (above all, takes new paths) and asserts himself or herself. Courageous, proud, energetic, strong-willed, enterprising, and passionate.

PROBLEM AREA: *The inconsiderate person.* Aggressive, egotistical, hurried, inconsiderate—above all, rude and destructive, even personally. Tolerates no frustrations. No ability to compromise, but a blunt either-or conduct. Tends to be arbitrary, violent, misuse power, or show off. Wants to go at everything head first.

IMAGE: I am the first.

FEELING TOWARD LIFE: Here I come! And: Let's get going!

APHORISM: Nothing ventured, nothing gained.

ATTITUDE TOWARD MARRIAGE AND PARTNERSHIP: Tends to experience a committed life partnership as confinement and imprisonment. Seeks the element of tranquillity in the relationship, but cannot enjoy it. Needs a serene and understanding partner to whom one can always return after excursions.

EXTERNAL APPEARANCE: Lean, muscular body. Thick, straight, sometimes jagged eyebrows. Prominent facial features. "Butting bumps" on the forehead. Decisive, intense movements. Goose-step.
Note: see also pages 106-107.

| ♉ | Taurus Ascendant | *The Connoisseur* |

| ELEMENT: Earth | TEMPERAMENT: Melancholic | RULER: ♀ |

THEME: Receiving, preserving, and enjoying.

STRENGTH: *The comfortable individual.* Loves what is familiar and lasting. Distinct taste and highly developed sense of forms. Artistic disposition. Lets things have the time they need to develop. Needs emotional and material security. Leisurely, persistent, relaxed, calm and stable, practical, full of feeling, and very sensual.

PROBLEM AREA: *The incorrigible creature of habit.* Tends to fall back into old habits despite an awareness of them and the desire to change. Uncomprehending stubbornness. Clings tightly to everything that is old and defiantly defends against any innovation. Greedy, excessive, lazy, self-indulgent, ponderous, and indolent.

| IMAGE: I am good-natured and stable. | FEELING TOWARD LIFE: If things would just stay as they are. |

APHORISM: Rome wasn't built in a day. Or: What the farmer doesn't know, he doesn't try.

AC

ATTITUDE TOWARD MARRIAGE AND PARTNERSHIP: Seeks and offers faithfulness and stability, therefore willing to commit to a relationship at a young age. Often difficult to tolerate since there is no express tendency to keep agreements that have been made. Frequent power struggles. Needs a strong partner who knows what the person wants, is willing to engage in conflicts, and makes life more exciting.

EXTERNAL APPEARANCE: Large, round eyes ("cow eyes"), warm or "violet" glance, sensual mouth with thick lips. Often pyknic figure with round nape of neck and round shoulders. Men have an inclination toward crescent-shaped balding.
Note: see also pages 106-107.

| ♊ | Gemini Ascendant | *The Changeable Individual* |

| ELEMENT: Air | TEMPERAMENT: Sanguine (optimistic) | RULER: ☿ |

THEME: Searching, finding, searching again, finding something new.

STRENGTH: *The intellectual.* Eternally en route, constantly searching, without exactly knowing what one's looking for. Curious, versatile, able to make friends easily, mentally flexible, adaptable, always well-informed and ready to converse. A butterfly that flies everywhere but only lands for a little while. Rhetorically skilled and never at a loss for words. Has a finger in every pie.

PROBLEM AREA: *The absentminded professor.* Always creates total confusion and appears to feel good when no one else knows what's going on. Nervous, restless, lack of concentration, talkative, unstable, sly, cynical, and double-dealing. Nasty manipulation of words.

| IMAGE: I know everything! | FEELING TOWARD LIFE: What I don't know bothers the hell out of me. |

APHORISM: Ah, two souls live in my breast!

ATTITUDE TOWARD MARRIAGE AND PARTNERSHIP: Longs for a partnership as the liberating element of tranquillity. Resigned to fate in the belief in a higher guidance that will bring one together with a partner. Yet, remains independent in one's innermost heart and shows curiosity and interest in a variety of contacts.

EXTERNAL APPEARANCE: Slender, delicately boned, sometimes ungraceful figure. Sharp, interested, observant glance. Wide forehead, straight eyebrows, small bridge of the nose. May also have narrow "greyhound" face. *Note: see also pages 106-107.*

| ♋ | **Cancer Ascendant** | *The Motherly Person* |

| ELEMENT: Water | TEMPERAMENT: Melancholic | RULER: ☽ |

THEME: Helpfulness, security, instinct.

STRENGTH: *The caring individual.* Sensitive, delicate, tends to be fearful but tough, persevering, and ambitious. Reacts and acts with emotion on the basis of strong instincts. Seeks and gives a feeling of safety and security within the circle of friends and family. Empathizing, romantic, and dreamy.

PROBLEM AREA: *The childlike person.* Refuses to grow up and hides behind a mask of childlike innocence. Shy, fickle, fearful, very moody, sulky, and extremely resentful. Pathological ambition because of strong feelings of inferiority. Emotionally tyrannical. Melancholy and full of self-pity.

IMAGE: I am willing to help.

FEELING TOWARD LIFE: Anything, except taking a straight path.

APHORISM: There's no place like home. Or: Why roam afield when good things are so close at hand?

ATTITUDE TOWARD MARRIAGE AND PARTNERSHIP: Not easily capable of living alone. Therefore, very willing to commit to a relationship or even hungry to do so. Searches for security, lasting protection, and safety with a rooted, imperturbable, and completely serious person who makes sure he or she has a way out (hermit crab). Once such a partner has been found, he or she feels liberated, open and willing to explore the entire world. Once entered into a relationship, he or she keeps it going as long as this is in any way possible.

EXTERNAL APPEARANCE: "Moon face," pale skin, dreamy glance, and round body forms. Sometimes timid, uncertain expression and startled look. Men have an inclination toward balding.
Note: see also pages 106-107.

AC

| ♌ | Leo Ascendant | *The Person Who is Confident of Victory* |

| ELEMENT: Fire | TEMPERAMENT: Slightly choleric | RULER: ☉ |

THEME: Self-confidence, showmanship, joy in living, being hard to please

STRENGTH: *The privileged individual.* Self-confident, proud, warmhearted, and a generous, natural type of authority. An optimist with the feeling of being a privileged individual and a child of fortune. Creative, very expressive, and successful. Full of momentum and rousing, exuberant joy in life.

PROBLEM AREA: *The braggart.* Overbearing, haughty, condescending, presumptuous, and power-hungry. Crude show-off and conceited bluffer. Tends toward silly, dramatic scenes.

IMAGE: I am wonderful!

FEELING TOWARD LIFE: Life is worth living.

APHORISM: Why settle for less?

ATTITUDE TOWARD MARRIAGE AND PARTNERSHIP: Maintains a high degree of freedom and independence in the life partnership. Allows the partner the same degree of freedom.

EXTERNAL APPEARANCE: Often very attractive. Well-built body—sometimes also very portly—with broad shoulders and a self-confident way of walking. Decorative, high, and wide forehead. Arched eyebrows and an open glance. Eyes appear to be set close together. Lion's mane.
Note: see also pages 106-107.

| ♍ | Virgo Ascendant | *The Careful Individual* |

| ELEMENT: Earth | TEMPERAMENT: Slightly melancholic | RULER: ☿ |

THEME: A clear eye for details, quick ability to differentiate, sense of what is practical, skillful at adapting.

STRENGTH: *The tidy person.* Concerned with health and inner and outer cleanliness. Able to adapt when life circumstances make it appear advisable and practical. With a sure instinct, one differentiates between what is useful and worthless, beneficial and harmful in the physical and emotional realm. Loves what can be comprehended at a glance. Systematic, methodical, critical, and down-to-earth.

PROBLEM AREA: *The perfectionist.* Overly cautious, obsessed with details and afraid of life, unfeeling, eternally finding fault, sly, upright, inhibited, prudish, narrow-minded, colorless, and endlessly pedantic, boring, and bureaucratic. With exaggerated fear, one avoids everything that could possibly be harmful. Very dependent on pure formalities.

| IMAGE: I am critical. | FEELING TOWARD LIFE: Practice makes perfect. |

APHORISM: It's better to be safe than sorry.

ATTITUDE TOWARD MARRIAGE AND PARTNERSHIP: Very critical attitude toward marriage, which above all means dividing the rights and doubling the obligations.[2] Often does not marry until late in life. However, one is then very concerned with sustaining the marriage—at least the outer semblance.

EXTERNAL APPEARANCE: Slender, well-formed body, often youthful appearance until old age, then very wrinkled. Tends to have knockknees. Trustworthy forehead. Frequently has straight eyebrows. Usually small eyes with a firm, critical look. Always has clean fingernails.
Note: see also pages 106-107.

AC

| ♎ | Libra Ascendant | *The Esthete* |

| ELEMENT: Air | TEMPERAMENT: Sanguine (optimistic) | RULER: ♀ |

THEME: Balance, peace, and beauty.

STRENGTH: *The diplomat.* Cheerful, calm, sensible, and well-groomed. Concerned with harmony and justice. Good eye for aesthetic forms. Diplomatic skills. Makes friends easily and is very oriented toward other people. More than others, one seeks and needs the encounter with others in order to be able to be reflected in them and find one's own standpoint. Able to make compromises, charming, and sociable.

PROBLEM AREA: *The conflict-avoider.* Often has great difficulties making decisions. Extremely exaggerated willingness to make compromises for the sake of peace. Lack of endurance and ability to assert oneself. Pleasure-seeker. Detached within one's innermost heart. Has only apparent interest in the superficially beautiful illusion.

IMAGE: I am charming.

FEELING TOWARD LIFE: The main thing is to do it with style!

APHORISM: It is not good for a person to be alone.

ATTITUDE TOWARD MARRIAGE AND PARTNERSHIP: Very much oriented toward a partner, cannot live well alone. However, one won't let oneself be driven out of one's mind by matters of love. Tends toward a relationship that is both a marriage of convenience and one of love. Very willing to compromise as long as independence is not threatened.

EXTERNAL APPEARANCE: Fine, delicate build. Graceful appearance. Sensitive skin. Usually has very straight eyebrows. Friendly but somewhat distant personality. In men, an inclination toward very wide balding (tonsure). *Note: see also pages 106-107.*

♏	Scorpio Ascendant	*The Mysterious Person*

ELEMENT: Water	TEMPERAMENT: Melancholic	RULER: ♇ and ♂

THEME: Secrecy, power of fascination, passion.

STRENGTH: *The hypnotist.* Strong powers of suggestion, strength of will, endurance, and determination. Extreme feelings of love and hate. Excellent observational powers. At the same time, mistrusting, clever, and capable of deep insights. Can also remain externally calm and restrained while very agitated inwardly. Healthy willingness to engage in conflict. Reserved and secretive. Understands how to draw other people out of their reserve. Sharp eye for weak spots.

PROBLEM AREA: *The omnipotent charlatan.* Hunger for power, overestimation of one's own capabilities, and feelings of omnipotence. Dependent on recognition and homage, therefore also very reliant upon surroundings, which one strongly manipulates. Ceaseless alternating between nasty needling (which leads to conflicts and rejection time and again) followed with an intense solicitation of sympathy. Vindictive, hateful, and maliciousness. Uncontrolled, vicious, and destructive. Extreme problems with sex drive and a tendency toward deep depressions. Bloodsucker, fake, and charlatan.

IMAGE: I am irresistible.	FEELING TOWARD LIFE: All or nothing!

APHORISM: The deeper, the better.

ATTITUDE TOWARD MARRIAGE AND PARTNERSHIP: Seeks a partner who does not permit himself or herself to be twisted around a finger and knows how to set clear limits. Secretly longs for a person who will show the (brutal) truth and can make one face the facts.

EXTERNAL APPEARANCE: Poker face. Very attractive or very ugly. Quite frequently a pyknic figure. Deep-set eyes with a sharp, piercing, and penetrating gaze (Mephistopheles), often with a prominent nose (hawk face). Women frequently have a seductive glance. Sturdy, sometimes disheveled hair with a low hairline.
Note: see also pages 106-107.

AC

♐ Sagittarius Ascendant — *The Optimist*

ELEMENT: Fire	TEMPERAMENT: Nervous-choleric	RULER: ♃

THEME: Idealism, freedom, justice.

STRENGTH: *The jovial person.* Cosmopolitan, enjoys travel, optimistic, liberal, enthusiastic, generous, and charitable. Striving for higher things (ideals, religion, education, professional and social position, etc.), religious, very concerned with justice and freedom. Exemplary.

PROBLEM AREA: *The arrogant preacher.* Overwrought zealot and obtrusive know-it-all. Self-righteous, unbearable arrogant and condescending, sensitive to criticism, presumptuous, conceited, and superficial. Without stability and pathetically moralizing. Slightly agitated because he or she always has to be good.

IMAGE: I am good (morality and qualitatively).	FEELING TOWARD LIFE: Things will turn out okay (trust in God).

APHORISM: If you do your best, you will be redeemed.

ATTITUDE TOWARD MARRIAGE AND PARTNERSHIP: Vacillates between freedom and commitment. As a result, postpones the decision for a lasting relationship as long as possible. Has greatest difficulties in deciding to marry because of fear of losing one's freedom. Ultimately always remains a bachelor at heart.

EXTERNAL APPEARANCE: Large, powerful, athletic body. High forehead and square chin. Cosmopolitan look and noble features. Inclined to have bald spots at the temples.
Note: see also pages 106-107.

| ♑ | **Capricorn Ascendant** | *The Dutiful Person* |

| ELEMENT: Earth | TEMPERAMENT: Melancholic | RULER: ♄ |

THEME: Discipline, stability, willingness to take responsibility.

STRENGTH: *The steadfast individual.* Tenacious, respectable, practical, thorough, patient, and ascetic, when necessary. Needs and creates clear structures. Very concentrated. Does not give up. Difficulties and obstacles only spur one on to more achievement. Skeptical to mistrusting.

PROBLEM AREA: *The naysayer.* The joyless careerist who is constantly subject to an inner pressure of having to do something. Pessimistic, denies everything, depressive, often conscious of guilt feelings, reserved, cold-hearted, hard, miserly, lacking in humor, and embittered.

IMAGE: I am reliable and competent.

FEELING TOWARD LIFE: There's no free lunch.

APHORISM: If you want to go to Rome, you shouldn't get caught up in the carnival in Venice.

AC

ATTITUDE TOWARD MARRIAGE AND PARTNERSHIP: Experiences the life partnership as a non-terminable contract with clear rights and obligations. Does his or her best to faithfully fulfill obligations and make every necessary sacrifice for the sake of adapting in order to maintain the relationship.

EXTERNAL APPEARANCE: Slender or lean figure. Sometimes deep wrinkles in the face. Serious look. Long nose. Sometimes very beautiful, clearly profiled face, but frequently also an appearance that has the effect of being scarred. Large hands and feet.
Note: see also pages 106-107.

≈   **Aquarius Ascendant** *The Eccentric, the Extraordinary Individual*

| ELEMENT: Air | TEMPERAMENT: Sanguine | RULER: ♅ and ♄ |

THEME: Originality, individualism, independence.

STRENGTH: *The free spirit.* Objective, independent, friendly, and open, while always remaining distant at the same time. Intellectual and practical abilities. Imaginative and inventive. Good judge of human nature. Does not even consider taking the normal path of development and enters through a side door instead.

PROBLEM AREA: *The eccentric.* Nonchalantly and arrogantly puts oneself above the general rules of the game. Full of scorn for the conformists (which is everyone else). Cold, isolated, distanced, and friendless. Reclusive and presumptuous. Torn by inner conflict and without endurance. Suffers because of one's state of being unusual, which only consists of not being able to consider oneself normal.

| IMAGE: I am really something quite special. | FEELING TOWARD LIFE: Let's go (where there's more freedom)! |

APHORISM: Above the clouds...

ATTITUDE TOWARD MARRIAGE AND PARTNERSHIP: Very carefully approaches a possible partnership and takes a long time to examine the possibility. Even in a long-lasting life partnership, experiences oneself with certain feelings of distance, strangeness, or unfamiliarity. Needs and expects warmth and momentum in life from the partner. Seeks an elite partner.

EXTERNAL APPEARANCE: Oval face, receding forehead, wide-awake eyes. Little erotic charisma, more of a "pal."
Note: see also pages 106-107.

| ♓ | **Pisces Ascendant** | *The Medium, the Sleepwalker* |

| ELEMENT: Water | TEMPERAMENT: Phlegmatic | RULER: ♆ and ♃ |

THEME: Inspiration, sensitivity, empathy.

STRENGTH: *The seismograph* Mobile sensitivity and uncanny sureness of instinct. Capable of devotion, intuitive, willing to help, flexible, and adaptable. Idealistic and dreamy. Artistic disposition.

PROBLEM AREA: *The overly sensitive. individual* Extremely oversensitive, great difficulty with setting boundaries. Selflessness that borders on giving oneself up. Starry-eyed, childish belief in miracles. Lives as in a trance and definitely doesn't want to be awakened. Fearful, moody, and easily impressed. Uncritical (esoteric) enthusiasm. Self-pity. Tends to play the role of the victim.

| IMAGE: Still waters run deep. | FEELING TOWARD LIFE: Everything is a dream. |

APHORISM: The essential things are invisible to the eye. Or: You wrangle your way through it all.

ATTITUDE TOWARD MARRIAGE AND PARTNERSHIP: Encounters the other person as if in a trance and suddenly finds oneself in a relationship (or just as easily on the other side of the door). Longs for a partner who will take care of the burdensome things of everyday life so that he or she can devote time to a personal dreamworld.

EXTERNAL APPEARANCE: Usually delicately boned and tall. Can also be fleshy and bloated. Indistinct facial features. Dreamy or deep glance. Often has slanted eyes ("fish eyes").
Note: see also pages 106-107.

AC

The Lowest Heavens or *Imum Coeli*

The *Imum Coeli* (IC) is the axis at the beginning of the 4th house, the lowest point (midnight) in the horoscope. It shows the home in the spatial sense (dwelling) and emotional sense (security). It also represents homeland and origins. The IC is the most mediumistic point in the horoscope. Planets in its vicinity (up to a distance of 5°) can make corresponding statements about mediumistic talents. The image of the mother has traditionally been associated with the IC and the adjacent 4th house. However, a newer interpretation primarily sees the image of the father, his role, and the process of coming to terms with him here.

The (partially unconscious) attitude toward security, deep feelings, and how one takes root emotionally, physically, and—in the figurative sense—also spatially (house, apartment, etc.) is shown in the table on page 122.

IC

IC in	Unconscious Attitude
♈ Aries	Rebellion and opposition, emotional dependence, constant chomping at the bit; in search for new shores.
♉ Taurus	Strong emotional need for security. Knows how to value the appeal of what has developed through the years, what is familiar and lasting. Needs solid ground under his or her feet.
♊ Gemini	Curious and restless. A nomad who can quickly pack the tents. Problems in coming to terms with deep feelings.
♋ Cancer	Longing for peace, security, and tranquillity. Strong attachment to the family. Great sensitivity and depth of emotion. Intensive dreams.
♌ Leo	The feeling of security combines with feeling grand. Firm belief in one's own talents. When deep feelings are expressed, it is done with intensity.
♍ Virgo	Great need for security. Also satisfied with a modest scope, as long as he or she feels secure. Sober to critical way of dealing with deep emotions.
♎ Libra	Seeks a harmonious and stylish home. Peaceable down to the bone. Esthetic, sometimes artistic expression of feelings.
♏ Scorpio	The secretive home. Enormous inner depths that are not accessible to others.
♐ Sagittarius	Cosmopolitan and very agile in the innermost heart. Willing to move far away. Deep, religious feelings.
♑ Capricorn	Depths of feeling to which it is difficult to find access. Inner toughness, great ability to see things through, need for emotional security. Needs constancy.
♒ Aquarius	Inner independence, eccentric feelings, unusual forms of security.
♓ Pisces	Extraordinary depth of feeling, strong inner emotion. Search for spiritual or mystical feelings of security.

The Descending Sign or Descendant

The Descendant (DC) is the sign that sets (Latin = *descendere*) on the western horizon at the time of birth. As a result, it is always the sign opposite the Ascendant. While the Ascendant represents the feeling of oneself and of self-expression, the Descendant reflects the experience in conjunction with the other person, which makes it an essential aspect of the partnership theme. The qualities of the signs and planets on the Descendant are frequently first activated and made conscious by life in a relationship. Because this is always the complementary opposite pole to the feeling of oneself that is embodied in the Ascendant, it is quite acceptable to use the common phrase "better half" to describe the Descendant.

Although the forms of relationships listed in the following chart are an important aspect of the partnership theme, it is just one aspect of the overall theme, which is usually quite complex. Further aspects result; for example, from the distribution of the elements and the position of the masculine (Sun, Mars) and feminine (Moon, Venus) lights and planets, as well as the planets in the 7th house.

DC

Descendant	Partnership Themes	Matching Ascendant
♈ Aries	The conflict relationship.	♎ Libra
♉ Taurus	The sensual relationship.	♏ Scorpio
♊ Gemini	Diversity of relationships.	♐ Sagittarius
♋ Cancer	Family warmth.	♑ Capricorn
♌ Leo	The luxury relationship.	♒ Aquarius
♍ Virgo	The orderly relationship.	♓ Pisces
♎ Libra	The egalitarian relationship.	♈ Aries
♏ Scorpio	The pact (the magical relationship).	♉ Taurus
♐ Sagittarius	The holy relationship.	♊ Gemini
♑ Capricorn	The solid, eternal relationship.	♋ Cancer
♒ Aquarius	The original, modern, free relationship.	♌ Leo
♓ Pisces	The dream relationship.	♍ Virgo

Theme of the Descendant	Finds "Better Half" in the Form of
Peaceableness, indecision, "cultivated paleness," refinement.	Willingness to engage in conflict, impulsive spontaneity, vitality, originality.
Profound feelings of omnipotence; destructiveness, mistrust.	Realism, clear boundaries, serenity, good-naturedness.
Unctuous holiness, gullibility, smugness, one-sidedness.	Irony and wit, nagging doubt, critical scrutiny, diversity.
Strictness and resolution, maintains boundaries, loneliness, sobriety, and toughness.	Softness, indulgence, safety and security, communion, sense of family, depth of feeling, dreaminess.
Eccentricity, bloodless rationalism, cool detachment.	Being at the center of attention, effusive vitality, momentum in life.
Mediumism, chaos, spirituality, improvisation.	Sobriety, order, science, perfection.
Egocentric, go-getter attitude, wildness and coarseness, inconsideration.	Focusing on the partner, clever strategies, esthetics and style, pronounced fairness.
Earthiness, gullibility, stubbornness, carefree sensuality.	Depths, slyness, extreme sensuality, provocation.
Doubt/despair, inner conflicts.	Strong convictions, "in"-sight.
Fickleness, need for protection, dependency on moods, naiveté.	Straightforwardness, feeling of security, discipline, resolution, willingness to take responsibility.
Showmanship, complacency.	Team spirit, exposure.
Sobriety, fastidiousness, clarity.	Dream and intoxication, creative chaos, boundlessness.

DC

The Midheaven or *Medium Coeli*

The *Medium Coeli* (MC) is the axis at the beginning of the 10th house, the highest point (midday) in the horoscope. Above all, it shows the themes, qualities, and tendencies that become increasingly important during the course of a lifetime and should be developed. In addition, it stands for occupation and calling, and can also describe the content as well as the type of professional work. The MC and adjacent 10th house traditionally have been associated with the image of the father. According to the newer interpretation, the image of the mother, her role, and the process of coming to terms with her is primarily depicted here. The following chart describes only the factors that become increasingly important in the life of the individual, both in general and professional terms. To find out what professions these themes relate to, look up same sign where it appears as the Sun sign.

MC in	Themes that Become Increasingly Important	Development
♈ Aries	Self-assertion, personal authority, conquest of new areas, willingness to engage in conflict, derring-do, accepting challenges and growing through them.	Development of fighting spirit and spontaneity.
♉ Taurus	Patience, stamina, security, tradition, enjoyment of life, sensuality, solidarity, developing an awareness of value.	Development of sensual pleasures and stability.
♊ Gemini	Diversity, variety, intellectual curiosity, communication and information, establishing and mediating contacts.	Development of curiosity and diversity.
♋ Cancer	Willingness to help, compassion, loving care, safety and security, home, homeland and family.	Development of femininity and depth of emotion.

MC in	Good Themes	Development
♌ Leo	Equanimity, success, recognition, generosity, grandness, leadership role, being at the center of attention, power.	Development of sense of self-worth and generosity.
♍ Virgo	Economy, methodology, precision, reliability, ability to be critical, thoroughness, health, easy adaptability to whatever is necessary.	Development of precise powers of discernment and love of detail.
♎ Libra	Esthetics, equilibrium, harmony, peace, art, elegance, refined style.	Development of sense of beauty and peaceableness.
♏ Scorpio	Everything enigmatic and unfathomable, concealed truths, taboos and their transgression, depths and abysses, secret powers (the gray eminence), comprehensive changes in favor of a deeper-lying truth.	Development of inner strength, powers of healing and suggestion.
♐ Sagittarius	High ideals, noble-mindedness, high level of education, justice, strong convictions, international connections.	Development of wide horizons and a deep feeling for relevance.
♑ Capricorn	Perseverance, resoluteness, structure, reliability, authority, performance of duty.	Development of resoluteness and willingness to take responsibility.
♒ Aquarius	Independence, originality, joy of experimentation, overcoming the old and bringing something new into the world.	Development of individuality and utopias.
♓ Pisces	Spirituality, transcendent experience, all-embracing love, resolution of solid structures.	Development of mediumistic ability and true brotherly love.

MC

The SUN, MOON, *and* PLANETS

in the HOUSES

The Energy of the Houses

⊙   Sun

The house where the Sun stands is the area of life involved with the central development of the self. It should never be neglected. The Sun imparts the greatest experience of happiness and feelings of deep fulfillment. Whenever life appears to be empty and meaningless, or the question as to the task in life is posed, the range of topics inherent to this house contain the essential answer.

☽   Moon

The Moon house covers that area into which a person feels instinctively prompted, where his or her wish for a feeling of security and other deep longings lie. However, since the Moon is also an expression of adaptability and permanent responsiveness, this house also contains themes to which the person is open at all times.

☿   Mercury

The house position of Mercury shows where the individual prefers to use the mind, intellectual agility and skill, and in which direction curiosity moves him or her. It also shows what he or she grapples with intellectually, and in what areas he or she is always willing to learn something new.

♀   Venus

The position of Venus' house allows us to perceive where the need for harmony, peaceableness, and good taste are expressed, where the wish for community predominates, and where flirtation, eroticism, and seduction play a role. The Venus house indicates where important acquaintances are made and, in many cases, where the encounter with the life partner takes place.

♂   Mars

The Mars house represents the area of life that requires the greatest expenditure of energy. It is the area that must be conquered, where the greatest willingness to engage in conflict is expressed, where the use of force can achieve great things, but also where conflict and destructive frenzy can destroy everything again.

♃   Jupiter

Jupiter's house shows where one feels rich and independent of all outside factors. These are the areas one enters with full trust, where one is given help (or allows help), where one knows how to master problems in a natural and easy manner, and where one grows and confidently looks to the future.

♄   Saturn

Saturn's house represents those areas in life where one feels impoverished, which one initially faces with a critical, suspicious, and mistrusting attitude, or which one would prefer to completely banish from life. But the tasks that no one can avoid are located at precisely this spot. Each individual—to vary-ing degrees—clashes with the themes of the Saturn house; but these themes are simultaneously the greatest opportunities for growth. If they are recog-nized and made use of, experience has shown that development takes place in the following steps:

1. INHIBITION: Rejection and contempt for the themes, which are usual-ly recognized and perceived only in other people at the start.

2. COMPULSION: Radical turnabout and compulsive living out (at any price) of the interrelated topics that had been despised before, whereby an expansion of the previous boundaries always occurs because new ground is being broken.

3. RESOLUTION: Relaxed and serene way of dealing with the previous problem area and its complete integration into the personality.

♅   Uranus

The house of Uranus reveals the themes which a person would like to be independent of, where he or she develops a free spirit, as well as a certain uniqueness, where striving for freedom causes fickleness or, when it comes to opinions, even a "traitor" who—much to his or her own surprise—breaks a promise or a solid agreement. The Uranus house is full of surprises, upheavals, lunacies, as well as being the area of great independence, inge-nious solutions, and eccentric ways of life.

♆   Neptune

The Neptune house represents the areas in which a person develops the finest feelers, sure of instincts and inspirations, possessing "cosmic anten-nae." This is the area in which he or she is guided, where all the important things come, or happen apparently without any effort of his or her own. However, unpleasant Neptune constellations can also indicate confusion, chaos, illusion, or addiction.

♇   Pluto

The Pluto house is primarily concerned with experiences of power and help-lessness, dependencies and entanglements, as well as total transformations on the basis of experiences—usually difficult ones—from which the person emerges changed to the core.

☊ ☋ Moon's Nodes

The house in which the North Node (Ascending Moon's Node) ☊ is posi-tioned shows the way to one's goal and the major points in life. In contrast, the Descending Moon's Node ☋ in the opposite house represents the ideas, manners of behavior, and qualities that are to be resolved.

1st House: *I Am*   Ascendant (AC)

ANALOGY:	RULER:	EXALTATION	DETRIMENT:
♈	♂	☉	♀

FALL:	ELEMENT:	QUALITY:	GENDER:
♄	Fire	Cardinal	Masculine

GENERAL: *The Appearance.* The basic mood in life, outer appearance, type, personality, vital energy, awareness of life, physical constitution, vitality, expression of self, temperament, power of assertion, independence, and way of approaching other people and plans.

POLARITY: The feeling for oneself in contrast to the experience of the other person in the 7th house.

☉   **Sun** in the 1st House   *Being at the Center of Attention*   Exaltation

THE CENTRAL THEME OF DEVELOPMENT OF THE SELF is the expression, the assertion, and affirmation of one's own personality. Tends to be masculine, frequently warm and generous personality.

STRENGTH: THE *Showman.* Full of vital energy, active and initiating. Shapes his or her own life and is always willing to approach something new. Experiences self as the natural focal point of the environment. Egocentric rather than egotistical. Strong-willed, open, cocky, free, direct, vigorous, independent, and convinced of self.

PROBLEM AREA: *The Obtrusive Attention-Seeker.* Overestimates capabilities; self-adulation; unpleasant self-centeredness. Constantly needs attention, which is either grabbed impudently or not taken directly; gets attention indirectly through trickery. Places self at the center of attention by being complicated, long-winded or uses illness and other afflictions. Sensitive to criticism and unable to criticize self, but has a distinct tendency to dish it out to others. Narcissistic, uncomprehending, naive, attention-craving, boastful, and tyrannical.

BEHAVIOR: Supreme style.

☽   **Moon** in the 1st House   *Willingness to Adapt*

STRENGTH: *The Empathetic Person.* Distinct sense of the surrounding world's expectations, connected with a willingness to accommodate and a preference for reacting instead of being active. Easy to talk to. Intuitive, sensitive, and possessing a sure instinct. Reacts strongly to impressions of the surrounding world, high level of emotional impressionability, great intuitive understanding and willingness to adapt. Often has a feminine aura.

PROBLEM AREA: *The Remote-Controlled Individual.* Lack of courage to trust Sun and develop its theme. Conforming attitude and lack of independence, uneven temper and moodiness, unstable, easily distracted, restless, susceptible and easily influenced by others. Dependent on fashion trends. Cowardly character. Inconsistent person who always takes sides with someone who is stronger.

BEHAVIOR: Careful, intuitive, willing to adapt.

☿   **Mercury** in the 1st House   *Tactics*

STRENGTH: *The Clever One.* Talented and clever in the way he or she presents self, looks after personal affairs and asserts self. Crafty, sharp as a tack, sociable, and quick to act. Tactically skilled and ready to adapt, if necessary. Well-pondered conduct. Intellectual behavior. Precocious thinker.

PROBLEM AREA: *The Calculating Mind.* Wily, sly, knows all the tricks of the trade, is cold as ice when it comes to own advantages; opportunistic, and too talkative. Phony and cunning. Never makes a mistake! Always claims to already have said what he or she just heard.

1st

BEHAVIOR: Smart, experienced, agile.

♀ **Venus** in the 1st House	*Charm*	Detriment

STRENGTH: *The Lovable Individual.* Friendly, gracious, likable, feminine aura and a winning, charming nature. Attractive appearance, often also striking beauty. Optimistic attitude toward life. Uninhibited, peaceable, able to adapt, diplomatic, and sociable. Is always popular and welcome everywhere. Often has artistic ambitions.

PROBLEM AREA: *The Beautiful Vacuum.* Nice at all costs and nothing more. Has little to offer except a well-behaved, beautiful facade. Greedily strives for attention, smug, vain, indolent, untruthful, and sensitive to criticism. Infantile innocent conscience.

BEHAVIOR: Charming, gracious.

♂ **Mars** in the 1st House	*Power of Assertion*	Dignity

STRENGTH: *The Lightning-Bolt.* Knows no hesitation, immediately gets down to business. Is quick, direct, appropriately aggressive and willing to engage in conflict when it comes to asserting, achieving, or conquering something. Vigorous, audacious, spontaneous, strong. Masculine aura.

PROBLEM AREA: *The Braggart.* Will go to any lengths to quarrel. Inconsiderate, egotistical, sometimes brutal and violent. Lack of ability to adapt and be level-headed. Starts fights easily. Hurts others without noticing it. Nasty troublemaker.

BEHAVIOR: Direct, impulsive, willing to engage in conflicts.

♃   Jupiter in the 1st House   *Trust*

STRENGTH: *The Confidant.* Is trusting and (therefore) wins the confidence of others. Noble nature, dignified aura, convinced of self and achievements. Cheerful, benevolent, jovial, and optimistic attitude toward life that rubs off on others. Charismatic behavior. Respectable appearance.

PROBLEM AREA: *The Reverend.* Condescending and intolerably arrogant, very high opinion of self, vain and lazy. Unable to criticize self or even admit errors. Smug guru who enjoys playing the illuminated one.

BEHAVIOR: Dignified, respectable, superior.

♄   Saturn in the 1st House   *Mistrust*   Fall

OBJECTIVE: Development of a positive sense of self-assertion.

INHIBITION: *The Reserved Individual, The Misanthrope.* Fear of being hurt. Deep sensitivity concealed behind a facade of self-control and apparent toughness. Or fear of conflicts causes person to appear selfless. Very little self-assurance, but mistrusting and skeptical about life. Suffers because of self and constantly sees self surrounded by a pack of wolves. Difficulties in getting started asserting self. Lifeless, dry, pessimistic, slow, without spirit and élan, joyless, depressed, serious, gloomy, shy, resigned. Often a loner. Constantly worrying. Twists things around until they become impossible to solve.

COMPULSION: *The Stiff Person.* Tries to forcibly overcome inhibitions, but gives the impression of being awkward, clumsy, rough, stiff, and sometimes even aggressive in the process. Being lively becomes a duty. Offense is considered the best defense.

1ˢᵗ

RESOLUTION: *The Great Thaw.* Sober and realistic attitude toward life. Willing to open up to new things after taking a critical, clever look at them. Then consistent, self-controlled, tough, responsible, straightforward, reliable, discreet.

BEHAVIOR: Inhibited, mistrustful, rigid.

♅ Uranus in the 1st House   *Uniqueness*

STRENGTH: *The Free Spirit.* Lives and loves freedom and uniqueness. Unconventional, original, quick to make decisions, full of ideas, and always open to everything new. Tolerates no constriction or imposed duties. Completely convinced of own uniqueness and importance. Only acts in accordance with own free will.

PROBLEM AREA: *The Troublemaker.* Cool, impenetrable, incalculable, impatient, erratic, and shows little willingness to integrate or even subordinate within a system. Seditious, rebellious, superficial, reclusive. Exaggerated need for freedom and extravagant sense of self-worth lead to blatant unreliability and the breaking of agreements, contracts, and commitments.

BEHAVIOR: Eccentric, alert, restless.

♆ Neptune in the 1st House   *Sensitivity*

STRENGTH: *The Guided Soul.* Mediumistic ability for sensing things that go beyond one's own identity and experiencing the border between self and non-self to be fluid. Sensitive intuitive understanding. Open to influences from the outside. Artistic, dreamy, enigmatic. Takes the right path with a sure instinct—as if remote-controlled.

PROBLEM AREA: *The Day-Dreamer.* Seducible, airy-fairy, and incapable of having a (self-)critical view of the world. Personality that is completely dazzling, but not predictable, with the tendency toward blind self-deception, as well as deluding others. Quickly becomes the victim of stronger personalities. Can easily become addicted, dependent, or enslaved to other people. Sometimes makes an absent-minded and incomprehensible impression, but often cannot be fathomed either. Tends to show the world the face that it wants to see. Severe identity problems. Ultimately does not know who he or she is.

BEHAVIOR: Sensitive, dreamy, entranced.

♇   Pluto in the 1st House   *Magnetism*

STRENGTH: *The Fascinator.* Strong charisma, captivating glance, and intensive, irresistible, magical power of attraction. Strong-willed, powerful, and influential. Self-determined, concentrated, and always willing to personally become involved in deep experiences or accompany others in such phases. At the same time, this person has a practically inexhaustible inner strength and an energy that overwhelms everything.

PROBLEM AREA: *The Power-Hungry Person.* Wants to control everyone else and make others dependent out of fear of being defeated or deserted. Inconsiderate and cruel assertion of will. Extremely headstrong, inflexible, and compulsive. Dark, somber, and impenetrable.

BEHAVIOR: Intensive, decisive, overwhelming.

☊   North Node in the 1st House

THEME: Conflict between development of self and striving for harmony, equilibrium, and accommodation in relationships. Tension between giving and taking.

TASK: *Independence.* Developing the courage to emerge from relationship dependencies, create a true relationship to yourself, and do what you personally find to be best for yourself. The development of self-sufficiency, self-confidence, and joy in your own power and strength. Also the willingness to face conflicts and fears of loss in encounters and relationships.

1st

DANGER: *Self-Abnegation.* Being overly adapted; the tendency to always and immediately offer assistance to others, even if this is in contradiction to own needs. Becoming too reliant on other people, too little personal initiative, and always being dependent on confirmation from the outside.

2nd House: *I Have*

ANALOGY:	RULER:	EXALTATION	DETRIMENT:
♉	♀	☽	♂ and ♇

FALL:	ELEMENT:	QUALITY:	GENDER:
♅	Earth	Fixed	Feminine

GENERAL: *Assets.* Assets in both senses of the word as the foundation of material, intellectual, and emotional security. Wealth and possessions, finances, social background, money-making and dealing with money, income and expenses, profit and loss, talents, abilities, physical awareness.

POLARITY: The tangible values in contrast to the subtle values in the 8th house.

⊙   **Sun** in the 2nd House   *Security*

THE CENTRAL THEME OF DEVELOPMENT OF THE SELF is security, which—in accordance with the background—is sought in material, intellectual, emotional, or spiritual areas. The development and expansion of assets in both senses, as property and talent, is vital here.

STRENGTH: *The Rich Man.* Person needs solid support ground; concerned with things that give security. Loves clear boundaries and staked-out territory. Likes to display satisfaction with life to the outside world. Realistic, practical, content, generous, epicurean. Not to be considered poor is, itself, a question of prestige.

PROBLEM AREA: *The Fanatic for Security.* Inner insecurity concealed by inappropriate means. Immoderate hoarding, greed and miserliness, as well as pretentiousness: showing off and spending money in a big way, squandering and dissipating everything.

WAY OF DEALING WITH MONEY: Supremely confident.

☽   **Moon** in the 2nd House   *Need for Security*   Exaltation

STRENGTH: *Financial Intuition.* Intuitive striving for possessions and stability. Sure instinct in dealing with things of value and a deep-rooted feeling of security. Emotional need to lavish care on and "mother" things that are cherished. Outside recognition and admiration of one's talents strengthen the feeling of self-worth and security considerably.

PROBLEM AREA: *Fluctuating Finances.* Great need for security together with very emotional way of approaching money. As a result—in accordance with the Moon sign—strongly fluctuating financial situation (ebb and flow). Existential fears and generous moods alternate with each other. Unstable feeling of self-worth. Leaving options open and not wanting to make commitments. Vanity that demands constant admiration.

WAY OF DEALING WITH MONEY: Emotional.

☿   **Mercury** in the 2nd House   *Business Acumen*

STRENGTH: *The Resourceful Person.* Wealth of ideas and skill in developing and dealing with everything that means security. Practical, economic way of thinking and a good sense of economic fluctuations. Feeling secure thanks to clever mind. Resourceful, experienced, and sharp in dealing with property assets.

PROBLEM AREA: *The Trickster.* Dubious, shady tricks in money-making. Cold-blooded, nasty, untruthful business practices. Financial trap-setter, as well as reckless and incautious approach to money. Losses as a result of presumptuous overestimation of one's own shrewdness.

2nd

WAY OF DEALING WITH MONEY: Clever.

♀ Venus in the 2nd House   *Goldfinger*   Dignity

STRENGTH: *The Lovely One.* Confidence in one's own taste as talent. Business acumen in dealing with art, jewelry, and everything that is beautiful, or that makes a person beautiful. Joy in comfortable surroundings and possessions. Seeks and loves emotional and material security. Likes to adorn herself and joyfully shows what she has. Equilibrium and prudence in dealing with money.

PROBLEM AREA: *The Vain Squanderer.* Egotistical, smug satisfying of one's own needs. Intemperance. Believes that one must measure love in dollars and cents or that one can buy love.

WAY OF DEALING WITH MONEY: Erotic attitude toward money.

♂ Mars in the 2nd House   *The Struggle for Money*   Detriment

STRENGTH: *The Money-Maker.* Conflict readiness and the will to assert self, as well as pure muscle power as basic disposition that signifies security. Struggles and works offensively at full power for the development of financial security since money means power and strength.

PROBLEM AREA: *The Speculator.* Arbitrary, self-righteous way of dealing with money. Would rather take a gamble than carefully weigh matters. Engages in foolish financial risks (test of courage!). Rivalry and fighting about money resulting in financial losses. Impulsive expenditures, which are ruinous in extreme cases.

WAY OF DEALING WITH MONEY: Spontaneous, arbitrary.

♃ Jupiter in the 2nd House   *Consciousness of Wealth*

STRENGTH: *The Money-Spinner.* Great trust in personal security and assets in the sense of ability and possessions. Feels rich—independent of actual bank balance. Lucky hand in money matters. Carefree, content, and full of trust in God that nothing will go wrong. Gives support to others and likes to let them share in his or her own wealth.

PROBLEM AREA: *The Self-Satisfied Person.* Lazy. Finds it natural to demand things without providing (an appropriate) service in return. Resting on one's presumed laurels. Conceit. Squanders and wastes money and property.

WAY OF DEALING WITH MONEY: Jovial.

♄ Saturn in the 2nd House   *Consciousness of Poverty*

OBJECTIVE: Development of a true feeling of self-worth.

INHIBITION: *The Short-Changed Person.* Fear of poverty; distinct mistrust of everything that could offer security. Feels impoverished—regardless of bank balance (Uncle Scrooge McDuck syndrome). Even with enormous assets, always concerned everything could be lost, stolen, dispossessed, destroyed, or eaten away by inflation. Insecure regarding personal value and abilities. Sells self for sake of security. Mistrustingly fearful and inhibited, allows self and others nothing. Envy, penny-pinching, stinginess (materially and intellectually) or exactly the opposite: vehement rejection of material values.

COMPULSION: *The Pseudo-Generous Individual.* Acts like he or she doesn't worry about money. Forces self to be generous, but gives impression of being clumsy and artificial (shakes when signing the check). Gets involved in risks and speculations in order to not be seen as stiff, fossilized, or antiquated.

RESOLUTION: *The Value-Conscious Person.* Realistic attitude toward everything that embodies security. Responsible, healthy, sober way of handling assets. Understands how to view talents and abilities as lasting values and inner possessions that are to be developed and cared for. Thorough, matter-of-fact, careful, conscientious, and prudent, confident, rich, emotionally free.

WAY OF DEALING WITH MONEY: Fearful, reserved, circumspect.

2nd

♅   Uranus in the 2nd House   *Financial Surprises*   Fall

STRENGTH: *The Financially-Independent Individual.* Imaginative and inventive in money matters. Strong urge for financial independence. Uncommon ways of making (and spending) money. Courage and joy in trying out and exploring unfamiliar things and new areas. Unusual talents. Strong and rapidly fluctuating bank balance. Financial fireworks.

PROBLEM AREA: *The Unpredictable Person.* Eccentric way of dealing with money. Blatantly disregards prevailing norms. Too special to have to earn money like everyone else, which frequently causes financial problems. Love of freedom is more important than reliability. Result is often breach of contract.

WAY OF DEALING WITH MONEY: Unconventional to crazy.

♆   Neptune in the 2nd House *Spiritual Security*

STRENGTH: *The Sustained One.* Inexplicable feeling of self-worth and security, regardless of outside factors. Deep consciousness of being sustained, being well looked-after and therefore withstanding all life's difficulties. Properly evaluating talents and abilities. Earning money through spiritual or mediumistic gifts. Having a sure instinct for financial matters and a good nose for lucrative transactions, but sometimes difficulties in approaching things systematically. Money-lending transactions.

PROBLEM AREAS: *The Anti-Business Person.* Vacillating, untrustworthy, unpredictable basis. Nebulous security. No feeling of self-worth and very dependent on other people's appraisals. Easy to encourage or discourage. No—or just a dull—feeling for financial matters. Irresponsible. Tendency toward secrecy, never showing others what he or she really possesses (materially, intellectually, psychologically). Obscure money transactions. Swindle and fraud.

WAY OF DEALING WITH MONEY: Visionary/illusionary or nebulous.

♇   **Pluto** in the 2nd House   *The Power of Money*   Detriment

STRENGTH: *Inner Wealth.* Deep-reaching transformations through financial crises or experiences of dependency. Earning money with spiritual powers (hypnosis, healing powers). Building on the basis of inner wealth. Feeling of deepest security.

PROBLEM AREA: *Financial Dependency.* Succumbing to the fascination of money. Making other people (financially) dependent on yourself or personally experiencing yourself to be helplessly dependent on money. Shamelessly demonstrating the power of money. "Buying" other people, opinions, and "love." Compulsively chasing after money. Greedy, stingy, petty, avaricious, and with a compulsive need to control when it comes to material things.

WAY OF DEALING WITH MONEY: Fascinated or obsessed.

☊   **North Node** in the 2nd House

THEME: Conflict between holding on tight and wanting to preserve something on the one hand and the forces of transformation and necessity to leave the old behind yourself on the other.

TASK: *Intrinsic Value.* Must accept the need for security, closeness, trust and intimacy, confidence and physicality. Recognizing own value, experiencing self as important, discovering possibilities and abilities, valuing self, and loving self. Development of talents and everything that means security: material security, inner security, and self-assurance.

DANGER: *Compulsive Need to Control.* Wanting to control everything as a result of great fears of loss. Seeking security, as well as confirmation that he or she deserves love and is important, through the questionable creation of dependencies. Abuses of sexuality and eroticism as instruments of power.

2nd

3rd House: *I Think*

ANALOGY: ♊	RULER: ☿	EXALTATION —	DETRIMENT: ♃
FALL: —	ELEMENT: Air	QUALITY: Mutable	GENDER: Masculine

GENERAL: *The Mind.* Healthy common sense. Learning, communicating, thinking, perceiving, differentiating. Exchange of thoughts, correspondence, everyday contacts, everyday experiences, intellectual abilities and the capacity to learn, logic, power of expression, business acumen—particularly trade, brokerage business, business trips, and short journeys.

POLARITY: Prosaic thought and the kind of newspaper reality valid for just one day in contrast to higher thinking and the true convictions in the 9th house.

⊙   **Sun** in the 3rd House   *The Eternal Student*

THE CENTRAL THEME OF DEVELOPMENT OF THE SELF is found in studying, communicating, absorbing knowledge and information and imparting it to others, as well as constantly exploring and learning something new.

STRENGTH: *The Knowledge-Sponge.* Enjoyment of learning that doesn't abate with age. Curiosity about everything with which the surrounding world is concerned. Desire to read and exchange thoughts with others. Mentally flexible, able to change and adapt. Sociable, thirsty for knowledge, full of ideas. Often quick-witted and intelligent. A good teacher and speaker.

PROBLEM AREA: *The Overly Intellectual.* Intellectual snobbishness. Feels (without reason) superior to others and tries to force the world to accept ideas. Condescending, chatty, and know-it-all. Contradictory.

SPEAKING STYLE: Personal, powerful, showman-like.

☽   Moon in the 3rd House   *The Curious One*

STRENGTH: *The Talkative Person.* The need to have a say and to communicate thoughts. Open, very talkative, eloquent, empathizing in conversations. Likes to hear himself or herself talk, and knows how to have a say everywhere. At the same time, does well at imitating others and talks with each person in his own language. A talent for appropriately stealing the spotlight in greatly differing social groups and at every opportunity. Tendency to record everyday life (in journals). Vivid manner of expression. Desire to learn to show others the knowledge gained.

PROBLEM AREA: *The Chatterbox.* Superficial in word and thought. Influenced by moods. Problems are intellectualized and talked to death. Plays the talented person, easily assumes other people's thoughts and considers them to be his or her own. Constantly changing interests.

SPEAKING STYLE: Emotional, vivid, relies very much on the listeners

☿   Mercury in the 3rd House   *The Inquisitive Individual*

STRENGTH: *The Articulate One.* Skillful in negotiations and discussions. Quickly and adroitly speaks the language of the person he or she is talking to. May easily persuade other people. Ability to show interest in the mental habits of another and beating him at his own game or coolly letting him trap himself. Never at a loss for arguments. Often has a special intellectual talent. Constant studiousness.

PROBLEM AREA: *The Sophist.* Hair-splitter for whom the discussion is of more significance than the content. More interested in rhetorical superiority than the truth. Superficial, flighty, and loquacious. Premature judgments.

3rd

SPEAKING STYLE: Objective, witty, lively.

♀   **Venus** in the 3rd House   *Beautiful Words*

STRENGTH: *Ms. or Mr. Popularity.* Lovely verbal expression. Spreads a cheerful, harmonious atmosphere. Is witty, optimistic, and very charming. Knows how to flatter and seduce with beautiful words. Maintains many contacts and has good relationships with siblings and the immediate environment. Is good at stealing the spotlight. Has a good understanding of how to mediate and settle conflicts.

PROBLEM AREA: *Beautiful Empty Phrases.* Melodic, magical words without any substance. Graceful, but horribly shallow. Superficial, trivial, and opportunistic contacts lacking in depth. Likes to play games with other people.

SPEAKING STYLE: Charming, winning, stylish.

♂   **Mars** in the 3rd House   *Sharp Wit*

STRENGTH: *The Talkmaster.* Can express strongly both verbally and in writing. Tends to sharply criticize the surrounding world and inconsiderately expose everything that is wrong, phony, or somehow inconsistent. Has the courage to stand up for self and show true colors, even at the risk of looking like a fool. Strong, but vacillating application of energy in learning.

PROBLEM AREA: *The Cantankerous Person.* Great gift (and desire) for making self unpopular. Is always looking for a fight. Constantly disgraces self without even noticing it.

SPEAKING STYLE: Offensive, quarrelsome, commanding.

♃   Jupiter in the 3rd House   *Wealth of Ideas*   Detriment

STRENGTH: *The Scholar.* Great intellectual grasp, likes to talk a lot and does it convincingly. Loves big words and epic embellishments. Brilliant, well-informed entertainer. Educated, popular, and respected. Learns quickly and easily and is good at imparting what has been learned.

PROBLEM AREA: *The High and Mighty.* Lazy about learning (would rather be a teacher than a student). Fear of looking like a fool. Is embarrassed about not knowing something and therefore secretly studies and skillfully bluffs with immature, superficial knowledge. Loud, disrespectful, presumptuous, self-righteous. Considers himself or herself to be better than others. Likes to play the judge, even if no one has asked him or her to do so. Getting his or her due is more important than being right.

SPEAKING STYLE: Exalted, didactic, convincing.

♄   Saturn in the 3rd House   *Methodical Thinking*

OBJECTIVE: Concentrated, consistent, profound thinking.

INHIBITION: *The Ponderous Person.* Slow and dense in conversations, as well as when reading and studying. Clings to each letter. Hangs on too tightly to everything, which also causes speech defects and expressive disorders (stuttering). Tends to be mistrustful and reserved in everyday life and in contacts with surroundings, initially at least. Strong doubt about own intellectual abilities and verbal skills. Inflexible thinking. The Cinderella of the family. Finds no open doors. Must constantly wait longer than other people (who are allowed to go first) wherever he or she is.

COMPULSION: *The Wind-Bag.* Communication at any price. The obtrusive person who always talks without having anything to say and who believes he or she knows everything. The phrase-monger who always just mechanically repeats everything he or she hears.

3rd

SOLUTION: *The Experienced Speaker.* The ability to think in a careful, profound, concentrated, objective, and serious manner without losing the red thread. Clear and practiced in verbal expression. Demosthenes symptom.[3]

SPEAKING STYLE: Structured, chronological, sober.

♅   Uranus in the 3rd House   *The (Unrecognized) Genius*

STRENGTH: *The Self-Taught Person.* Original, imaginative, but completely erratic thinking that is frequently a step ahead of its time or other people. Sudden ideas, perceptions, and inventions (Eureka effect[4]). A free-thinker. The impromptu speaker who doesn't follow any type of speaking concept. An autodidact who quickly comprehends and learns in accordance with a personal—mostly unusual—manner. Spreads a lively atmosphere. Eternal desire to learn.

PROBLEM AREA: *The Recluse.* An eccentric, even among siblings. Isolated, mysterious, unappreciated, which frequently results in tormenting self-criticism. Crazy, high-flown thinking that often disregards all the norms. Suffers strongly under the customary school system that imposes too many standards, demands too many restrictions, and progresses much too slowly. Not concentrated, restless, has too many irons in the fire (tries to think several thoughts at the same time).

SPEAKING STYLE: Spontaneous, original, lively, capricious.

♆   Neptune in the 3rd House   *Knowledge from the Depths*

STRENGTH: *The Seer.* Thinking inspired from the depths. Imaginative, vivid in manner of expression. Led from within when thinking, writing, speaking, and lecturing, and therefore often does not even know where words will take him or her. The same applies to the way in which her or she learns. Empathy and identification with immediate environment. Quickly finds the way anywhere. Good at slipping into various roles. Master of the art of persuasion; actor. Writes anonymously, under a pseudonym, as a ghostwriter.

PROBLEM AREA: *The Illusionist.* Boundless, hazy thinking and unclear manner of expression. Constantly goes off on a tangent. Loses self in a fictitious reality. Already incomprehensible to siblings during childhood. Problems with the truth, becomes victim of untruths or spreads tall tales and daydreams which are considered to be true. Often has difficulty in differentiating between personal thoughts and opinions and those of other people. Distracted and confused.

SPEAKING STYLE: Inspired, imaginative, pictorial, seductive.

♇   **Pluto** in the 3rd House   *The Penetrating Mind*

STRENGTH: *The Spirit of Research.* Profound thinking and search for background reasons without compromise. Can be fascinated by a thought and nearly get completely embroiled in an idea. Strong power of expression and persuasion. Understands the power of thoughts and knows how to use them effectively.

PROBLEM AREA: *The Demagogue.* Wants absolutely to assert personal viewpoints and opinions. Misuses the suggestive power of words in order to win over other people. One-track thinking, fixed ideas, and compulsion to talk. Difficult, dark, destructive train of thought.

SPEAKING STYLE: Overwhelming, insistent, suggestive, demagogic.

☊   **Ascending Moon's Node** in the 3rd House

THEME: Conflict between the search for objectivity, broad knowledge, lively communication and exchange of information, as well as the insistence on a strongly subjective view of things and retreat into an elitist, intellectual world with solidly anchored standpoints and extremely prejudicial convictions and commandments.

TASK: *Interpreting.* Expressing complex correlations, lofty convictions, and great thoughts in the everyday language. Translating spiritual knowledge into practical living and conveying it to the immediate environment in a generally understandable manner. Making clear the relationship between noble perceptions, philosophical ideas, as well as ethical and religious values, in everyday life. Imparting practical knowledge through writing and speaking. Looking after immediate matters.

3rd

DANGER: *Dogmatism.* Getting stuck in rigid patterns, convictions, and prejudices. Maintains a fundamentalist attitude in a myopic and stubborn manner. Doesn't budge an inch from acquired convictions or personal view of the world.

4th House: *I Feel* Imum Coeli (IC)

ANALOGY:	RULER:	EXALTATION:	DETRIMENT:
♋	☽	♃ and ♆	♄

FALL:	ELEMENT:	QUALITY:	GENDER:
♂	Water	Cardinal	Feminine

GENERAL: *The Soul.* The depths of the soul, premonitions and dreams, the origins, the home, the need for a feeling of security, well-being, homeland and homesickness, the evening of life, family roots, the image of the father, tradition, the way of living

POLARITY: The origin in contrast to the goal in life in the 10th house.

⊙ Sun in the 4th House   *Depths of the Soul*

THE CENTRAL THEME OF THE DEVELOPMENT OF THE SELF is the home, the family, the homeland, as well as the experience of the inner world, the depths of one's own soul.

STRENGTH: *Emotional Strength.* Creative confrontation with the images of the unconscious as psychologist, interpreter of dreams, or artist. Strives for a harmonious connection between the inner world and the outer environment. Rooted in native soil, home-loving. Deeply rooted in family tradition and proud of family heritage. The responsible patriarch as dignified bearer of the family name. Intuitive. Intensive feelings and frequently introverted. Mediumistic gifts if the Sun is located close to the IC (up to 5°).

PROBLEM AREA: *The House Tyrant.* Does not manage to detach from the family and the home grounds, or has difficulty in doing so. Remains in the parental house or quickly establishes own family. Develops nasty patriarchal airs and forces own—usually—narrow-minded formulas for explaining the world upon environment. Fearful, sentimental, reserved, egotistical, tyrannical, dependent on others, depressive. Relates everything to self.

IMAGE OF THE FATHER: Self-confident, exemplary, strong.

☽ **Moon** in the 4th House   *Attachment to One's Native Land*   Dignity

STRENGTH: *Emotional Wanderlust.* Instinctive search for emotional security and intimacy. Needs a clear feeling of belonging, a genuine home, yet is still quite mobile and likes to travel like a rolling stone. However, can adapt to a strange environment with astonishing ease. Strong relationship to the unconscious mind, the past, and origins. Fine intuitive sense of other people's needs and feelings. Imaginative, creative, artistic talent. Mediumistic gifts if the Moon is located close to the IC (up to 5°).

PROBLEM AREA: *The Person Without a Home.* Cannot develop any feelings of inner belonging. Restless, constantly on the road. Remains emotionally infantile, dependent on other people, and self-destructive.

IMAGE OF THE FATHER: Protective-emotional, the father in the role of the mother, or possibly unstable, moody, and unreliable.

☿   **Mercury** in the 4th House   *Thinking Along Familiar Lines*

STRENGTH: *Sensitive Thought.* Deep understanding of the image language of the soul. Good interpreter of dreams, fairy tales, and symbols. Imaginative storyteller. Likes to work at home. Mediumistic gifts if Mercury is located close to the IC (up to 5°).

PROBLEM AREA: *The Intellectually Retarded.* Uncritically assumes the thought patterns and conceptual world of the family. Aversion to outside ideas. Narrow-minded, old-fashioned, unimaginative way of thinking.

4th

IMAGE OF THE FATHER: Clever, smart, skillful.

♀   Venus in the 4th House   *Peace of Mind*

STRENGTH: *The Beautiful Home.* Makes sure there is peace and a pleasant atmosphere in the domestic area. Builds a love nest there. Great emotional romanticism. Deep sensual and motherly tendencies. Has great emotional powers and strives for inner peace. Love of homeland.

PROBLEM AREA: *The Little Woman.* Too emotionally attached to parental home. Doesn't develop a sense of independence. Gets stuck on the parent of the opposite sex as the searching image. Imitates the parents' marriage.

IMAGE OF THE FATHER: Loving, attractive.

♂   Mars in the 4th House   *Emotional Uproar*   Fall

STRENGTH: *The Watchdog.* Is alert and ready to fight at any time when it comes to sheltering or protecting the home, the family, or the parents against attacks. Early and distinct striving for independence. If Mars is located close to the IC (up to 5°), this means a distinctly good feeling for emotional energies and a talent for working with spiritual energies.

PROBLEM AREA: *The Center of Unrest.* Rebellion, strife, and opposition in the parental home, particularly against the father. Humiliations, restriction of freedom, and experiences of helplessness usually lead to an early detachment from the parental home. Pent-up aggression and deep-seated, concealed, paralyzing rage lead to greater inner unrest with considerable emotional tensions that are difficult to bring to the surface and integrate. Frequent fights at home.

IMAGE OF THE FATHER: Strong and powerful or aggressive and hot-tempered.

♃ Jupiter in the 4th House   *The Good, Splendid Home*   Exaltation

STRENGTH: *The Aristocrat.* Proud of own descent. Strong trust in roots. Feels self to be the high point of the line of ancestors. Enjoys living in elegant, comfortable housing. Relatively simple to find a corresponding residence even under difficult external conditions. Spiritual wealth. Certain of, and trust in, being led by the inner voice. Mediumistic gifts if Jupiter is located close to the IC (up to 5°).

PROBLEM AREA: *Class Conceit* Arrogance in dealing with people of supposedly lower status. High-handed house tyrant.

IMAGE OF THE FATHER: Wonderful, dignified, good.

♄ Saturn in the 4th House   *The Meager or Cold Home*   Detriment

OBJECTIVE: Development of inner stability and independence.

INHIBITION: *The Unwanted Individual.* Difficult childhood, painful feelings of not being safe and secure, emotional injuries, rejection, repression, not being loved, frustrations, and emotional insecurity. Being deeply stricken by life. Wishes he or she had never been born. Fear of intimacy and closeness. Difficulties in permitting and expressing feelings. Sees self as being very weighty, serious, and important. Shifts the search for emotional security to the outside world, such as through the acquisition of real estate as a substitute. Has a hard time finding a place to live. Usually lives below means, sometimes even spartanly (the eternal student's pad) or in cold, impersonal, comfortable surroundings.

COMPULSION: *Emotional Exhibitionism.* Violent attempt to express feelings and permit closeness. Group experiences or other "training grounds" as a mandatory program.

RESOLUTION: *Genuine Inner Security.* When inner inhibitions have been reduced and mistrust toward intimacy and closeness has melted away, trust in one's own inner security gradually grows. The deeply understood insight that only the person who deserts himself or herself has been deserted by everyone leads to the grateful feeling of inner security without outer support.

IMAGE OF THE FATHER: Strict, reserved, authoritarian, or absent.

4th

♅   Uranus in the 4th House *The Homeless or Stateless Individual*

STRENGTH: *The Person With No Strings Attached.* Leaves home at an early age and then goes own way completely. Needs the feeling of absolute freedom, particularly from family ties and obligations within the clan. Only likes to join forces with kindred spirits on own accord. Lives in a highly individualistic, original environment. Always mobile. Surprising moves.

PROBLEM AREA: *The Test-Tube Baby.* As a child, often doubts whether parents are really his or her own. Distanced relationship to the family, homeland, and tradition. Often feels like he or she doesn't belong, but is rather an alien element. Therefore no feeling of obligation to parental home or homeland. The family suddenly loses its hold. Without a homeland, uprooted, completely alienated. Vagabond.

IMAGE OF THE FATHER: Original, but unreliable and unpredictable.

♆   Neptune in the 4th House   *Family Mists*   Exaltation

STRENGTH: *The Sensitive Person.* Natural, intuitive access to the images of the unconscious mind. Sensitive and emotional. Instinctive understanding of dreams and symbols. Can only slowly and passively detach from the parental home. "Dreams" way out of it and looks for an environment in which the vibrations are good (house on the ocean). Can also live alone in a spiritualized manner, completely untouched by environment. Mediumistic gifts if Neptune is located close to the IC (up to 5°).

PROBLEM AREA: *Hazy Origins.* Unclear origins, blurry family relationships. No chance of identifying with parents, family, or homeland. Constant theme of dissolution. Feels driven, without solid ground or boundaries. Feelings of homesickness without clear idea of where this longed-for homeland should be.

IMAGE OF THE FATHER: Idealized, unreachable or intangible, sometimes also absent.

♇   **Pluto** in the 4th House   *Family Power Struggle*

STRENGTH: *Clean Sweep.* Radical and relentless renewal wherever it is seen as necessary. Willingness to cut off decaying roots and fundamentally change oneself inside and out. Profound transformations often occur through confrontations within the family or living conditions. Mediumistic gifts if Pluto is located close to the IC (up to 5°).

PROBLEM AREA: *The Emotionally Shackled.* Extremely strong, fated bonds to the family and/or the family heritage. Power struggles within the family. Feels obligated or coerced into fulfilling the parent's expectations instead of living own life. Vehement inner rage and aggression, but greatest difficulties in freeing self and going own way.

IMAGE OF THE FATHER: Felt to be powerful, influential, decisive, controlling, and manipulative; frequently unconscious, erotic relationship.

☊   **North Node** in the 4th House

THEME: Conflict between family and profession, home and public life, closeness and distance, inner experience and outer obligations.

TASK: *Emotional Strength.* Seeking and finding happiness and fulfillment in the home, the family, in your own inner life. Becoming involved with your own origins, the clan, the nation, and the homeland. Turning to the inner world, the images of the soul, your own feelings and emotional needs. Searching for possibilities of expressing your own solicitude: in the family, as a physician, therapist, etc.

4th

DANGER: *The Rover.* Keeping away from domestic life and occupation with the inner world through external, professional assignments and obligations. Concentrating entire ambition on performance and outer recognition instead of developing inner peace and emotional security.

5th House: *I Show Myself*			
ANALOGY: ♌	RULER: ☉	EXALTATION: ♀	DETRIMENT: ♄ and ♅
FALL: —	ELEMENT: Fire	QUALITY: Fixed	GENDER: Masculine

GENERAL: *Self-Expression.* The joy of showing who you are, what you have, and what you can do. You do everything for fun and not because it's your duty. Self-expression and joy in life. The inner child. Play and pleasure, from playing with children to gambling for money, acting, and the game of love. Flirting, eroticism, sexuality, love affairs, children, creative expression, speculation, hobbies.

POLARITY: Emphasis on self and self-expression in contrast to the integration in a group in the 11th house.

⊙   **Sun** in the 5th House   *The Player*   Dignity

THE CENTRAL THEME OF DEVELOPMENT OF THE SELF is the joy of one's own powers of creation and procreation, self-realization, showmanship, as well as the playful depiction of what a person is capable of.

STRENGTH: *Awareness of Personal Effect on Others.* Likes to show what he or she can do in a heartfelt manner and of own accord. At the same time, doesn't like to be bound to duty. Prefers to experience life and love as one big game. Is always perfectly conscious of the effect made when he or she appears on any type of stage. Great abilities in areas of creativity and design that— above all in artists—can lead to true creative ecstasy. Stands fully in the limelight. Independent, spontaneous, positive, cordial. The eternally youthful, dynamic, sensual, creative person.

PROBLEM AREA: *Dependence on an Audience.* Must constantly try out effect on other people, particularly effect on the opposite sex. Dependent on applause. Needs much recognition in order to cover up deep feelings of inferiority.

ATTITUDE TOWARD CHILDREN: Fatherly, big-hearted, benevolent.

☽ Moon in the 5th House   *The Participant*

STRENGTH: *The Playful Person.* Instinctive urge to behave playfully in order to express feelings, emotions, and skills. Being willing to open up to things that are playful, new, and exciting at any time and simply being a part of things. Joy of life and enjoyment of playing, above all the eternally new game of love. Loves the enjoyment of the moment: impulsive, playful, creative, poetic, dramatic, passionate. Harmonious connection between feelings and development of the self. Artistic and musical disposition. Good teacher. Fond of children.

PROBLEM AREA: *The Gambler.* The game is important, but the fellow player or players can be replaced at any time. Gets involved in senseless risks in the process. Too playful. "Plays away" life. Unstable, arrogant, insecure, without self-assurance.

ATTITUDE TOWARD CHILDREN: Motherly, caring, fond of children.

☿ Mercury in the 5th House   *Playful Thinking*

STRENGTH: *Creative Thoughts.* Can easily be preoccupied with a number of things at the same time. Creative in thought and action. Likes to show everything he or she knows. Quickly overcomes interim failures. Very clever at playing. Knows all the tricks of the trade, particularly in the game of love. Physical and intellectual agility.

PROBLEM AREA: *The Con Man.* Unscrupulous gambler, shrewd, foolhardy, mean, arrogant. Skillful imitator of thought and action, but without individuality.

5th

ATTITUDE TOWARD CHILDREN: Promotes intellectual inclinations.

♀   Venus in the 5th House   *Enamored by Love*

STRENGTH: *The Flirt.* Great willingness to be happy. Deep gratitude for all the beauty in the world. Always prepared to overlook what is ugly for the sake of beauty. Loves love and flirting. Knows how to place himself or herself in the best light and make an enchanting impression. Can yield to the intoxication of beauty from the bottom of his or her heart. Artistic disposition. Fond of children.

PROBLEM AREA: *The Playboy.* Superficial, vain behavior. Calculating, heartless playing of trumps. Can only live in very high spirits or states of ecstasy. Undignified and foolish when older.

ATTITUDE TOWARD CHILDREN: Promotes abilities in the fine arts.

♂   Mars in the 5th House   *Game with High Stakes*

STRENGTH: *The Radiant Victor.* Impetuous conqueror, valiant and passionate lover. Loves competitive games, likes to get involved in high wagers, and shows that he or she is the greatest, capable of doing everything better. Wants to assert personal interests and wants to be autonomous and independent. Highest stakes in love and play. Joy of life, zest for living, fiery, very passionate sexuality, and out to conquer. Natural authority.

PROBLEM AREA: *The Quarrelsome Gambler.* Likes to place all the bets on one card and plays with risky stakes. Tends to grossly exaggerate. Passionately loves to wager, but doesn't know how to lose. Always picks a quarrel instead. Erotic ambition, narcissistic disposition, sadomasochistic, violent, jealous, overbearing.

ATTITUDE TOWARD CHILDREN: Promotes interest in sports.

♃ **Jupiter** in the 5th House   *Lucky at Love and Play*

STRENGTH: *Optimist.* Enjoyment of life, love, and art. A fundamental trust in one's own abilities, conduct, and the idea that simply everything in life can be achieved. Lucky at love and play. Strong attraction for others. Good actor.

PROBLEM AREA: *Vain Dilettante.* Superficial, sensitive to criticism, smug, irresponsible. Likes to depend on others. Gambler personality, pleasure-seeker, indolent. A Don Juan with countless love affairs and an easily injured self-esteem.

ATTITUDE TOWARD CHILDREN: Good-natured, indulgent, supportive.

♄ **Saturn** in the 5th House   *Stage Fright or "Playing Prohibited!"*

OBJECTIVE: Trust in one's own self and one's own center. The willingness to put in an appearance and show oneself.

INHIBITION: *The Unlucky Devil.* Always takes everything too hard, too seriously, and too tragically. Every game (and each flirt) immediately turns into something serious and usually turns out badly. Secret feelings of guilt and (unconscious) desire to be penitent. Keeps betting on the same card even in hopeless cases and after the game is lost. Lack of recognition and admiration. Believes one is not lovable or even likable. Fear of showing oneself or making an appearance (stage fright). Unapproachable, shy, reserved, strict, stiff, envious, petty, cold. Disappointments in love.

COMPULSION: *Playing as a Duty.* Tries with all one's might to come on strong and not take life seriously. Frantically attempts to step nonchalantly into the limelight or become a carefree, cheerful master of the art of living and playing.

RESOLUTION: *Sensible Behavior.* Has learned to give in to the unpredictable turns of a game. Shows what he or she can do, but not without adequate practice and preparation. Stands behind personal mistakes and doesn't need to be perfect. Aware of personal uniqueness; likes to spontaneously open up and express self in an uninhibited manner. Plays prudently—instead of doggedly—with a high degree of endurance. Warm-hearted, open, congenial.

ATTITUDE TOWARD CHILDREN: Serious, responsible, or possibly fearful, disapproving, strict.

5th

♅   **Uranus** in the 5th House   *Personal Rules of the Game*   Detriment

STRENGTH: *The Fireworks of Love.* Loves craziness, variety, and flirting, but above all personal freedom and personal rules in the game of love and life. Always has something dazzling. Tends to make original, spontaneous appearances, but can only participate if personally interested. As a result, tends to avoid routine and obligations of every sort. Experiences many surprises.

PROBLEM AREA: *The Disappointed One.* Cannot stick to one thing faithfully or for a long time. Doesn't like to get completely involved with one person or one plan. Never succumbs to intoxication to the point of being out of control. Knows that sooner or later every experience results in disappointment or separation. Maintains own inner independence and distance toward everything and everyone. Leaves the other person or people quickly, before being deserted (or thrown out). Mistrustful and suspicious. Never completely trusts and loves. Ultimately always disappointing, disappointed, and lonely.

ATTITUDE TOWARD CHILDREN: "Progressive" and changeable. Children are often also experienced as burdensome and restricting.

♆   **Neptune** in the 5th House   *The Art of Seduction*

STRENGTH: *The Romantic Flame.* Imaginative and entrancing when it comes to flirting and seduction. Longing and willingness to let oneself be transfigured and swept away by love. Deep intuitive understanding or even identification with one's environment. Great talent for giving or conveying to others what they secretly expect—up to the point of selflessly surrendering the ego. Must lose him- or herself in another human being or in love in order to find self. Artistic touch, creative potential, connection of spirituality and eroticism (Tantric sex).

PROBLEM AREA: *The Cheater.* Cannot adhere to the rules of the game because he or she keeps forgetting them. Extremely easy to seduce. Very passive. Is drawn into a relationship or affair and then dreams his or her way out of it. Afterward, doesn't really know what actually happened and what just took place in dreams. Also victim of own deceptive images. Eroticism stimulated through aphrodisiacs or drugs.

ATTITUDE TOWARD CHILDREN: Vague, idealizing, nostalgic.

♇   **Pluto** in the 5th House   *Magical Power Games*

STRENGTH: *The Fascinating Player.* Charismatic personality and magnetic powers of attraction when in the limelight, but also an emotionally compelling force in the game of life and love. Wins thanks to extraordinary powers of suggestion. Strong sexual energy.

PROBLEM AREA: *The Obsessive Gambler.* Risks everything and loves to gamble for all or nothing. Misuses powers of suggestion and forces others to participate in games that give them chills up and down their spines. Also gets caught up in dependencies and becomes entangled in own spider web. Dangerous liaisons and passions.

ATTITUDE TOWARD CHILDREN: Mutual dependence and (subtle) power games.

☊   **North Node** in the 5th House

THEME: Conflict between passionate, sensual, erotic love, and the pure love of friendship, between ego-centered showmanship and the consciousness of belonging to a group.

TASK: *Creative Genius.* Playfully and enjoyably providing a means of expression for your own creativity. Showing what you are capable of and thereby making room for your hopes, wishes, dreams, and thoughts, letting them become reality. Standing on stage or otherwise attracting attention and admiration for yourself. Understanding life to be a playful challenge.

5th

DANGER: *The Peripheral Figure.* Placing yourself at the edge instead of in the center. Remaining so rooted in group feeling that no clear feeling for the self can be created. Dissipating your energies. Wanting to have a say everywhere, to provide assistance for everyone else and thereby squander your own strength and initiative. Not wanting to prove yourself.

6th House: *I Integrate Myself*

ANALOGY:	RULER:	EXALTATION:	DETRIMENT:
♍	☿	☿	♃ and ♆

FALL:	ELEMENT:	QUALITY:	GENDER:
♀	Earth	Mutable	Feminine

GENERAL: *Health and Work.* Physical health, the relationship between body and mind, consciousness of health, disposition to illness, traditional and alternative medicine. Everyday working life, place of work, work contents, way of working, working methods, and result of work. Class-consciousness. Social integration and adaptation.

POLARITY: The integration of the self in contrast to the self-sacrifice in the 12th house.

☉	Sun in the 6th House	*Integration*

THE CENTRAL THEME OF DEVELOPMENT OF THE SELF is the smooth interplay of all components in an organism or community (human being, company, or nation) of united organs as the necessary precondition for the health of the whole.

STRENGTH: *The Structurer.* Is aware of the necessity of hierarchies and makes sure that every wheel in the mechanism functions. As a result, looks after the health of the respective system and likes to integrate oneself well. Brings order to the chaos. Creates clear, transparently smooth structures. Promotes achievement and develops systems for preventing damage. Practical, skillful, tenacious, concentrated, independent. Work in the field of public health.

PROBLEM AREA: *The Prestige-Hungry Person.* Always concerned with own prestige. Puts too much pressure on self (and subordinates) to produce results. Fear of failure and inferiority complexes. Therefore conformist and horribly normal. Hypochondriac self-observation because of exaggerated fear of illness.

WORKING STYLE: Very personal, completely involved, leadership quality.

☽   Moon in the 6th House   *Professional Adaptation*

STRENGTH: *The Indispensable Individual.* Instinctive urge to work, live a healthy life, and remain fit. Knows how to integrate oneself into the area of work in such a manner that existing gaps are filled, impulses are taken up and translated into action so that sooner or later one becomes indispensable. Needs and seeks work that offers variety. Constantly concerned with doing everything correctly and well and improving it. Good sense in matters of poor health.

PROBLEM AREA: *The Opportunist.* No backbone at all. Is burdened with every task and takes care of it with servility. Fear of rejection, injury, and punishment. Moody, irritable, and unpredictable. Able to withstand little strain, restless, shy, overly sensitive. Tends to have psychosomatic disorders.

WORKING STYLE: Adaptable, imaginative, caring, intuitive.

☿   Mercury in the 6th House   *Cleverness at Work*   Dignity & Exaltation

STRENGTH: *The Useful Person.* Easily becomes familiar with any field of work and quickly makes oneself useful. Easily copes in all areas. Can also move in a great variety of social circles without any effort, which often makes one an excellent advisor. Flexible mind that is always open and cleverly analyzes. Finds skillful solutions, suggests astounding improvements, and makes crystal-clear decisions.

PROBLEM AREA: *The Man with a Price.* (Quickly) betrays own principles. Lives according to the motto of: "I dance to the tune of the piper that pays me!" Values and convictions are—if the money is good enough—adapted to the respective environment in a flash.

6th

WORKING STYLE: Quick, clever, with business acumen, skilled at negotiations.

♀   **Venus** in the 6th House   *Friendliness on the Job*   Fall

STRENGTH: *Ms. or Mr. Sunshine.* Promotes harmony at the place of work. Friendly, cordial nature. Tactful and obliging. Good team spirit. Very popular with fellow workers. Enjoys creating a beautiful design of things. Social commitment (charity events). Fosters peace on the job.

PROBLEM AREA: *The Life of the Party, The Love Affair.* Sociableness is more important than the result of the work. Love affairs on the job. Employs erotic charisma in a cold and calculating manner in order to achieve success. Is always self-controlled. Only falls in love when it is really clever to do so.

WORKING STYLE: Esthetic, cooperative, harmonious, peaceful, friendly.

♂   **Mars** in the 6th House   *Rivalry*

STRENGTH: *Competition.* Loves to compete against others professionally to be the best, the fastest, or the strongest. True zeal, considerable perseverance, and clear powers of assertion. Brash, ambitious, decisive, willing to engage in conflict, venturesome. Pushes ahead.

PROBLEM AREA: *The Arguer.* Doesn't fit into any team. Sees oneself just surrounded by enemies. Tends to take irresponsible risks. Rebels against superiors, argues with colleagues, and tyrannizes subordinates. Incautious, impatient, overly sensitive. May also be whiny. Tends to fight out conflicts dealing with work on the level of the body. Vehement, acute health disorders. Inconsiderate toward colleagues and others. Argumentative and scheming.

WORKING STYLE: Powerful, quick, aggressive.

♃ Jupiter in the 6th House	*Success on the Job*	Detriment

STRENGTH: *The Respected Careerist.* Self-assurance and a good deal of success in everyday working life. Leadership qualities that sooner or later lead to a leadership position. Exemplary, generous, dignified, incorruptible, willing to help, and motivating. Respected and highly esteemed. Good health. Excellent healer, doctor, or therapist.

PROBLEM AREA: *The Prestige-Oriented Jerk.* Has an overall feeling (but particularly in terms of the job) of being better than other people. Little tendency to be concerned with details. Prefers to disdainfully and condescendingly delegate them to others. By way of contrast, quite keen on collecting objects of prestige, titles, and medals. Well-behaved conformity and snobbish "government-official" mentality. Excesses endanger health.

WORKING STYLE: High standards, purposeful, successful.

♄ Saturn in the 6th House	*The Crisis at Work*

OBJECTIVE: Developing true integrity and inner cheerfulness, even in fulfilling "lowly" tasks as well (the happy street-sweeper).

INHIBITION: *The Drudge.* Is always ordered to do the most difficult tasks, has to do work no one else wants to do, and is even assigned something else when the others have long gone home. Has no sense of trust in one's professional position. Fears that resistance would cause one to become unemployed. Prefers to cling to the familiar misery. Joyless drudgery, caught in routine and apathy. Escapes into illness. Resigned, subservient, dissatisfied, dependent, as well as tyrannically controlling others. Fear of inner chaos. Not a good boss.

COMPULSION: *The Highflier.* Works on career with a grim smile. Lets no one help and especially doesn't permit anyone to give anything. Is merciless with self and hard on others. Represses and covers up signals of poor health.

RESOLUTION: *The Conscientious Worker.* Accepts every task—no matter how much prestige value it has—reliably, with humor or inner cheerfulness. Has a sense of work rituals and therefore doesn't shy away from "boring" assignments. Tenacious, with an eye for detail. Responsible, a good boss, incorrigible examiner, and experienced specialist.

WORKING STYLE: Diligent, concentrated, tenacious.

6th

♅   **Uranus** in the 6th House   *Innovation*

STRENGTH: *The Creative Self-Motivator.* Contributes original ideas and problem solutions, but needs a great deal of space to do so. For this reason, it is better if one works freelance. Develops new concepts, creates progressive working conditions, and has a good antenna for the spirit of the times and future trends. Can very purposively draw attention to human and social grievances and put a finger on sore points.

PROBLEM AREA: *The Squabbler.* Just simply can't be like the others. Doesn't adhere to the rules of the job. Always needs something extra. Not able to withstand any type of strain. Quickly irritated and rebellious. Unreliable.

WORKING STYLE: Intuitive, crazy, changeable, imaginative.

♆   **Neptune** in the 7th House   *Sensitive Work*   Detriment

STRENGTH: *The Prophet.* Has a good nose for future developments (politics, art, culture, fashion, stock market) and lets this knowledge flow into work. But also has a distinct sense for problems and needs of the physical and psychological body. Thin-skinned, open, sensitive, and permeable for outside influences. Can also work extremely well as a healer in subtle areas. However, doesn't succeed in sticking to a solidly structured framework. Delicate health. Vague symptoms.

PROBLEM AREA: *The Slob.* Ranges from dreamy to drowsy, sloppy, unpunctual, and unreliable at work. Easily becomes the "victim" of having job rationalized out of existence. Physical and psychological instability. Withdraws from the requirements of the surrounding world and lets self drift. Avoids concrete, clear, and binding decisions. Mock conforming. Open to bribery, corruption, or fraud in particularly difficult cases. Never knows if he or she is healthy or ill. Imaginary diseases, vague health disorders, or suffering from someone else's illness.

WORKING STYLE: Spiritualized, dreamy, mediumistic, or chaotic.

♇   **Pluto** in the 6th House   *Wealth of Influence*

STRENGTH: *The Effective Individual.* Develops great powers of persuasion and influence at the place of work. Doesn't give in and knows how to get to the bottom of things. Is totally committed to a chosen task (the obsessive scientist). Experiences health problems as basis of deepest transformation. Healing abilities.

PROBLEM AREA: *The Workaholic.* Power politics and chicanery at the place of work. Playing on dependencies and fear of one's own dependency. Gets stuck in a task like a fixed idea and then works oneself to death on it. Tries to drag in others and patronize them in the process.

WORKING STYLE: Profound, passionate, obsessive, maniacal.

☊   **North Node** in the 6th House

THEME: Conflict between the rational and the irrational, between dream and reality, between adaptation of the self and self-sacrifice.

TASK: *Integration.* Becoming concrete. Confrontation with the daily routine, reality, and the obligation to work. From imagination, withdrawal, and introspection to activity and performance of duty in everyday life. Expressing transcendent experiences in daily life. Taking leave of (spiritual) seclusion and becoming an integrated, active member of society.

6th

DANGER: *Forlornness.* Getting lost in boundlessness instead of contributing mediumistic abilities to society. Withdrawing from everything, not clearly obeying obligations, being unreliable and forgetful, isolating self. Withdrawing from the world in an airy-fairy or fanciful way.

7th House: *I Commit Myself* Descendant (DC)

ANALOGY: ♎︎	RULER: ♀	EXALTATION ♄	DETRIMENT: ♂
FALL: ☉	ELEMENT: Air	QUALITY: Cardinal	GENDER: Masculine

GENERAL: *The Partnership.* The ability and willingness to commit, marriage, lasting relationships, partnership (also professional), working together, associates. Willingness to adapt within a partnership. Giving and taking in interpersonal relationships. The other person as a surface for projection. Conflict and reconciliation.

POLARITY: The "victim of accommodation" in contrast to unlimited development of the self in the 1st house.

☉ Sun in the 7th House	*Willingness to Commit*	Fall

THE CENTRAL THEME OF DEVELOPMENT OF THE SELF is the encounter with the other person and becoming wrapped up in a partnership.

STRENGTH: *The Suitor.* Always ready to become involved in a relationship. Can't imagine life without an intimate partner. Needs the partner as the focus of life and catalyst in order to discover, develop, and realize potential. Likes to get married. Open, sociable, and concerned with harmony.

PROBLEM AREA: *The Freedom-Lover.* High ideals of freedom despite all the willingness to commit to a relationship, which makes one unstable in relationships or concerned with one-sided advantages and special rights. However, afraid of being alone at the same time. Thoughtless. Short-sided and fickle in willingness to commit.

IDEA OF PARTNERSHIP: "Solidarity in action," or the relationship as a mirror.

☽   **Moon** in the 7th House   *Adaptation to the Partner*

STRENGTH: *Someone Ready to Get Involved in a Relationship.* Strong desire for partnership and instinctive urge to commit to a relationship. Experiences own feelings above all in contact with the intimate partner. Feels deep happiness in truly being connected. Distinct sense for all common interests. Always willing to become involved with the other person, to take care of and be there for that person. Great willingness to adapt and high level of intuitive understanding. Wishes the same from the partner.

PROBLEM AREA: *The Love-Starved Individual.* Believes he or she can't live without a relationship, yet frequently is unable to really get involved in one. Constantly changing, noncommittal, superficial relationships that are all lived as if they were (now truly and finally) lasting. Great fear of rejection. Excessive conformity.

IDEA OF PARTNERSHIP: The relationship as a nest.

☿   **Mercury** in the 7th House   *Relationship Talk*

STRENGTH: *The Good Mixer.* Can easily start relationships and knows how to discover the other person anew time and again. Experiences diversity in the partner's many facets. Needs a lively intellectual exchange in the partnership. Is also good at bringing other people together (match-making).

PROBLEM AREA: *The Eternal Fiancée* Likes to talk about relationships and think about the various forms they can take. But isn't in a hurry to go beyond the intention to marry. Seeks variety through contacts to further partners. Is coldly calculating, insincere, unfaithful, and commits breach of contract in difficult cases.

7th

IDEA OF PARTNERSHIP: The business relationship.

♀   Venus in the 7th House   *Lover's Bliss*   Dignity

STRENGTH: *Eager to Get Married.* Great need for contact and exchange with an intimate partner. Always open for a loving encounter. Gladly willing to enter into a lively relationship, swear eternal faithfulness, and marry. Romantic, optimistic, capable of devotion, willing to adapt, and faithful.

PROBLEM AREA: *Disenchanted.* Too carefree in attitude toward a relationship. Enters recklessly into a partnership and underestimates the demands inherent in it. After the initial phase of being high, quickly becomes sober, superficial, reckless, unstable, jealous, and critical. Possibly also distinct material interests in the partnership.

IDEA OF PARTNERSHIP: The happy relationship.

♂   Mars in the 7th House   *Tension in the Relationship*   Detriment

STRENGTH: *Bundle of Energy.* Brings much momentum and vivacity into the relationship. Takes a direct approach to the partner. Immediately settles differences and provides a clarifying thunder storm. Full of go and always ready to battle with the partner—both with or against. Much conflict and much reconciliation. Lively, exciting, as well as strenuous relationships.

PROBLEM AREA: *The Rival.* Sees the mate as a rival who must be subjugated. No willingness to adapt whatsoever. Aggressive, destructive conduct in interpersonal relationships. Tends to take rash actions. Likes to put self in the foreground and drive the partner up against the wall. Tough, inconsiderate, despotic, mistrustful, insulting, or feels insulted.

IDEA OF PARTNERSHIP: The competition.

♃ Jupiter in the 7th House   *Richness of Relationship*

STRENGTH: *Rich in Relationships (Qualitatively).* Experiences the deep wealth of a relationship. Encounters the partner full of trust and generosity. Has high relationship ideals and is seriously willing to enter into a committed, lively partnership of equal rank. Wants to be proud of the relationship.

PROBLEM AREA: *Rich in Relationships (Quantitatively).* A "wealth of relationships" can be interpreted to be "more is better," or, "If you are not with the one you love . . ." This person is smug and much too comfortable to assume duties and responsibilities of a relationship or adapt to it. Separates when things get uncomfortable and goes into new, more convenient relationships.

IDEA OF PARTNERSHIP: The grand relationship (to show off).

♄ Saturn in the 7th House   *The Serious Relationship*   Exaltation

OBJECTIVE: Trust in a responsible, mature relationship.

INHIBITION: *The Orphan.* Lacking in contact; reserved and cautious in relationships for fear of closeness or being hurt; afraid of being lonely. Strong mistrust of the other person. As a result, avoids relationships or always comes a moment too late. Only falls in love in hopeless cases, waits a long time in vain for the desired person, and quickly backs down if the tide should actually turn in his or her favor. Can't believe he or she is loved on own account. Searches for guarantees and proof of love. Will unconditionally try to maintain the outer form even if the relationship has long been dead in terms of emotions. Regiments and dominates the partner.

COMPULSION: *The Fake Don Juan.* Breaks out of personal reserve and plays Don Juan. At the same time, is always in control, remains cold on the inside, and only opens up to short encounters in which no true closeness is created.

RESOLUTION: *The Responsible Person.* Sees through own avoidance strategy that led to earlier disappointments. Carefully and slowly grows into a relationship and continually gains deeper confidence in it. Overcomes old fears and develops steadfastness. Is responsible, caring, faithful, reliable, patient.

IDEA OF PARTNERSHIP: The solid relationship.

7th

♅   Uranus in the 7th House   *The Free Relationship*

STRENGTH: *The Bird of Paradise.* Lives and loves an original partnership of own accord, without limiting obligations. Tolerates no chains or cages for they would cause death like bird of paradise. Doesn't let self be "enslaved" by saying "I do" and signing his or her name. Can stay in a lasting relationship and remain faithful, as long as it is voluntary and all the doors are open. Brings a great deal of liveliness, variety, and excitement into any relationship.

PROBLEM AREA: *The Island.* Very difficult relationship problems. Unwilling and unable to commit to a relationship. Strives for complete independence. Considers self something special and looks down on conventional ideals of relationships, which are meant for the "broad masses" at best. Always stays single, even within the scope of a possible marriage. Immediately breaks all agreements and promises if feelings of freedom are infringed on too much. Unreliable. Can't be held onto!

IDEA OF PARTNERSHIP: The single relationship; the companionable relationship.

♆   Neptune in the 7th House   *The Dream Relationship*

STRENGTH: *The Soul Mate.* Highest relationship ideals. Deep intuitive grasp of the partner, kindred souls, and inner harmony. Inexplicable encounters. Is guided into the right relationship without any effort. Great willingness to adapt and sacrifice. Also tends toward platonic relationships.

PROBLEM AREA: *The Disappointed Person.* Extravagant, unrealistic ideals of relationship and partnership. Longing for redemption. Hunger for love and desire to become one with the other person. Very easy to seduce. Constant expectation without fulfillment. The other person is often not tangible, disappears, "dissolves," or becomes elusive. Bitter disillusionment on the basis of unfulfilled expectations leads to disappointed rejection of all concepts of a solid relationship in some cases.

IDEA OF PARTNERSHIP: Merging into one, mystical unity.

♇ Pluto in the 7th House   *The Extreme Relationship*

STRENGTH: *The Powerhouse.* Strong magnetism and a willingness to enter into an intensive, exclusive, and irrevocable relationship with a strong person. Transformation and far-reaching profound change also in a relationship through extreme feelings of helplessness and being at the other person's mercy, of domination and subjugation.

PROBLEM AREA: *The Cruel Heart.* One-sided experiences of power and dependency that—in various relationships—can sometimes be experienced as the victim and sometimes as the perpetrator. Compulsive relationship with extremely painful experiences, emotional entanglements, blackmail, physical threats, and sadomasochistic rituals.

IDEA OF PARTNERSHIP: The indissoluble pact.

☊ North Node in the 7th House

THEME: Conflict between striving for harmony, equilibrium, and adaptation in the partnership, as well as consciousness of self and powers of self-development.

TASK: *Orientation toward the Partner.* Becoming involved in a committed partnership. Opening up to the other person's needs. Developing devotion, understanding, consideration, and sensitivity in a relationship. Cultivating self-confident willingness to adapt instead of selfishly demanding the sacrifice of conformity from the other person alone.

7th

DANGER: *Egocentrism.* Being unable to go beyond your own self-centeredness. The great fear of becoming lost in close commitments, not being taken into account enough, or having to sacrifice personal individuality and independence.

8th House: *I Probe*

ANALOGY:	RULER:	EXALTATION	DETRIMENT:
♏	♂ and ♇	♅	♀

FALL:	ELEMENT:	QUALITY:	GENDER:
☽	Water	Fixed	Feminine

GENERAL: *Life's Enigmas.* All taboos and their transgression, borderline experiences, death and rebirth, deepest experiences of sexuality, orgasm as the experience of death and birth, overcoming oneself, transformation, the ability to regenerate, crises about the meaning of life and overcoming them, everything that is cryptic and profound, inheritances, other people's possessions and money.

POLARITY: The assets of the soul in contrast to the concrete assets in 2nd house.

⊙   Sun in the 8th House   *The Alchemist*

THE CENTRAL THEME OF DEVELOPMENT OF THE SELF is the exploration of life's secrets, everything that is enigmatic and concealed, as well as the descent into one's own darkness.

STRENGTH: *The Cellarman.* Willing to descend down into (one's own) depths and become involved with the dark and difficult, tabooed or ostracized aspects of life and one's own personality. Intensive confrontation with psychoanalysis, death, shamanism, magic, sexuality. The Faustian person. Can keep other people's secrets. As a result, often advisor or administrator in the money matters of others. Can make money out of "dirt." Frequently late bloomer—introverted in youth, but increasingly sociable with age.

PROBLEM AREA: *The Unscrupulous Person or Mr. Clean.* Taboo-breaker who makes money from questionable deals without scruples. Cold-blooded profiteer in times of crisis, earning money on other people's losses. The little or big Mafioso, the profiteer in the red-light district, the dealer, as well as all the shady figures who misuse the money or dependence of other people. But also the extreme repressor who fearfully suppresses the dark side, then unconsciously lives it out in the worst way. Chasing after stubborn notions.

IMAGE OF DEATH: The person who lives with death.

☽ Moon in the 8th House	*Magical Power*	Detriment

STRENGTH: *The Good Witch.* Instinctive desire to air secrets, violate taboos, explore everything forbidden, hidden, cryptic, and otherworldly, and probe the dark depths of the soul. Early interest in the meaning of death, as well as magical and esoteric themes, and shamanism. Can develop strong powers of healing and suggestion. Premonitions of the future. Need for great emotional security. Sexual response. Very good nose for things and intensive dreams.

PROBLEM AREA: *The Bewitched.* Danger of losing self in the labyrinth of the esoteric and magical, or becoming entangled in power games. Extreme forms of hatred, passion, and jealousy, as well as depression, confusion, and longing for death. Must die many emotional deaths. Fascinated with everything forbidden and dubious. The barmaid.

IMAGE OF DEATH: Death as the return home.

☿ Mercury in the 8th House	*Profound Thought*

STRENGTH: *The Solver of the Mystery of the Universe.* Inquiring mind and Faustian thinking. Loves to spy and discover what is concealed. Urge to perceive and interpret images of the depths. Distinct intuition and sureness of instinct. Ability to think in contradictions and express the profound in paradoxes. Can give words a magical power.

PROBLEM AREA: *The Pigheaded.* Narrow-minded, dogmatic, compulsive thinking. Has a rigid notion of reality and tyrannizes everyone else with it. Refuses to realize that reality is much more complex than the personal concept of it and the way other people look at things can be just as justified and correct as one's own. Resentful, scheming, and mean.

8th

IMAGE OF DEATH: Death as an object of curiosity, as a business, or as a teacher.

♀   **Venus** in the 8th House   *Love Magic*   Detriment

STRENGTH: *Beautiful Sin.* The attraction of what is forbidden, the beauty of the macabre, the faded, the morbid. The romanticism of what is broken, and the temptation of the eerily beautiful. Often still sleepy during youth, becomes increasingly pleasure-loving with time. Seductive erotic aura. Passionate, intense interpersonal relationships. Fine feeling for the right moment, hidden fantasies, and desires. The magic of love and the love potion.

PROBLEM AREA: *Dangerous Liaisons.* Calculating, manipulative, playing on sexual charms. Perverse tendencies and depths of eroticism. Gaining power and making money out of subjection and sexual dependence. The business of "love." Jealousy and greed. Self-deceptive.

IMAGE OF DEATH: The peaceful death or dying for love.

♂   **Mars** in the 8th House   *Danger*   Dignity

STRENGTH: *The Death-Defier.* Goes into dangerous areas and borderline situations. Boldly fights against death, sometimes under life-endangering conditions (doctor, rescuer). Iron will, fearless, total dedication of energy. Enjoys taking risks that go all out. Strong sexuality and sense for practicing sexual magic.

PROBLEM AREA: *The Enemy of Life.* Inconsiderate toward self and merciless with others. Criminal energies, such as the brutal use of violence, torture, rape, and death threats. Playing with one's own life, as well as the lives of others. Destructive inner tension. Misanthropy.

IMAGE OF DEATH: Death as the enemy.

♃ Jupiter in the 8th House   *Richness of the Depths*

STRENGTH: *The Fisher of Souls.* Successfully draws on inner images, exploring concealed regions and taboo zones. Seeks the depths of the soul. Eager to bring insights won in this manner into harmony with a higher purpose. Doesn't lose self-respect. Remains proud and full of dignity, even in times of bitter crisis and great poverty. Blessing in disguise.

PROBLEM AREA: *The Shady Guru.* Overextension of the ego, self-aggrandizement, and misuse of strong emotional powers. Creates dependencies and, as a self-proclaimed healer, lives as an energetic and material burden on followers.

IMAGE OF DEATH: Kind, dignified death and death as a friend.

♄ Saturn in the 8th House   *Fear of Death*

OBJECTIVE: Overcoming the fear of death and developing emotional stability

INHIBITION: *The Stick-in-the-Mud.* Unable to really let go because of an (unconscious) fear of death. Fear of deep emotions and overwhelming, uncontrollable (sexual) experiences, as well as the fear of failure. Inwardly self-conscious, stiff, standoffish, inhibited, hardened, always unsatisfied, and often awkward. Emotional coldness, impotence, or frigidity. Increasing fear of inexplicable phenomenon and magical powers. Fear of falling into a crisis about the meaning of life. Fear of poverty in old age and loss of control. Incapable of simply letting important things happen.

COMPULSION: *The "Perfect" Lover.* The active player in the area of sexuality. Perfect on the physical level, but cut off emotionally. Compulsive erotic ideas and actions. Promiscuity as an obligation. Also compulsive confrontation with previously avoided (but always tempting) taboo areas.

8th

RESOLUTION: *Emotional Strength.* Insight into reality. Overcomes the fear of death (through crises in life) to allow outer hardening to become an inner strength of character. Has made peace with the imponderables of life. Can open up and let go. Emotionally capable of devotion. Open, and inwardly deeply willing to have overwhelming, ecstatic, spiritual, and/or sexual experiences. At the same time, responsible, resolute, and trustworthy.

IMAGE OF DEATH: Death as a bitter truth and ultimately a serene certainty.

⛢   Uranus in the 8th House   *The License*   Exaltation

STRENGTH: *The Self-Liberator.* Is intensively concerned with one's dark side in order to purposefully free self from unconscious compulsions and the violence of one's own shadow. Struggles for autonomy from sexual drives. Strong confrontation with death and very independent attitude about this last, inevitable necessity. The alchemist's search for the elixir of life. Very reserved and withdrawn in one's inner depths. Quickly comes to the point of needing to retreat and permits no one admission to innermost feelings or even one's soul.

PROBLEM AREA: *The Immortal.* Believes one has the license to do everything. Feels completely independent and even freed of the most fundamental conditions and necessities of life. Makes use of every sexual freedom and recklessly disregards the threshold of all taboos. Also wants to liberate self from the inevitability of death and only die through own free will. In extreme cases, even considers oneself too special to even have to die at all.

IMAGE OF DEATH: The sudden death and death as liberation.

♆   **Neptune** in the 8th House   *Trance*

STRENGTH: *The Spiritual Individual.* Has mediumistic and clairvoyant abilities. Strong powers of the soul that can be used as healing powers. Longing for complete transformation. Deep certainty of being guided along the path through inner abysses or external crises. Rich world of dreams and good feeling for the language of dreams. Great deal of sexual fantasy. Desires to merge with another and be redeemed. Strives for spiritual, ecstatic sexuality (Tantra, Tao, trance) or dissolution of sexual energies. Very intuitive and good feeling for what is concealed and unspoken. Mystification of death and only minimal fear of death.

PROBLEM AREA: *The Intoxicated Person.* Irresistible yearning for overwhelming experience alternates with fear of dissolution and, above all, fear of the irrational and invisible world. Tendency toward drugs or intoxicants as substitute for true trance. "Transfigured" rejection of sexuality or the opposite extreme of boundless debauchery. Easy to seduce. Lacks in critical powers. Unfaithful. In danger of losing the self in diffuse feelings and horror visions, as well as becoming crazy. Longing for death.

IMAGE OF DEATH: Death as deliverance.

♇ Pluto in the 8th House	*Magic*	Dignity

STRENGTH: *The Magician.* Extraordinary powers of the soul, hypnotic abilities, healing powers, and enormous but totally subtle influence on others. The urge to explore the secrets on the dark side of life. Fascinated by everything that is taboo or forbidden. Deep experiences of transformation. Strong sexuality that awakens at an early age, with radical experiences of power and helplessness. Very willful, tenacious, ambitious, and unyielding in following goals that have once been set. Understands upheavals and crises as opportunities for renewal.

PROBLEM AREA: *The Devil.* Misuse of power for reasons of calculation or because of powerlessness in the face of strong, dark drives from one's personal depths. Creates emotional, physical, or sexual dependencies and lives out one's primitive drives and sexual obsessions on the victims. Suffers from (sexual) obsessive ideas that can assume the character of possession. Primitive greed and sadistic tendencies.

IMAGE OF DEATH: Fascinating, uncanny death and powerlessness in the face of death.

☊   North Node in the 8th House

THEME: Conflict between material possessions and those of the soul, between knowledge of transience and the greed of wanting to hold onto something.

TASK: *Depth.* Reconciling with the transience of all being and recognizing death as the great teacher. Instead of building on or betting on false external values, unearthing the immaterial treasures of the depths. Becoming willing to engage in conflict and violate social conventions and taboos instead of persisting in pleasant innocuousness. Finding the deepest opportunities of experiencing sexuality, which conceal a genuine spiritual experience beyond all sensuality and passion within them.

8th

DANGER: *Avarice.* Compulsive clinging to material goods, to what is accustomed, proved, and secured. "Selling" oneself in order to fulfill material desires. Seeing values in terms of monetary values and not forging ahead to the actual, deeper-rooted values. Avoidance of conflicts in order to minimize problems.

9th House: *I Believe*

ANALOGY: ♐	RULER: ♃	EXALTATION —	DETRIMENT: ☿
FALL: —	ELEMENT: Fire	QUALITY: Mutable	GENDER: Masculine

GENERAL: *Higher Thinking and the Worldview.* The expansion of horizons through inner and outer journeys, finding a purpose, and one's own philosophy of life. Search for truth and meaning, faith, religion, and the personal image of God, ethics, higher values and perceptions, higher education, insight, intuition and inspiration, ideals, metaphysics. Long journeys and experiences in foreign countries.

POLARITY: Deep convictions and fundamental conceptions of values in contrast to the sober and objective information in the 3rd house.

☉   Sun in the 9th House   *The Religious Human Being*

THE CENTRAL THEME OF DEVELOPMENT OF THE SELF is the search for meaning in life and the development of one's own religious view of the world.

STRENGTH: *The Cosmopolitan.* Great interest in philosophy and religion, as well as distant cultures, exotic customs, and everything that expands one's own horizons. Educated and well-versed in many areas. Likes to travel for the purpose of developing and experiencing the self. Guided by a religious view of the world and supported by a personal experience of meaning. Ethically strong, contemplative, idealistic, tolerant, farsighted.

PROBLEM AREA: *The Bigoted Sectarian.* Religious megalomania and contemptuous despising of poor sinners and people who are ignorant. Hypocritical piety. Tends to force own strict moral standards on others.

IMAGE OF GOD: God the Father.

☽   **Moon** in the 9th House   *Wanderlust*

STRENGTH: *The Globetrotter.* Instinctive urge to roam afield. Fond of travel. Likes to be on the go without knowing where he or she will end up tomorrow. Longs for new horizons, but without a distinct goal. Inner certainty of being guided by a higher power. Trust in ability to find the meaning of life. Deep religious feelings and desire for higher ideals. Tends to settle down far away from home.

PROBLEM AREA: *Holier-Than-Thou.* Strongly vacillating religious moods. Parroting of pious phrases without coming to terms with the content. Hypocritical, presumptuous, dogmatic, and narrow-minded.

IMAGE OF GOD: God the Mother.

☿   **Mercury** in the 9th House   *Religious Thinking*   Detriment

STRENGTH: *The Tour Manager.* Likes to be on the road. Skillful at organizing trips. Good at orienting oneself while traveling and making oneself at least adequately understood in the foreign language. Desire to discover something while traveling and show it to others. This also applies to the inner journey in the figurative sense. Interest in culture, philosophy, religious issues, and higher education in general.

PROBLEM AREA: *The Phrasemonger.* Empty words instead of the experience of meaning. Wanting to missionize others with hollow platitudes. Profiteering without scruples in questions of faith. Quickly changing "convictions." Also empty talk in questions of culture and general education.

9th

IMAGE OF GOD: Logos as the divine child and the rational and provable God.

♀   **Venus** in the 9th House   *Holy Love*

STRENGTH: *The Hymn of Love.* High ideals of love and holy feelings of love. Love as the sense of life. Philosophy of joy, optimism in life, and the gift of awakening a positive feeling of self-worth in other people as well. Seeks love in distant places and while traveling. Foreign marriage.

PROBLEM AREA: *Idolatrous Love.* Peculiar veneration of saints or idolatrous enthusiasm for a guru. Problems with drives because holy love must not be dirtied. Repression of conflict and compulsive tendency to always see everything in a positive light.

IMAGE OF GOD: God is love.

♂   **Mars** in the 9th House   *Chivalry*

STRENGTH: *Courage of Convictions.* Representing one's own convictions with commitment and courage, advocating high ideals, and mercilessly denouncing grievances. Use of all energies in order to achieve a high level of education in social, philosophical, or religious areas. Achievement of long-range goals.

PROBLEM AREA: *The Militant Do-Gooder.* Intolerance, fanatic opinions, and an audacious know-it-all attitude. Persecuting and fighting against deviationists and people of a different faith in the name of a holy idea. Glorification of violence. Dissatisfied and deeply pessimistic. Tends toward serious self-reproach.

IMAGE OF GOD: The warlike, avenging God.

♃ **Jupiter** in the 9th House *Priestly Dignity*	Dignity

STRENGTH: *The Scholar.* A person with wide horizons, a high level of education, and true religious values. Supported by a clear sense of meaning and strong powers of faith. Well-versed in art, culture, philosophy, and literature. Loves distant journeys in order to constantly receive new impulses. Good adviser and wise friend.

PROBLEM AREA: *The Sermonizer.* Overbearing sense of superiority toward other people. Considers his or her truth to be the only correct one. Self-satisfied view of the world and concepts of values, in which personal viewpoint comes off looking like the best.

IMAGE OF GOD: The kind God.

♄   **Saturn** in the 9th House   *Religious Crises*

OBJECTIVE: Finding one's personal view of the world beyond all doubts and imponderables, and having a deep experience of meaning

INHIBITION: *Limited Vision.* Fixed view of the world with extremely rigid concepts and values. Black-and-white categories. Strict, inhuman religious values that constantly lead to a bad conscience, feelings of guilt, and depression. Serious self-reproach because of one's own shortcomings. Losing the faith and feeling oneself to be mercilessly at the hands of life's absurdity. Mistrusting everything that can't be explained. Failing in the question of meaning. Rejecting everything that is unfamiliar.

COMPULSION: *The Dogmatic Atheist.* Believing in nothing at all anymore and advocating atheism or nihilism with religious fervor. Or joining a movement or sect in which extremely strict morals and difficult rituals are practiced with prescribed penance exercises hostile to life itself.

RESOLUTION: *Strength of Faith.* A mature, clear view of the world, free of superficialities or Baroque varnish. Standing as firm as a rock in a deep faith with simplicity, earnestness, and humility.

IMAGE OF GOD: The strict God.

9th

♅   Uranus in the 9th House   *Religious Freedom*

STRENGTH: *The Free Spirit.* Progressive view of the world on the principles of freedom, equality, and brotherhood. Very individual, unconventional idea of the meaning of life. A freethinker who never joins a larger religious movement but always takes his or her own path, seeking and finding a personal philosophy of life. Open for modern or even utopian ways of looking at the world. Reform-oriented concepts of raising children, education, religion, and philosophy.

PROBLEM AREA: *The Anarchist.* Glorification of rebellion and subversion of all values just for the hell of it. Mad, eccentric ideas are fermented into a smart-alecky pseudo-religious standpoint. Crazy self-glorifying esoteric beliefs and fantasies about being the chosen one.

IMAGE OF GOD: The individual God.

♆   Neptune in the 9th House   *Spirituality*

STRENGTH: *The Mystic.* Turns away from logic while on the religious quest and is guided by inner eye like a blind pilgrim. Doesn't find concept of the world or God in personal striving, but lets oneself be found. Feels drawn to mysticism and spiritual exercises that lead to another state of consciousness (trance). Willing to go beyond own boundaries for the sake of religious experiences.

PROBLEM AREA: *The Religious Screwball.* Misled and unworldly. Has been taken in by a Fata Morgana and clings ecstatically to the supposed truth. Very uncritical, which is why one easily becomes the victim of dumb, but beautiful-sounding pseudo-wisdom and esoteric ideas that are crazy. Quickly falls for a guru and becomes dependent on the guru's promises of healing and deliverance. Pseudo-religious drug abuse.

IMAGE OF GOD: The God who sacrifices himself.

♇   **Pluto** in the 9th House   *The Magical View of the World*

STRENGTH: *The Merlin.* Philosophy of the world colored by an unadulterated religiousness that is close to nature (Druid/witch). Fascinated interest in alchemy, old shamanic rituals, magical circles, occult orders and lodges. Seeks original experiences at the places of power. Image of God that is characterized by deep, personal experience in life and transformation (conversion as in the Damascus experience[5]). Intensive struggle for deeper truths.

PROBLEM AREA: *The Black Magician.* Religious misuse of power. Glorification of violence and shameless exploitation of the emotionally dependent. Purposive use of magical powers to harm others (curse). Black masses, Satanism, destructive forms of sexual magic.

IMAGE OF GOD: The dark, omnipotent God.

☊   **North Node** in the 9th House

THEME: Conflict between higher thought and everyday truisms, between profane perceptions and holy values, between intellectual doubts and religious convictions.

TASK: *True Education.* Finding genuine meaning behind various ideas and appearances. Achieving a personal, religious worldview through studies, travel, and spiritual pilgrimage. Trust in one's own opinion and developing one's own standpoint. Attaining higher perceptions and ethical values beyond the truth as it stands in the newspaper. Emerging from the narrow, familiar environment to discover new possibilities and contemplate long-range, significant goals.

9th

DANGER: *Dissipation.* Getting lost in an abundance of knowledge. Not being able to differentiate between the diversity of information and evaluate it. Getting stuck in superficiality and failing in the search for meaning.

10th House: *I Feel That I Am Called* Medium Coeli (MC).

ANALOGY:	RULER:	EXALTATION	DETRIMENT:
♑	♄	♂	☽

FALL:	ELEMENT:	QUALITY:	GENDER:
♃ and ♆	Earth	Dry	Feminine

GENERAL: *Catching the Public Eye.* Vocation and calling, public recognition, social position, fame and honor, life objective, success in life, career, power and authority, responsibility, achievement, popularity. Things that become increasingly important in the course of a lifetime.

POLARITY: The crown of the Tree of Life as a counterpart to the roots in the 4th house.

☉   Sun in the 10th House   *Attention*

THE CENTRAL THEME OF DEVELOPMENT OF THE SELF is creating and striving for a goal in life. The effect in the public eye and self-realization in vocation and calling.

STRENGTH: *The Appointee.* Strong urge to be in the public eye. Wrapped up in profession. Strives for recognition and authority. Charismatic personality. In most cases, leadership quality, sense of responsibility, and will to succeed. Dignified conduct in full consciousness of receiving attention.

PROBLEM AREA: *The Acclaim-Addict.* Likes to bask in own glory and tends to considerably overestimate abilities. Authoritarian, vain, sensitive, and presumptuous. Unpleasant little dictator. Striving for power that is without scruples and inconsiderate of others.

IMAGE OF THE MOTHER: The mother in the role of the father.

☽   **Moon** in the 10th House   *Popularity*   Detriment

STRENGTH: *The Celebrity.* Need for recognition and popularity. Instinctively senses what the audience, the public, and the people want. Can easily make oneself popular and is good at dealing within other people in the scope of working life. Likes to have profession and the public as one's family. Often has the ambition of making the theme of the Sun house one's vocation. Wins followers easily. The born representative.

PROBLEM AREA: *The Narcissist.* Is enthusiastic and uninhibited about adorning self with borrowed plumes. Overly exaggerated need for admiration and reckless approach to responsibility. Tends to make decisions that don't help the matter as a favor to someone else because of a craving to be liked. Frequently changes professions.

IMAGE OF THE MOTHER: Strong identification figure and close emotional ties.

☿   **Mercury** in the 10th House *The Talent for Everything*

STRENGTH: *The Jack-of-all-trades.* Can easily train for any profession and quickly make oneself useful in it. All-round talent. Professional agility. Skillful organizer and work-simplifier. Has a good grasp of how to delegate. Likes to employ intellectual and verbal fluency for professional purposes (as an expert, reviewer, editor). Is well-informed about everything and good at giving advice. Loves contact with the public.

PROBLEM AREA: *The Weather Vane.* Can't decide on any profession (because one can imagine doing them all). Overestimates both abilities and possibilities. Tends to be superficial and not really on the ball. Cold and calculating when it comes to own advantage.

10th

IMAGE OF THE MOTHER: Clever and well-versed, perhaps also moody.

♀   **Venus** in the 10th House   *Popularity*

STRENGTH: *The Charmer.* Talented at making, maintaining, and developing contacts. Charming, popular, reliable, and faithful. Would like to bring happiness or beauty into the world within the scope of her profession. Artistic ambitions or doing business with things that make life more beautiful. Good representational figure. Sense for charity.

PROBLEM AREA: *The Schemer.* Specifically makes use of one's charm in order to exploit others for own interests. Egotistic, calculating, pushy, and power-hungry. Overrates status and power.

IMAGE OF THE MOTHER: The beloved, attractive mother, as well as the mother as competitor.

♂   **Mars** in the 10th House   *Rivalry*   Exaltation

STRENGTH: *The Fighter.* Always ready to fight for matters that concern one, push through unpopular steps, and swim against the current. Great ambition to reach the top, willingness to engage in conflict, enormous endeavors in the professional area. Seeks confrontations and likes to compete against rivals. Many enemies, much honor.

PROBLEM AREA: *The Machiavellian Prince or Princess.* Scorns other people's opinions and inconsiderately disregards justified interests and claims within the scope of the profession. Attacks others out of the blue and continually infringes on the professional rules of the game and agreements. Unscrupulously oversteps competencies and likes to "govern" one's way into other people's areas of responsibility. Power-hungry, unpredictable, greedy for success.

IMAGE OF THE MOTHER: Strong, dangerous, aggressive.

♃   Jupiter in the 10th House   *Success*   Fall

STRENGTH: *The Boss.* Great trust in the abundance of professional opportunities. Luck and good connections favor professional advancement. Gains support from other people. Needs a dignified, respectable function; easily achieves leadership positions. Radiates trust; good at motivating others. Has an excellent understanding of how to represent an enterprise to the outside world.

PROBLEM AREA: *The Minion.* Has no scruples in exploiting advantages and relationships. Attracts envy and ill will. Self-satisfied, egoistic, concerned with own interests. Exaggerates on the way to the top, sometimes loses one's breath (but not the success). Also the lazy, smug fatso in the executive chair.

IMAGE OF THE MOTHER: The good, highly esteemed mother.

♄   Saturn in the 10th House   *Staying Power*   Dignity

OBJECTIVE: Overcoming fear of failure; willingness to assume responsibility; the ability to measure achievements by more than just external factors.

INHIBITION: *The Walking Disaster.* Deep mistrust in the possibilities of professional advancement. Receives no support whatsoever because no one can help. Feels inadequate; has a great fear of failing. Only registers what one has been unsuccessful at. Stubborn and unpopular. Much bad luck and weak achievements. Inflexible, unsuccessful, dictatorial, authoritarian, and inconsiderate.

COMPULSION: *The Downtrodden.* Makes it a point of great honor to fight one's way doggedly up the ladder alone and with one's own strength despite all resistance. In the process, enslaves oneself to the utmost degree. Joyless career person. Easily gets dizzy because of the heights for fear of a sudden fall.

10th

RESOLUTION: *The Master.* Succeeds in gradually developing enough trust in the idea that the rungs of the ladder of professional success will also hold him or her. Dedicates self to a task with total consistency and develops—even against all opposition—true mastery there. Responsible, dutiful, objective, honest, ambitious, just, fatherly, consistent, decisive.

IMAGE OF THE MOTHER: Reliable, dominating, hard, strict, cold, restrictive.

♅   **Uranus** in the 10th House   *Professional Individualism*

STRENGTH: *The Freelancer.* Professionally very creative and inventive. Needs the greatest possible amount of free space for the development of these talents. Often works freelance, independent and free. Has a great aversion to everything that is prefabricated and to limits on general conditions. Has a very personal touch in everything and is therefore always determined to be irreplaceable. Extraverted behavior.

PROBLEM AREA: *The Center of the Storm.* Creates chaos and uncertainty through an exaggerated tendency toward originality and renewal. Cannot stick to one thing. Erratic in one's way of thinking, but also in changing both assignment and profession. Quickly loses interest in a project when one cannot contribute any more new ideas. Imaginative and inventive, but impatient and bad at carrying things out.

IMAGE OF THE MOTHER: The freedom-loving, fickle mother.

♆   **Neptune** in the 10th House *The Dream Profession*   Fall

---

STRENGTH: *Ms. or Mr. Pseudonym.* Lets self be found by one's profession and true calling. Has an excellent nose for the trend of the times and future developments. However, doesn't want to step into the foreground. As a result, prefers to work under a pseudonym. Is professionally at home in the area of mediumism, as well as media.

PROBLEM AREA: *The Professional Haze.* Despite all one's will, can't find a profession and lets oneself drift. Great difficulties in choosing a vocation, as well as in taking clear positions in working life. Lets oneself be quickly swept away by moods, but also loses interest and orientation just as abruptly. Dazzling personality, camp follower, afraid of taking responsibility, not trustworthy.

IMAGE OF THE MOTHER: Overly idealized, difficult to comprehend, spiritual or crazy: the martyr who sacrifices herself.

♇   **Pluto** in the 10th House   *The Position of Power*

STRENGTH: *The Statesman.* Strong striving for power and influence connected with the willingness to become completely wrapped up in one's calling. Great commitment, as well as far-reaching transformation through experiences in working life. Constant striving to penetrate more deeply into the task in life and comprehend its profound significance. Professional confrontation with the dark, suppressed sides of life and the society.

PROBLEM AREA: *The Godfather.* Shamelessly demonstrates one's power. Makes sure that others become dependent in order to be able to manipulate and blackmail them. Dark business deals with shady characters.

IMAGE OF THE MOTHER: Powerful, possessive, jealous and often dark; can feel like her serf for entire lifetime.

☊   **North Node** in the 10th House

THEME: Conflict between professional career, public obligations, as well as domestic life and the family and searching one's own heart.

TASK: *Coming to the Fore.* Going beyond the domestic area and family to enter the public eye. Becoming mature and assuming responsibility. Developing discipline, consistency, and straightforwardness. Detaching oneself from dependencies in the area of family and emotions. Being able to lower one's personal expectations.

10th

DANGER: *Remaining a Child.* Emotional dependency on profession, obligations and status, or even complete adherence to the protective security of the family. Expecting affection, consideration, and protection instead of risking the step out into raw reality. Not developing any sense of personal responsibility, and immediately looking for someone to blame for every mishap.

11th House: *I Make Friends*

ANALOGY: ♒	RULER: ♄ and ♅	EXALTATION —	DETRIMENT: ☉
FALL: ♇	ELEMENT: Air	QUALITY: Fixed	GENDER: Masculine

GENERAL: *The Circle of Friends.* Experience of friendship, group experiences, team spirit, affinity, hospitality, patrons, spiritual brotherhoods, cosmopolitanism, support of humanitarian goals. Spirit of the times, reforms, emancipation.

POLARITY: Community spirit and cooperation in contrast to the competition and domination of the self in the 5th house.

☉ Sun in the 11th House	*Community Spirit*	Detriment

THE CENTRAL THEME OF DEVELOPMENT OF THE SELF is the experience of friendship, life with and within a group that has been created of its own accord, as well as supporting reforms and humanitarian goals.

STRENGTH: *The Cosmopolitan.* Ignores all national boundaries, racial barriers, and social differences and has a distinct awareness of connection with all human beings as a citizen of the Earth. Strong development in friendships and good sense of group consciousness. Knows how to lead a group. Joining together voluntarily (affinity) is more important than family ties. Oriented toward the future. Imaginative and visionary. Advocate of social and cultural reforms.

PROBLEM AREA: *The Isolationist.* Expectations of friendship that are too high and sometimes tyrannical, followed by corresponding disappointments and friendships being broken off. Intensely dependent on whether other people like him or her. Too selective in friendships. Retreat into proud resignation with increasing isolation.

ROLE IN THE GROUP: The trendsetter.

☽   **Moon** in the 11th House   *Feelings of Friendship*

STRENGTH: *The Good Friend.* Need for friendly relations and spiritual affinities. Gladly willing to enter into a friendship, be there and fulfill the friend's expectations. Adaptable, changeable, and sociable within a circle of friends. Must always know what others think about one and how they see one.

PROBLEM AREA: *The Fickle Friendship.* Easily irritated, restless, superficial, feelings of friendship that go through extreme changes. Only commits self until changing his or her mind. Unreliable and moody.

ROLE IN THE GROUP: The participant.

☿   **Mercury** in the 11th House   *The Travel Companion*

STRENGTH: *The Clever Friend.* Very good mixer, sociable and entertaining. Establishes friendships easily, but these aren't always necessarily deep and tend to be more rational than emotional. Like to share experiences, seeks and gives clever advice and exciting impulses. Likes to be with people of the same convictions. Loves obvious agreements (clear scores = good friendship).

PROBLEM AREA: *The Business Friend.* Cool, calculating, and reserved. Community of interests or loyalty toward colleagues instead of friendship. Benefit of friendship stands in the foreground and not the friend. Problems are ignored. No room for familiarity or true sympathy.

11th

ROLE IN THE GROUP: The (detached) observer, mediator, or wise guy.

♀   **Venus** in the 11th House   *The Friendly Flirt*

STRENGTH: *Friendship Plus.* Deep solidarity and feeling of happiness in the friendship. Flirtation with erotic slant that doesn't always make the boundary between friendship and dalliance clear. Romantic coloration of the friendship. Peace-loving, faithful, and obliging. Seeks connection to artistic or cultural groups.

PROBLEM AREA: *The Flatterer.* Intensely avoids all encumbrances from friendships. Ingratiates oneself and is always vulnerable to flattery. Uncritical of friends. Danger of dependency. Insatiable thirst for adventure.

ROLE IN THE GROUP: The popular, peaceful, and connecting person.

♂   **Mars** in the 11th House   *The Fighting Team*

STRENGTH: *The Strong Friend.* Committedly supports one's friends and is willing to go through thick and thin with them. Also demands the same from them. Fights for the group and its goals. Loves male friendships and fighting teams. Is willing to fight for progress. Seeks contacts in sports clubs.

PROBLEM AREA: *The Quarreler.* Has difficulties in conforming and integrating oneself into the group. Very sensitive to antipathies. Demands great proof of friendship. Unpredictable and hard to get along with. Tends toward rivalries and competitive attitude. Threatens to break off the friendship with a constant "either-or" stance.

ROLE IN THE GROUP: The troublemaker.

♃   Jupiter in the 11th House   *The Noble Friendship*

STRENGTH: *Mr. or Ms. Hospitality.* The good, generous, and trustworthy friend and patron who gives friends help and support, but also receives it from them. Clearly differentiates between truly trusted and more distant friends. Loves to have friends around him, is very hospitable, and would like friends to be friends with each other as well. Seeks connections within or with religious communities or respected social contacts.

PROBLEM AREA: *The Elitist.* Distinct class consciousness. Judges others according to background and social role. Seeks important friends. Not really interested in friends' personal and emotional problems. An overbearing, conceited friend.

ROLE IN THE GROUP: The group leader, the guru, the aristocrat.

♄   Saturn in the 11th House   *The Solid Friendship*   Dignity

OBJECTIVE: Overcoming distance and coldness in the encounter with others, becoming trusting beyond fears of closeness, and starting up friendships.

INHIBITION: *The Lonesome Wolf.* Mistrust of potential friends. Fear of not being accepted, not being good enough for a friendship, or not being able to give enough. Retreat into isolation. Painful feelings of loneliness, but frequently with a resigned pride. Fear of groups.

COMPULSION: *The Proper Companion.* Violently forces oneself to change, is present at all social occasions, and also invites others to one's home. Very proper, but always somewhat standoffish and far from developing true feelings of friendship.

RESOLUTION: *The Steady Friend.* Has overcome mistrust of people and placed deep trust in a few good friends. Sincere and honest in friendship. Seeks mutuality and reliability. Is faithful, steadfast, and serious. Tends to be modest and thankful. Seeks connections with and within serious communities—such as a Zen brotherhood.

ROLE IN THE GROUP: The scapegoat, the supervisor.

11th

♅   **Uranus** in the 11th House   *The Crazy Friendship*   Dignity

STRENGTH: *The Peculiar Friend.* Seeks the highly individualistic, original, exotic friendship. Has an enriching and stimulating effect on others. Always remains very independent and individualistic. Strictly rejects all friendship rituals. Can't truly commit to a friendship, but can be a good friend for life of one's own accord. Seeks free connections with kindred spirits, such as world brotherhoods.

PROBLEM AREA: *The Flaky Friend.* Eccentric, unpredictable, and unable to make any adaptations in friendship. Completely numb and inconsiderate toward the wishes and standards of a friend. Comes and goes when and as one pleases. Puts a strain on one's very frequently changing friends.

ROLE IN THE GROUP: The eccentric, the eternal exception, the agitator.

♆   **Neptune** in the 11th House *The Spiritual Friendship*

STRENGTH: *The Sensitive Friend.* High, idealistic concepts of friendship. Strong feeling of solidarity and great willingness to adapt to the other person. Kindred souls in the circle of friends. The sensitive, caring, loving, understanding, and self-sacrificing friend. Longs for mystic friendships with spirits and seeks connection to spiritual groups.

PROBLEM AREA: *The Two-Faced Friend.* A naive and starry-eyed approach lead to deception, illusion, and betrayal in the friendship. Danger of being drawn into the aura of dubious societies or questionable friendships and not being able to get away from them anymore. Tendency toward becoming victim of a false friendship, as well as the danger of being a false friend.

ROLE IN THE GROUP: The invisible one, the victim, the prophet.

♇   **Pluto** in the 11th House   *The Powerful Friendship*

STRENGTH: *The Sworn Friend.* More a pact than a friendship. The feeling of karmic connection to the friend and compulsion to live through all the highs and lows with this person. Experiences of power and helplessness with deep-reaching transformations through the experience of friendship. Tendency to join secret societies and groups involved with magic.

PROBLEM AREA: *The Spooky Friend.* Difficult friendships with mysterious figures. Friendship problems on the basis of sexual tensions, danger of abuse, dependence, vulnerability to blackmail, violence, and dangerous struggles for power.

ROLE IN THE GROUP: The mysterious person, the secret (uncanny) leader.

☊   **North Node** in the 11th House

THEME: Conflict between egocentric showmanship and a necessary group consciousness, between platonic love or the love of philosophy and a passionate, sensual-erotic experience.

TASK: *Community Spirit.* Viewing life from a superordinate point of view and not just paying attention to satisfying the ego. Developing community spirit, advancing the consciousness of cosmopolitanism, supporting the breakdown of social differences, and being committed to new ideas and reforms.

11th

DANGER: *Self-Adulation.* Putting yourself at the center of attention all the time and everywhere and claiming a special role. Demanding attention, recognition, and admiration. Openly and primarily always thinking of yourself.

12th House: *I Dream*			
ANALOGY: ♓	RULER: ♃ and ♆	EXALTATION ♀	DETRIMENT: ☿
FALL: ☿	ELEMENT: Water	QUALITY: Mutable	GENDER: Feminine

GENERAL: *Seclusion from the World.* Transcendental experiences, mysticism, trance, ecstasy, purification, sacrifice, transfiguration, withdrawal from the world. Secrets and clandestine enemies. Voluntary isolation (hermitage, monastery) or involuntary isolation (hospital, prison). Longing for the "roof of the world." Configurations in this house are shown to outer world with shyness—if they are shown at all. They can also be experienced as nonexistent for a long time, yet still develop in silence. Or they can be discovered and developed in seclusion.

POLARITY: All things incomprehensible and boundless and dissolution in contrast to the order, clarity, and limitation in the 6th house.

⊙   **Sun** in the 12th House   *Spiritual Mastery*

THE CENTRAL THEME OF DEVELOPMENT OF THE SELF is the retreat into seclusion (on the roof of the world) in order to collect mystical and transcendental experiences, come into contact with other worlds, and encounter the images of one's own unconscious mind.

STRENGTH: *The Liberated Soul.* Has become independent and free by overcoming one's own suffering. Strongly spiritualized, fine personality. Willing to help others, and has a deep love of humanity. Withdrawn, creative, empathetic, intuitive, wise, illuminated. Knows how to work with subtle materials and energies (Bach flower essences, homeopathy).

PROBLEM AREA: *The Prisoner.* Feels excluded. Defiant, but ineffective, rebellion against the feeling of being a prisoner. Loud preacher of freedom. Chameleon. Full of complexes, timid, emotionally ill, inwardly very lonely, self-destructive, and, in extreme cases, confused and asocial. The eternal victim. Flight out of and from reality. Problems with addiction.

FINDS IN SECLUSION: What is essential.

☽   **Moon** in the 12th House   *Longing for Redemption*

STRENGTH: *The Sensitive Spirit.* Great sensitivity for everything that "lies in the air." Frequently occurring tendency to withdraw into seclusion and stillness in order to meditate, collect mystic and transcendental experiences, and come into harmony with oneself. Feels strongly drawn to everything that is vast, eternal, and irrational. Great yearning to be redeemed.

PROBLEM AREA: *The Emotionally Numb.* Is not conscious of emotions and only senses numbness when one asks oneself what one feels. Perhaps even has the impression of having no feelings at all or consciously keeps them hidden (even from oneself) so one is not hurt. Extremely unwilling to suffer. Remains a mystery to oneself for a long time. Cannot mature emotionally and remains very naive and infantile on this level. Danger of uncontrolled intoxication because of vast but conscious desires for deliverance.

FINDS IN SECLUSION: One's dreams and feelings.

☿   **Mercury** in the 12th House   *Exploring Chaos*   Detriment & Fall

STRENGTH: *The Paradoxical Thinker.* Great spiritual intuition. May do well at thinking in apparent contradictions and expressing deep insights in a paradoxical, allegoric, or symbolic manner. Can reconcile greatly varying schools of thought. Understands how to beat the opponent in confrontations with their own weapons (the other person's logic). Very scholarly. Good nose when it comes to revealing secrets, but also well-versed in search for transcendental experiences.

PROBLEM AREA: *The Plagiarist.* Engages in intellectual thievery without necessarily noticing it. Often has the impression of having known everything at a much earlier point in time. Also intellectual timidity, secrecy, and illusionary thinking.

12th

FINDS IN SECLUSION: Clear thoughts and good ideas.

♀   **Venus** in the 12th House   *The Dream of Love*   Exaltation

STRENGTH: *Selfless Love.* Great longing for merging and becoming one with another person. Absolute ability to be dedicated, idealistic, selfless, willing to make sacrifices. Love as a deep, spiritual experience and boundless, divine rapture. Artistically inspired.

PROBLEM AREA: *Secret Love.* Longing for a love that can never become reality because it must remain in the realm of fantasy not to do damage. Repressed femininity and concealed eroticism, unrequited love, or secret liaisons that never come into the public eye. Peculiar, sometimes anonymous loves: encounters without mentioning names, enamored correspondence between strangers, or love of someone in prison.

FINDS IN SECLUSION: Her ability to love and worthiness of love.

♂   **Mars** in the 12th House   *The Washout*

STRENGTH: *The Knight of the Holy Grail.* Powers of assertion, the will to con-quer, and initiative are strongly influenced by spiritual and unconscious forces. With the appropriate, spiritual exercise (such as Tai Chi, Aikido, archery in the spirit of Zen), the highest degree of effectiveness develops. Committed willingness to help. Defender and champion of the underprivi-leged (Robin Hood). High level of spiritual striving.

PROBLEM AREA: *The Bluff.* Chronically dissatisfied. Can get terribly excited about everything but only creates a storm in a teacup. Never really takes action. Plans, practices, tests, and then misses the opportunity. Complicated sexuality and repressed sexuality. In particularly difficult cases, criminal energy.

FINDS IN SECLUSION: Courage, resoluteness, and powers of assertion.

♃   **Jupiter** in the 12th House   *The Concealed Meaning*   Dignity

STRENGTH: *Happiness in Silence.* Happy experiences in solitude and silence. Finding meaning in reclusion after withdrawal from the outside world. The knowledge that true wealth is not of this world. Finding deep, inner wealth in meditation and spiritual exercises. Enriching inspiration and help from the unconscious mind.

PROBLEM AREA: *Secret Glory.* Absence of happiness (as long as it is sought in the outside world or hoped for from an outside source). Getting lost in a dream world and abandoning oneself to fantasies of personal greatness, heroics, and fame.

FINDS IN SECLUSION: Meaning and happiness.

♄   **Saturn** in the 12th House   *The Old Soul*

OBJECTIVE: Growing trust in being upheld by higher forces.

INHIBITION: *The Helpless or Unstable Individual.* Lack of stability and firmness. Uncanny fear that something unknown and incomprehensible could dominate or destroy life. Dread of loneliness, chaos, loss of the self, and above all, fear of the irrational. Fear of losing control over oneself and of ending up in isolation or imprisonment. Inexplicable feelings of guilt.

COMPULSION: *The Grim One.* Tries to pull oneself together with total stubbornness and toughness and prove that one can master life. Takes a spiritual path as the "best pupil" with steely single-mindedness and an ambitiously lowered gaze.

12th

RESOLUTION: *The Steadfast Person.* Overcomes the fear of fear and gradually opens up to what is vast, unknown, and the chaotic depths of one's own unconscious mind. In silent exercise, finds inner strength and trust in the forces that uphold human beings. Humble and capable of honest service, selflessness, and devotion. Experiences aloneness as "all-one-ness."

FINDS IN SECLUSION: Structure and resolve.

♅   Uranus in the 12th House   *Longing for Freedom*

STRENGTH: *The Lucid One.* Surprising inspirations and clear vision of future developments. Particularly receptive to new religious, political, and spiritual currents. Must exercise the art of comprehending the meaning of images that suddenly emerge from the unconscious mind.

PROBLEM AREA: *The (Secret) Escapee.* Rebels against any form of limitation on freedom. Wants to force open all walls, freeing oneself (and others) from isolation and imprisonment, as well as being free of all secrets and "having" to do something in secret. The opposite is also possible: someone who only permits oneself clandestine liberties.

FINDS IN SECLUSION: True freedom.

♆   Neptune in the 12th House   *Nirvana*   Dignity

STRENGTH: *The Transparent or Transcendent Individual.* Responsive to voices and images from the unconscious so that one is constantly led by strong invisible powers to everything important in this life. Inexplicable certainty of being "found" by nirvana. Artistic talent.

PROBLEM AREA: *The Confused Person.* Can be overwhelmed by the forces of the unconscious because of repression or simple ignorance of mediumistic abilities. Lives beyond all limits and structures. "Knows" that only the illusion is not an illusion.

FINDS IN SECLUSION: Visions.

♇   **Pluto** in the 12th House   *Unconscious Powers*

STRENGTH: *The Transformed.* Transformed in a far-reaching manner through intensive experience of powers of the unconscious. Opens oneself to the forces of deepest renewal in meditative stillness and seclusion.

PROBLEM AREA: *The Distressed.* A victim of power fantasies and fears of help-lessness. Inexplicable fears of the powers of the unconscious and the primitive forces in one's own depths. Experiencing oneself as helpless in the face of illness and emotional suffering and becoming isolated.

FINDS IN SECLUSION: Inner healer.

☊   **North Node** in the 12th House

THEME: Conflict between transcendental striving and everyday reality, between chaos and order, between mediumism and rational thinking.

TASK: *Spirituality.* Emerging from the confines of the explicable and abandoning oneself to experiences of the transcendental and boundless. Developing powers of imagination and a spiritual consciousness through rational, analytic work. Exploring so-called chaos. Withdrawing from busy activity into seclusion. Developing the will to sacrifice and brotherly love.

12th

DANGER: *Clinical Purity.* Clinging tightly to utilitarian thinking. Fear of things that have not been planned. Compulsive rejection and avoidance of everything that is unorganized and inexplicable. Obsession with cleanliness, addiction to orderliness, or the mania of having to control everything.

The ASPECTS

Key Words for Aspect Combinations

☉ SUN	☽ MOON	☿ MERCURY	♀ VENUS	♂ MARS
Essence	Disposition	Mind	Relationship	Fight
Life	Fantasy	Orientation	Art	Sexuality
Heart	Stomach	Nerves	Balance	Muscles
Center	Feeling	Astuteness	Style	War
Light	Homeland	Learning	Taste	Violence
Consciousness	Soul	Tricky	Love	Conquest
Will	Instinct	Idea	Eroticism	Strength
Development	Darkness	Thoughts	Grace	Action
Content	Presentiment	Combining	Devotion	Desire
Father	Mother	Theory	Beauty	Brutality
Creation	Impression-	Way of	Peace	Competition
Aura	abilty	expressing	Sociability	Inconsiderate-
Spirit	Security	Thinking	Powers of	ness
Magnanimity	Fertility	Intellect	attraction	Assertion
Vitality	Dream	Logic	Harmony	Advancement
Zest for Life	Affect	Reason	Charm	Potency
High standards	Sixth sense	Calculating	Temptation	Drive
Equanimity	Willingness to	Perceiving	Gentleness	Wildness
	adapt	Cunning	Softness	Aggression
		Theory	Favor	Heat
			Solidarity	Dynamics

♃ JUPITER	♄ SATURN	♅ URANUS	♆ NEPTUNE	♇ PLUTO
Belief	Death	Freedom	Dream	Power
Ideals	Boundary	Flash	Longing	Magic
Liver	Bones	Utopia	Haze	Hypnosis
Virtue	Form	Independence	Intoxication	Healing
Values	Structure	Distance	Addiction	Shadow
Meaning	Tradition	Upheaval	Mysticism	Transformation
Morality	Duty	Revolution	Vastness	Dependence
Happiness	Lack	Crazy	Dissolution	Powerlessness
Wealth	Mistrust	Eccentric	Imagination	Regeneration
Trust	Deprivation	Rebellion	Deception	Possession
Exaggeration	Illness	Original	Reception	Pact
Growth	Asceticism	Flash of genius	Seduction	Entanglement
Justice	Earnest	Fickleness	Mediumism	Rearrangement
Conviction	Sobriety	Betrayal	Weakness	
Generosity	Bitter	Individuality	Trance	
Success	Poverty		Enthusiasm	
Honor	Standard		Supernatural	
Nobility	Pessimism		Incomprehen-	
Optimism	Experience		sible	
Expanse	Narrowness		Victim	
Kindness	Humility			
Ethics	Reality			
Opulence	Hardness			
	Responsibility			
	Coldness			
	Ritual			
	Failure			

In order to receive an impression of the many possibilities of an aspect's meaning, the key words listed here can all be combined with each other as desired in an aspect of connected planets.

Aspects of the Sun

☉-☽   **Sun-Moon:** *Mind and Soul*

ARCHETYPE: The King and the Queen

SHADOW: The Dazzler and the Evil Witch

COMPARISON:

☉	—	☽
Father		Mother
Will		Wish
Reason		Feeling
Active		Passive
Adult		Child
Conscious		Unconscious
Mind		Soul
Waking consciousness		Dream consciousness

GENERAL: The interplay of wishes (☽) and wanting (☉), of conscious striving (☉) and instinctive urge (☽), of the masculine (☉) and the feminine (☽), of the conscious (☉) and the unconscious (☽), of the waking consciousness (☉) and the dream consciousness (☽), of individuality (☉) and family heritage (☽).

HARMONY: *The Well-Balanced Individual.* Harmonious accord between taking action and the willingness to simply let things happen. Finds the right mixture between wanting and wishing, between masculine and feminine portions of her nature, between the childhood self and the adult self. Well-balanced, satisfied, optimistic, cheerful, vigorous, emotionally stable.

DISCORD: *The Tense Person.* Vehement conflict between the heart and mind, conscious striving and instinctive urge, above all in the group of themes that correspond to the sign position of the Sun and Moon. Experiences self in the battle of the sexes. Problems with the parental home and family. Torn back and forth between the efforts of becoming oneself and a passive attitude of letting oneself drift. Intense mood fluctuations, developmental crises, and identity problems. Uncontrolled emotional outbursts and depressions. Frustrated, self-satisfied, and subjective.

☉-☿	Sun-Mercury: *Cleverness*

ARCHETYPE: The Smart King and His Herald	SHADOW: The Boss and His Wily Attorney

COMPARISON:

☉ — ☿

Mind	Reason
Organization	Tactic
Venturing	Calculating
Courage to face life	Agility
Will to live	Orientation

GENERAL: Perceiving, understanding, thinking through, ordering, and formulating (all ☿) what is essential (☉). The distance between critical perception (☿) and subjective wanting (☉). Self-criticism (☉-☿). Making oneself understood (☿). *Since the Sun and Mercury are never more than 28° apart from each other, there are no tension aspects between these two planets. Their concurrence is judged by other criteria:*

If the Sun and Mercury are in different signs, this increases the objectivity of the thoughts because thinking (☿) can take another standpoint than the will (☉). If they are in the same sign, thinking loses the critical distance to the character and is subjectively colored by the will.

The most favorable distance between the Sun and Mercury is considered to be an interval of 3° to 8° because here—expressed in images—Mercury's power of thought can develop in the Sun's best light. If the distance is less, it is called a "combust Mercury": it no longer produces any achievements of its own but stands completely in the Sun's service, exclusively concerned with justifying the Sun's activities. The crass subjectivity of this conjunction is also valid if the two planets are not located in the same sign.

☉☿

☉-♀	Sun-Venus: *Charm*

ARCHETYPE: The Master and the Muse	SHADOW: The Beau and the Flatterer

COMPARISON:

☉ — ♀

Essence	Grace
Creative will	Formability
Individual nature	Sense of community
Independence	Desire for connection
Core	Packaging
Personality	Charm
Inner beauty	Outer beauty
Willfulness	Striving for harmony

GENERAL: The connection of personality (☉) and content of life (☉) for a person with style (♀), outer beauty (♀), and personal charm (♀). A sympathetic/likeable (♀) and peaceable (♀) nature (☉). *The Sun and Venus are never more than 48° apart from each other. This is why conjunctions, semisextiles, and semisquares are the only possible aspects.*

HARMONY: *The Likable Person.* Pleasant aura. A person who has a beneficial effect on others by just being there. Popular, charming, and usually erotic and seductive. Sociable, able to adapt, a good mixer, diplomatic, peaceable. Knows how to value elevated style, a cultivated atmosphere, luxury, and good taste. Frequently distinct interest in art and culture.

DISCORD: *The Coquette.* According to the position of the signs of the planets, cold-blooded tactics with erotic charms or crude ingratiation. False, sometimes extravagant expectations of happiness. Lapses of taste and excessive desire for pleasure.

☉-♂	**Sun-Mars**: *Bravery*

ARCHETYPE: The Courageous King and His General	SHADOW: The Tyrant and His Torturer

COMPARISON:

☉ — ♂	
Leading	Implementing
Strength of will	Muscle power
Conscious wanting	Instinctive desiring
Will	Instinct
Development of self	Power of assertion
Man	Youth
Masculinity	Virile power

GENERAL: Courage and power (♂) to believe in oneself (☉), assert (♂) the personality (☉), and penetrate (♂) through to the development of the nature (☉) of the world. The struggle (♂) for existence (☉).

HARMONY: *The Dynamo.* Characteristics and assertive force combine harmoniously into a clear, self-confident determination. Aggressiveness is directed outwardly in a healthy, appropriate manner. Distinct, sometimes imposing masculine traits and well-assessed willingness to take risks. Active, dynamic, goal-oriented, energetic. Pronounced willfulness and considerable strength of ego.

DISCORD: *The Self-Destruct Mechanism.* At variance with oneself. Inwardly torn and contradictory masculinity. Hothead who restlessly takes on challenges without thinking them over and frequently endangers oneself in the process. Conflict between will, use of energy, and goal. Aggressiveness is sometimes angrily directed at the outside world and then again directed in a destructive manner against one's own self. Energy is wasted and used at the wrong point in time, creating a ruinous exploitation of one's own powers and unpredictable energy eruptions. Has a difficult time reducing and controlling instinctual tensions. Erratic, irritable, impatient, frustrated, opinionated, stubborn, and aggressive.

☉-♃	Sun-Jupiter: *Self-Assurance*

ARCHETYPE: The Noble-Minded King and the High Priest	SHADOW: The Megalomaniac and the Self-Righteous Man

COMPARISON:

$$☉ — ♃$$

Essence	Meaning
Will	Success
Magnanimity	High-mindedness
Fame	Honor
Development of the self	Development of meaning

GENERAL: Self-assurance (☉-♃). Designing one's life (☉) with optimism and confidence (♃). Going through life (☉) with luck and success (♃). The meaning (♃) of life (☉).

HARMONY: *The Respectable Person.* A talent for happiness and the feeling of being chosen. Optimistic feeling for life that is full of self-assurance and also passed on to others. Always interested in expansion, improvement, growth, and promotion. Creative, capable of enthusiasm, tolerant, trustworthy, demanding, generous, kind, and humane. Inner and outer dignity, noble sentiments, and always concerned with living and acting in an ethically faultless manner.

DISCORD: *The Fat Soul.* Self-satisfied in judging oneself and one's own achievements. Is too good and fine for everything. Pomposity, wastefulness, and smugness that can be intolerable because of a constant concern about appearing in the light of the imaginary greatness. Emotional and physical fatness. Unreliable, indolent, conceited, demanding. Exaggerated attitude of expectation toward life. Con games. Collects all attributes that promise to increase one's own value.

☉-♄	Sun-Saturn: *Integrity*

ARCHETYPE: The Solemn King and His Wise Advisor	SHADOW: The Sick King and the Embittered Old Man

COMPARISON:

☉ — ♄

Essence	Form
Development	Boundary
Inner stability	Outer stability
Liveliness	Repose
Self-assurance	Self-doubt
Lightness	Heaviness
Zest for life	Asceticism
Consciousness	Conscience
Joy	Earnest
Demands	Humility
Wanting	Being compelled to

GENERAL: The boundary (♄) of growth (☉). The form (♄) and its content (☉). Slow (♄) but lasting (♄) development of the personality (☉). Learning to become humble (♄) in life (☉). Overcoming (☉) the fear of embarking on something new (♄). Inhibitions (♄) about believing in oneself (☉).

HARMONY: *The Builder.* Prefers slow but lasting growth in contrast to hasty, half-baked leaps. Needs and creates order and structure. Willing to recognize clear boundaries and look reality in the eye. Earnest, mature, and reliable personality. Respectable, competent, responsible, dutiful, strong, diligent, humble, and modest.

DISCORD: *The Stooped Individual.* Difficult authority conflicts. Lack of self-confidence, massive doubt about one's own value, and the persistent feeling of not being good enough. Inexplicable feelings of guilt. Seeks recognition, yet at the same time is incapable of "putting up with" praise and applause. Always has to prove oneself for fear of failure. In extreme cases, rigid and inflexible, clinging to proven norms and familiar misery. Fear of change and the step beyond the previous boundaries. Doesn't actually consider oneself worthy of love and therefore entertains deep (if secret) doubt even about declarations of love that are meant honestly. Strong inhibitions about showing oneself as one is. Has difficulties believing in oneself.

☉♄

☉-♅	Sun-Uranus: *Eccentricity*

ARCHETYPE: The Liberal King and the Court Jester	SHADOW: The Irresponsible Person and the Traitor

COMPARISON:

☉ — ♅

Essence	Individuality
Focus of attention	Outside
Creativity	Upheaval
Development	Mutation
Equanimity	Rebellion

GENERAL: The free (♅) person (☉). Consciousness (☉) of uniqueness (♅). The original (♅), crazy (♅), or eccentric (♅) mind (☉).

HARMONY: *The Casual Individual.* Great striving for independence, autonomy, and the freedom to live a completely individual life. Very interested in experimenting. Imaginative and inventive. Sometimes ingenious and often ahead of the times. Can easily adapt to new ideas, plans that have changed suddenly, unfamiliar situations, and new relationships. On the other hand, tolerates no type of routine, constricting structures, or restrictions of one's independence.

DISCORD: *The Self-Sufficient Person.* Exaggerated, sometimes problematic striving for independence that sooner or later experiences every form of contractual obligation or verbal agreement as an intolerable prison. As a result, more often than not commits a breach of contract out of "emotional self-defense" because personal freedom is always more important than any type of responsibility. Inwardly restless and torn. Constantly seeks change. Sudden and radical break with old habits in life, people, or attitudes. Unpredictable, egocentric, cold-blooded, impersonal, willful, and seditious.

☉-♆	Sun-Neptune: *Mediumism*

ARCHETYPE: The Spiritual King and the Seer	SHADOW: The Addicted King and His Tempter

COMPARISON:

☉ — ♆

Active actions	Letting oneself be guided
Searching	Being found
Consciousness	Illumination
Perception of reality	Vision
Waking consciousness	Trance
Sobriety	Intoxication

GENERAL: Being guided (♆) by a guardian angel (♆) on the path of life (☉). Expanding or befogging (♆) the conscious mind (☉) through mystic vision (♆), trance (♆), or state of intoxication (♆). Boundless yearning (♆) to be released (♆) from the confines of the body (☉) or from consciousness (☉).

HARMONY: *The Visionary.* Extremely sensitive to all moods and currents. Good sense for the spirit of the times and trends. Sure instinctual judgment on the basis of frequently inexplicable but solid inner certainty. Visionary gifts and great intuitive understanding. Often a strongly developed interest in spiritual experiences, mysticism, trance, and everything that helps exceed the boundaries of consciousness. Strong fantasy and dream life. Mediumism in the sense of spirituality, as well as interest in media like film, television, newspapers, etc.

DISCORD: *The Seducible Person.* Driven by boundless longing to leave the prison of the body; in danger of taking the wrong paths. Satisfies the yearning for the Holy Spirit rashly with the spirit of wine or other intoxicants. In danger of addiction, which is why—in some cases—one is strictly abstinent, even in the most difficult aspects. Has a hard time turning a deaf ear to the insinuations or expectations of others. Without distinct goals of one's own, can easily be seduced. No clear feeling of self. Easily becomes the victim of a false self-image. In some cases, feels only numbness in one's body. Has no problem slipping into a great variety of roles (chameleon), but also becomes the plaything of others. Without any backbone, insincere, and undependable; in difficult cases, completely insecure, corrupt, addicted, sordid, and depraved.

☉♆

☉-♇	Sun-Pluto: *Power*

ARCHETYPE: The Mighty King and the Sorcerer	SHADOW: The Despot and the Gray Eminence

COMPARISON:

☉ — ♇

Ego	Shadow
Foreground	Background
Light	Dark
Creation	Rearrangement
Aura	Magnetism

GENERAL: Experience and consciousness (☉) of power (♇) and helplessness (♇). The encounter of the self (☉) with its shadow (♇). The transformation (♇) of the personality (☉).

HARMONY: *The Shaman.* Enormous powers of the soul—frequently unconscious to a large degree—that can be used for both the benefit and the destruction of others: powers of suggestion, healing powers, hypnotic abilities, and the subtle but highly effective power of magnetically attracting, fascinating, and captivating other people, as well as causing situations and events to occur on the basis of enormous powers of desire. Strong interest in depth psychology, magical and occult knowledge and practices, archaic and shamanic rites, and all the taboos of a society, particularly death and sexuality.

DISCORD: *The Possessed Soul.* Dark, dubious character that is not strong enough to resist the temptations of power. Tries to bind others to oneself, make them dependent and enslaved in order to control and exploit them in an emotional, physical, and/or material way. Possessed by a thirst for power. But often also the helpless victim of own striving for power or the power of others. Extreme all-or-nothing maxims. Obsessed by fixed and compulsive ideas, above all regarding interpersonal relationships and sexuality. Self-glorification, strong powers of destruction, and tendency toward depression.

☉-☊   Sun-North Node

CONJUNCTION: The connection of the Sun with the Moon's Node places a very special accent on the sign and the house in which this conjunction is located. The related abilities, potentials, and tasks can and should be given the opportunity to blossom more intensely.

HARMONY: Good association of vital energy and direction in life. Helpful, powerful, and useful support by the Sun sign. However, occasionally also the expression of convenience and missed opportunities.

DISCORD: Constantly recurring conflicts and tensions between the demands of the Sun sign and the tasks of the Moon's Node that are to be fulfilled. As a result, lack of clarity about the path in life, inner conflict, inhibitions, laziness, difficulties in making decisions, and delays in the development of the personality.

☉-AC   Sun-Ascendant

HARMONY: *The Uninhibited Individual.* Positive, strong, more masculine expression of the personality. Spontaneous, powerful, natural, strong-willed. Can show who one really is without any timidity or effort. Strong trust in own abilities, great self-confidence, and a healthy feeling of self-worth.

DISCORD: *The Masked Person.* External appearance and inner nature are poles apart. As a result, inhibitions of personal expression and frustrated confrontations with the outer world. Shyness about showing true nature. Hides behind a socially acceptable mask.

☉-MC   Sun-Medium Coeli

HARMONY: *The Success.* Professional success, social climbing, and impression made in the public eye are an essential part of the development of the self. Conscious planning and active creativity in the realization of life's objectives and the professional career. Claim to leadership and leadership qualities.

DISCORD: *The Contradiction.* Relationship to public eye full of conflicts. The development of the self and the professional career—sometimes also the objectives in life—appear difficult to reconcile and may even run counter to each other. Overcoming these contradictions is the primary task.

Aspects of the Moon

☽-☿	**Moon-Mercury**: *Feeling Thought*

ARCHETYPE: The Clever Queen and Her Herald	SHADOW: The Babbler and the Liar

COMPARISON:

☽	— ☿
Disposition	Intellect
Feeling	Thinking
Dreaming	Seeing clearly
Instinct	Reason
Unconscious	Conscious
Fantasy	Logic
Image	Word
Associating	Combining
Guessing	Calculating
Sensing	Perceiving

GENERAL: The interplay of thinking (☿) and feeling (☽). Understanding (☽) and interpreting (☿) dreams. Expressing (☿) feelings (☽). Telling (☿) fairy tales (☽).

HARMONY: *Healthy Common Sense.* Good interplay between thinking and emotional depth. Sure instincts in assessing and judging situations and people. Having a good nose for things. Being intellectually agile and able to adapt. Very imaginative, yet always realistic. Vivid, graphic manner of expression. Quick-witted and good at languages. Excellent memory, healthy common sense, and good powers of observation.

DISCORD: *The Trivial Talker.* Conflict between disposition and intellect. Lack of orientation. Childish wishful thinking and dangerous rewriting of reality into the respectively most pleasant version. Or embarrassingly unsuccessful analyzing and complicated explaining of feelings. Superficial, trivial talk. Empty promises, bragging, lies, and gossip. Emotional, easily excited, hurtful, sharp-tongued, and slanderous. Pure assumptions become supposed facts in the wink of an eye.

☽-♀	**Moon-Venus:** *Peace of Mind*

ARCHETYPE: The Graceful Queen and the Lady-in-Waiting	SHADOW: The Moody Woman and the Vain Lady

COMPARISON:

☽ — ♀	
Loving care	Eroticism
Disposition	Sensuality
Closeness	Flirtation
Security	Temptation
Feeling	Taste
Atmosphere	Style
Mother	Young woman
Watching over	Enticing
Longing	Willingness
Family	Couple
Motherly love	Erotic love
Soul	Peace

GENERAL: Longing (☽) for love (♀) and a feeling of security (☽). Dreaming (☽) of love (♀) and eroticism (♀). A good feeling (☽) in matters of taste (♀), style (♀), and art (♀). Harmonious (♀), loving (♀), and peaceful (♀) feelings (☽).

HARMONY: *The Charmer.* Harmony between disposition and erotic aura. Charming, very feminine, lovable, and always willing to fall in love. Great desire for love and tenderness. Capable of deep, genuine love, devotion, and sympathy. Friendly, tender, gentle, affectionate, and loving with a sure sense of what is right and the right moment in a relationship. Doesn't like confrontations.

DISCORD: *The Unfulfilled Person.* Torn back and forth between the wish for emotional security and the enticing call of desire. Both at the same time are apparently not satisfying. As a result, an uneven temper, dissatisfaction, extreme sensitivity, moodiness, jealousy, and unpredictably passionate: sometimes lustful, sometimes inhibited. Also a tendency toward secrets and vicarious satisfaction like erotic or sweet things. Difficulties in marriage and relationships. Conflict between family sense and relationship with partner, as well as in the roles of mother and beloved.

☽♀

☽-♂	Moon-Mars: *Daring*

ARCHETYPE: The Brave Queen and Her Protector	SHADOW: The Haughty Lady and the Tormentor

COMPARISON:

☽	— ♂
Feminine	Masculine
Passive	Active
Wish	Deed
Passion	Courage
Powers of the soul	Muscle power
Mother	Son
Longing	Greed
Homeland	War

GENERAL: Passionate (☽) desire (♂). Acting (♂) on the basis of feeling (☽). Becoming emotionally (☽) excited (♂). Conquering (♂) or defending (♂) her nest (☽). Fighting (♂) for one's own or an entrusted brood (☽).

HARMONY: *The Spunky Person.* Spontaneous, courageous actions based on an emotional impulse. Good sense of the right point in time. The more vehement and holy the feelings, the greater the intrepidity. Committed champion of those who have been entrusted to one, and the needy. Or the fervent protector of nature. Decisive, passionate, direct, and open.

DISCORD: *The Uncontrolled Individual.* Severe tensions between disposition and aggression, anger and instinctual desire as the cause of massive problems with aggression like destructive frenzy and acts committed in the heat of passion, as well as stomach problems resulting from "swallowing" anger. Deeply injured, churned-up feelings lead to explosive outbursts of passion, vindictiveness, uncontrolled instinctive behavior, and chronic irritability. Constant inner unrest and hastiness. Aggressive feelings toward everything that is motherly. Fighting, repressing, or devastating what could provide a feeling of security.

☽-♃ Moon-Jupiter: *Wealth of Emotion*

ARCHETYPE: The Wise Queen and the Nobleman

SHADOW: The Arrogant Lady and the Condescending Man

COMPARISON:

☽	♃
Simplicity	Dignity
Instinct	Wisdom
Emotional values	Ethical values
Search for a feeling of security	Search for meaning
Physical nourishment	Intellectual nourishment
Fertility	Growth

GENERAL: Holy (♃), happy (♃), noble (♃), rich (♃) feelings (☽). Happy (♃) everyday life (☽). Desire (☽) to travel (♃). The happy (♃) woman (☽).

HARMONY: *The Kind-Hearted Individual.* Confident feelings and deep self-assurance. Likeable, winning, benevolent, lovable nature. Generous, convivial, epicurean. High spirits. Able to trust others. Great wealth of emotion. Deep respect for everything that is motherly and feminine. Enthusiasm for high ideals, noble convictions, and feelings that impart meaning. Skillful hand in everyday matters.

DISCORD: *The Pampered Person.* Considerable insincerity toward oneself. Courts applause and cheap flattery that supports overestimation of the self. Great plans that are never carried out. Spoiled mother's darling, feigned nonchalance toward life, emotional exaggerations. Lazy, indolent, comfort-loving, but also arrogant and demanding.

☽♃

☽-♄	**Moon-Saturn:** *Serious Feelings*
ARCHETYPE: The Unpretentious Queen and the Council Elder	SHADOW: The Embittered Lady and Her Adversary

COMPARISON:

☽ — ♄

Dream	Reality
Indulgence	Toughness
Wish	Fact
Desire	Duty
Affect	Control
Mood	Framework
Wish for the feeling of security	Reliability
Running wild	Limiting
Soft	Brittle

GENERAL: Stable (♄), controlled (♄), and/or serious (♄) feelings (☽). Resolute (♄), disciplined (♄), and sober (♄) in everyday life (☽). Feelings (☽) of guilt (♄). The earnest (♄) woman (☽).

HARMONY: *The Conscientious Individual.* Committed, stable feelings. Great staying power, prudence, faithfulness, and performance of one's duty, even under difficult conditions. Willing and able to tolerate hardships, deprivation, and necessary renunciation. Very composed, even in sorrowful situations. Inwardly willing and able to tighten one's belt and be modest, leave, or let go when necessary. Clear feeling for what is feasible and enjoyment of what has been achieved. Willing to take responsibility. Serious and dependable.

DISCORD: *The Hardhearted Person.* Merciless with oneself and others. Inhibited, emotionally withdrawn, lonely, or even embittered. Personal feelings and wishes are repressed and those of others are held in contempt or viewed with suspicious mistrust. Sometimes absurd envy of others. Can't express oneself emotionally. Lacks feeling of security, feels unloved and often worthless. Can't let go, and therefore remains bound even to situations that are unbearable, hopeless, and self-destructive. Extreme, insatiable need for a feeling of security. Leaden emotions.

☽-♅   **Moon-Uranus:** *Emotional Dynamite*

ARCHETYPE: The Unique Queen and the Court Jester

SHADOW: The Noncommittal Woman and the Agitator

COMPARISON:

☽ — ♅	
Closeness	Distance
Patience	Impatience
Dependence	Independence
Feeling of security	Freedom
Emotion	Idea
Monopolizing	Taking flight

GENERAL: Surprising (♅), unpredictable (♅), vacillating (♅), crazy (♅) feelings (☽). Longing (☽) for freedom (♅) and independence (♅). Tension between closeness (☽) and distance (♅). The spirit of departure (♅-☽). Electrifying (♅) feelings (☽). Sudden emergence (♅) of unconscious powers (☽). Emotional (☽) fireworks (♅).

HARMONY: *The Genius at Improvising.* Can spontaneously and easily adjust and adapt to new situations and people. Remains inwardly very flexible and always open for what is new. Yet, still capable of adequately integrating the need for a feeling of emotional security and the demand for independence and freedom. But tolerates neither closed doors nor demands placed on one. *Must* always do everything voluntarily (a compulsion in itself). Very bright, lively, quick-witted, and imaginative. Has a strongly distinct intuition, and sometimes even clairvoyant abilities.

DISCORD: *The Individual Incapable of Commitment.* Need for freedom that takes on a compulsive character. Can never really open up to anything on the emotional level. In any type of agreement, always keeps at least one (inner) loophole open. Hates all words of limitation like "never" and "always" and therefore tries to keep at least one option open at all times and in all places. For this reason, prefers to fall in love in "harmless cases," which means in people who are quite certain to be unreachable. Hysterical and easily excitable. Tends to have stage fright. Contradictory, strongly fluctuating, and easily irritated emotions. Quickly feels harassed, coerced, restricted, unfree, and then tears away abruptly and curtly. Chronic dissatisfaction with the present. Tends to have solitary ways.

☽♅

☽-♆	**Moon-Neptune**: *Feelings of Presentiment*

ARCHETYPE: The Sensitive Queen and the Blind Seer	SHADOW: The Airy-Fairy Lady and the Ghost

COMPARISON:

☽	—	♆
Dream		Vision
Presentiment		Inspiration
Devotion		Self-sacrifice
Longing for a feeling of security		Longing for vastness

GENERAL: Boundless (♆) feelings (☽). Longing (☽) for deliverance (♆), trance (♆), and mystic experience (♆). Fine (♆) antennas (☽). Artistic (♆) sense (☽).

HARMONY: *The Medium.* Can be easily and deeply touched on the emotional level. Finest antennas of the soul that convey knowledge about what is unspoken, unfamiliar, and the future. Great ability to be devoted to an ideal or a person, with a tendency toward exaggerated enthusiasm. Uncanny certainty in evaluating unfamiliar situations and people. Insatiable hunger for love, affection, attention, loving care, and great longing to become one with another person. This is connected with the fear of being deserted and left alone. Mystic tendencies.

DISCORD: *The Escapist.* Yearns for deliverance and lives in a fantasy world far from reality. Unfulfillable expectations of life and love, which—to be on the safe side—are usually not even tried out in the real world. Instead, flight into a dream world, hallucinations, intoxication, and addiction alternating with dissatisfaction, disappointment, loneliness, depression, and melancholy. In some cases, completely numb feelings. Great danger of being deluded, seduced, or cheated by others, as well as cheating, seducing, or deceiving others.

| ☽-♇ | **Moon-Pluto:** *Depths of the Soul* |

ARCHETYPE: The Irresistible Queen and the Sorcerer

SHADOW: The Spooky Queen and the Black Knight

COMPARISON:

☽ — ♇

Love	Power
Mothering	Seizing power
Helping	Healing
Empathizing	Seeing through
Preserving	Transforming
Attracting	Fascinating
Soul	Shadow

GENERAL: Longing (☽) for what is hidden (♇) and forbidden (♇). Emotional (☽) entanglements (♇). Desire or thirst (☽) for power (♇). Deepest transformation (♇) through feelings (☽) and/or emotional suffering (☽). Feelings (☽) of power (♇) and helplessness (♇). Extreme (♇) emotions (☽). The urge (☽) to go into the depths (♇).

HARMONY: *The Spy.* Enormous, lasting, sometimes fanatic urge to keep going in a certain direction once it has been decided on, and to air secrets, break taboos, and spy on things that are hidden and forbidden. Delving into the depths of one's own feelings with fear and fascination in order to explore one's self, one's own motives and drives, as well as those of other people. Great powers of the soul.

DISCORD: *The Power-Hungry Person.* An urge, difficult to control, to seize power over other people's souls and make them dependent. Also one's own feelings of helplessness toward others who bear emotional power (mother). Extreme emotional states like all-or-nothing or: if you are not for me, you are against me. Tremendous feelings of jealousy and manic need to control others. Enormous problems in giving the necessary freedom to people one is responsible for.

☽-☊	Moon-North Node

HARMONY: Instinctive urge to progress on the path shown by the North Node. Intuitive, partly unconscious and instinctually sound acceptance and evaluation of the possibilities connected with the house and sign of the Moon's Node. Feelings are in harmony with the goal's direction.

DISCORD: The yearnings of the Moon and its demands for a feeling of emotional security and attention are in contradiction to the position of the Moon's Node and related tasks in life. Feelings of unhappiness, inner indecision and irritability, dissatisfaction, and vexations on the path in life.

☽-AC	Moon-Ascendant

HARMONY: *The Obliging Individual.* Sensitive, imaginative, impressionable, cautious, usually reacts, tends to have a feminine form of expression. Willingness to adapt and be compliant.

DISCORD: *The Touchy Person.* Difficulties in showing feelings and putting one's own wishes into practice. Emotionally blocked in the manner of expression. At the same time, moody and touchy toward others. Tends to get involved in misunderstandings.

☽-MC	Moon-Medium Coeli

HARMONY: *Ms. or Mr. Popularity.* Instinctive urge to be in the public eye. Needs to be able to express one's feelings, perceptions, emotions, or artistic abilities in professional life. Good sense for what the pubic wants. Can make oneself well-liked. Popularity aspects.

DISCORD: *The Day-Dreamer.* The emotional area is in conflict with professional goals, the career, or the goals in life. Strong feelings of reluctance and mood vacillations disturb professional development. Difficult persistence of naive ideas about the dream job. Inhibitions and timidity about showing oneself in public and "exposing" the inner self.

Aspects of Mercury

☿-♀   **Mercury-Venus**: *The Esthete*

ARCHETYPE: The Smartie and the Muse

SHADOW: The Liar and the Circe

COMPARISON:

☿ — ♀	
Logic	Erotic
Thinking	Feeling
Reason	Esthetic
Word	Color
Practicality	Sense of beauty
Concept	Image
Writing	Painting
Business	Art
Cunning	Charm

GENERAL: Stylish (♀) expression (☿). Beautiful (♀) words (☿). Doing business (☿) with beautiful things (♀): galleries, cosmetic salons, the fashion industry, gastronomy.

HARMONY: *The Esthete.* Pleasant manner of expression, abilities in the fields of writing and art. Charming, graceful, harmonious, skillful, and diplomatic social manner. Optimistic thinking. Conversations can have an erotic effect. Wants to learn, be inspired, and stimulated by relationships.

DISCORD: *The Phony.* Using tactics with emotions and hypocritical feelings. Relationships that are "too sensible." Calculating "love," cunning flattery, swindle in relationships. Affected behavior.

☿
♀

☿-♂	**Mercury-Mars**: *Keen Perception*

ARCHETYPE: The Merchant and the Warrior	SHADOW: The Counterfeiter and the Scoundrel

COMPARISON:

☿ — ♂	
Thinking	Drive and urge
Reason	Instinct
Cunning	Muscle power
Tactic	Violence
Talking	Acting
Planning	Performing
Clever	Primitive
Skilled	Rough

GENERAL: Keenness (♂) of thought (☿), connection of thinking (☿) and acting (♂), power (♂) to make decisions (☿), the word (☿) duel (♂), stratagem (☿-♂).

HARMONY: *Quick Wits.* Asserting oneself in a tactically clever and skilled manner. Crystal-clear argumentation. Sharp, analytical mind. Extreme quick-wittedness. Fighting by using brains and words. The attorney, the literary critic, the chess-player. Enjoyment of discussion. Insight into one's own instinctive nature and deliberate actions.

DISCORD: *The Sharp Tongue.* Testy, destructive thinking. Irritable, loose tongue. Provokes verbal confrontations. Nasty mouth. Irrational acts. Nervous, restless, edgy. Danger of dissipating one's strength. Not respecting other people's opinions: disrupting, interrupting, arguing like a hothead. Mean criticism or slander.

☿-♃	**Mercury-Jupiter**: *Wealth of Thought*

ARCHETYPE: The Merchant and the Scholar	SHADOW: The Chatterbox and the Conceited Fool

COMPARISON:

☿ — ♃	
Intellect	Conviction
Knowledge	Education
Doubt	Faith
Science	Religion
Wording	Significance of words
Concept	Meaning
Teaching	Preaching
Secular	Holy
Student	Teacher
Purpose	Significance
Persuading	Convincing

GENERAL: The search (☿) for meaning (♃). Spacious (♃) thinking (☿). The good (♃) idea (☿). Roaming (☿) afield (♃). Positive (♃) thoughts (☿). Prestige (♃) thinking (☿).

HARMONY: *The Scholar.* Great thirst for knowledge and striving for higher education. Interest in philosophy. Good ability to learn. Wants to bring meaning and purpose into harmony with each other. Talented at languages. Striving for higher perceptions.

DISCORD: *The Conceited. Fool* Reckless, smug, and arrogant way of thinking. Puffed-up, hollow thoughts. Exaggerations and phrasemongering. Mentally lazy and presumptuous at the same time. Likes to play the scholar. Completely uncritical when it comes to one's own thoughts and perceptions.

☿♃

☿-♄	**Mercury-Saturn:** *Depth of Thought*

ARCHETYPE: The Student and the Hermit	SHADOW: The Smartie and the Villain

COMPARISON:

☿	—	♄
Curiosity		Experience
Theory		Practice
Idea		Reality
Flexible		Resolute
Nimble		Rigid
Idea		Form
Quick		Slow

GENERAL: Systematic (♄), critical (♄), formally resolute (♄), structured (♄) way of thinking (☿). Serious (♄) thoughts (☿) and mature (♄) perception (☿). Thoughts (☿) of departure (♄). Thinking (☿) something through to the end (♄).

HARMONY: *Realistic Thinking.* Talent of thinking in clear, logical, reasonable structures. Consistent and critical thought. Ability to have objective perceptions from a distanced perspective. Crystalline perceptions gained by hard brainwork. Not losing the red thread in deliberations and speeches. Sometimes slow and circumspect but also thorough, tactical, and clever. The search for substantiated perceptions. Inexorable striving for truth. Silent certainty.

DISCORD: *The Mental Block.* Doubt about one's intellectual abilities. Destructive, pessimistic, embittered, close-minded thinking. Gloomy thoughts and constant brooding. Getting stuck in negative ideas. Depressive, self-destructive thoughts. Being slow on the uptake. Inhibitions about expressing oneself verbally or boring, tiring monotony in manner of expression. Difficulties in learning. Speech impediments, ponderousness, or even blackouts in thinking. Dullness. Constantly has to reassure oneself.

☿-♅	**Mercury-Uranus:** *Freedom of Thought*

ARCHETYPE: The Intellectual and the Enlightener	SHADOW: The Know-It-All and the Madman

COMPARISON:

☿	♅
Logic	Intuition
Exploring	Inventing
Student	Revolutionary
Thought	Sudden inspiration

GENERAL: Lucid (♅), wide-awake (♅), willful (♅) thinking (☿). Unconventional (♅) perceptions (☿) and erratic (♅) thinking (☿). Unique (♅) ideas (☿). Sudden (♅) insights (☿).

HARMONY: *The Bright, Fast Thinker.* Extremely quick intellectual grasp. Has the right idea at the right moment. May think a number of thoughts at the same time. Witty, original, inventive, flexible. Independent, sometimes eccentric standpoints. Unbiased, independent, progressive thinking. Full of ideas, but without any particular love of details. Enlightened intellect. Bursts conventional systems of thought. Speed-reader, fast-learner, high-speed talker. Constantly likes to discuss things with oneself.

DISCORD: *The Scatterbrain.* Eccentric leaps from one idea to another with sudden, abrupt, and hardly understandable turns. Extreme impatience, hastiness, and exaggeration in thinking. Poor listener (particularly for people who speak slowly), impatient student. Ingenious ideas and intrepid assertions, but without or inadequately thinking them through. Sometimes confused states with the feeling of being an intellectual "live wire." Quick, short-lived thoughts. Disconnected, inconsequential, tactless statements. However, enormous accuracy of spontaneous ideas and solutions even in difficult aspects.

☿ ♅

☿-Ψ	**Mercury-Neptune:** *Search for the Vision*

ARCHETYPE: The Thinker and the Mystic	SHADOW: The Liar and the Day-Dreamer

COMPARISON:

☿ — Ψ

Thinking	Sensing
Knowledge	Fantasy
Perceiving	Dreaming
Clever	Mediumistic
Rational	Irrational
Sobriety	Intoxication
Physics	Metaphysics

GENERAL: Being able to understand (☿) and express (☿) arising images (Ψ). Imaginative (Ψ), sensitive (Ψ) thinking (☿). Visionary (Ψ) thoughts (☿). Understanding (☿) spiritual experiences (Ψ). Dream (Ψ) interpretation (☿). Search (☿) for the vision (Ψ). Hazy (Ψ) thoughts (☿).

HARMONY: *The Inspired Individual.* Creative imagination, good sense in thinking, poetic fairy-tale language, artistic disposition. Strives for balance between the rational and irrational, sobriety and intoxication. Seeks access to what is visionary, unspoken, and concealed. Good sense of intuition for trends and future developments.

DISCORD: *The Illusionist.* Thoughtlessness, nebulous thinking, or missing words. Wishful thinking and flight into fantasy. Often can't differentiate between what is truth and lies, what is genuine and artificial. A master liar who shamelessly lies through one's teeth. Is flooded by fantasies and may translate the inner images into a language that isn't understandable or can hardly be understood. Likes to forget unpleasant things.

☿-♇	**Mercury-Pluto:** *Inquiring Mind*

ARCHETYPE: Faust and Mephistopheles	SHADOW: The Rogue and the Reactionary

COMPARISON:

☿ — ♇	
Distance	Intensity
Objective	Committed
Superficial	Cryptic
Cunning	Power
Lightness	Depth
Intellect	Magic

GENERAL: Analytic (♇) and profound (♇) thought (☿). Power (♇) of persuasion (☿) and the fixed (♇) idea (☿). The magic (♇) of words (☿) or thoughts (☿).

HARMONY: *Uncompromising Thought.* Good powers of observation. Analytical, critical, probing mind. The gift and desire to convince the surrounding world of one's own opinions and perceptions. An urge to closely scrutinize, explore, and—without consideration of possible consequences—relentlessly reveal everything. Sharp observation that doesn't miss a thing.

DISCORD: *The Fixed Idea.* Compulsive need to talk and communicate. Dogged and obsessive thinking. Not being able to let go of a thought once it has come into existence. Persuading others in a dogmatic manner. Brutal openness without consideration of ethics or morals. Misuse of power. Intolerant, underhanded, and selfish.

☿-☊	Mercury-North Node

HARMONY: Intelligence and a good orientation on the path in life. Scrutinizing one's own motives, critical-creative confrontations with one's own personality, and openness in sharing thoughts with others. Capable of criticism and conflict. Perceiving and mastering the task in life with the help of analytical, logical thought.

DISCORD: Difficulties in orientation on the path of life. The intellect finds "good reasons" to distract from the actual direction of the goal time and again. As a result, partly stubborn and dogged defensive attitudes and unteachable insistence on detrimental positions.

☿-AC	Mercury-Ascendant

HARMONY: *The Nimble Individual.* Skillful and nimble in behavior. Enjoys contacts and communication. Diplomatic and entertaining. Intellectual touch.

DISCORD: *The Cunning Person.* Difficulties, insincerity, and slyness in communication with the surrounding world. Deceives, outsmarts, and slanders other people. Also becomes a victim. Many misunderstandings, exaggerated criticism, and gossip. Untiring spirit of contradiction.

☿-MC	Mercury-Medium Coeli

HARMONY: *The Clever Professional.* Seeks and needs a professional environment that is mentally stimulating, offers a certain intellectual kick, or challenges in a business sense. Can very quickly become familiar with assumed fields of activity. Very crafty in climbing the career ladder.

DISCORD: *The Sly Fox.* Unlikable. Concerned with "collecting professional points" in a one-sided and cold-blooded manner. Tense relationships to authority figures, but with colleagues as well. Sly and dishonest.

Aspects of Venus

♀-♂	Venus-Mars: *Passion*

ARCHETYPE: The Graceful Lady and the Conqueror	SHADOW: The Whore and the Brute

COMPARISON:

♀	—	♂
Love		Violence
Temptation		Lust
Eroticism		Sexuality
Peace		War
Reconciliation		Dispute
Fine		Rough
Gentle		Brutal
Cultivated		Primitive
Indecisive		Spontaneous
Cautious		Impulsive
Giving		Taking
Goodwill		Greed

GENERAL: Satisfying (♀) lust (♂). Fighting (♂) for what a person loves (♀). The erotic (♀) and sexual (♂) tension between man (♂) and woman (♀).

HARMONY: *The Sensual Individual.* Sensual-erotic powers of attraction. Carefree, natural relations with the opposite sex. Sure instinct in selecting a partner. Experienced passion and satisfied sexuality. Good feeling for rhythm, good taste, and the right tone.

DISCORD: *The Eternally Dissatisfied.* Strong sexual desire—demanding, aggressive, and tactless—yet, always unsatisfied. Permanent discord between graceful eroticism (♀) and raw sexuality (♂). Violent, brutal, aggressive, as well as self-destructive. Sexual insecurity and mistrust toward the opposite sex. Dramatic, emotionally-charged relationships. Little willingness to be devoted to another person.

♀♂

♀-♃   **Venus-Jupiter:** *Happiness*

ARCHETYPE: The Artist and the Patron

SHADOW: The Vain Lady and the Pompous Fool

COMPARISON:

♀ — ♃

Concord	Abundance
Harmony	Happiness
Eroticism	Morals
Art	Religion
Beauty	Nobility
Sensuality	Meaning
Love	Virtue
Taste	Value

GENERAL: Trust (♃) in love (♀). Great (♃) and small (♀) happiness. Art (♀) or love (♀) as the revelation of meaning (♃). Sense (♃) of beauty (♀).

HARMONY: *The Lucky Devil.* Pleasant aura and good ability to make contacts. Optimistic, popular, warmhearted, enthusiastic, charming. Pampered by luck. Likes to give and win trust in personal contacts. Confidence in matters of love. Artistic talent. Cheerfulness.

DISCORD: *The Dissipater.* Immoderate and reckless. Challenges one's good fortune, overestimating the streak of luck in the process. Goals that are set too high, exaggerated craving for recognition, and never being satisfied with what has been achieved. Extravagant demand to be pampered in one's love life. Very indolent, self-indulgent, conceited, and selfish.

♀-♄	**Venus-Saturn**: *Commitment*

ARCHETYPE: The Young Girl and the Wise Old Man	SHADOW: The Heartless Woman and the Embittered Man

COMPARISON:

♀	—	♄
Grace		Severity
Playful		Responsible
Light		Heavy
Love		Duty
Affectionate		Tough
Pampered		Austere
Open		Closed
Erotic		Ascetic
Says "yes"		Says "no"
Carefree		Mistrusting
Cheerful		Serious

GENERAL: Simple (♄) beauty (♀). Enjoyment (♀) of clear forms (♄) and structure (♄). The beauty (♀) of the bare (♄)—the winter landscape. The peace (♀) of stillness (♄). Not permitting (♀) oneself anything (♄).

HARMONY: *The Dutiful Individual.* Caring, responsible, faithful, and steadfast in friendship and partnership. Sobriety and earnest in matters of love. Seeks a mature partner. Great loyalty within the relationship. Can—when it appears to be necessary—love in strict asceticism. Love that blossoms under particularly difficult, modest, or impoverished circumstances. Believing in a partner who is difficult, ill, or marked by destiny.

DISCORD: *The Unhappy Person.* Difficulties making contact. Feels lonely and unloved—with and without a relationship. Mistrustful, stiff, and usually disapproving about matters of love and toward everything feminine. Can't believe that one is truly loved and continuously demands new guarantees and proof of love in a relationship. Inability to enjoy, or embitterment causes asceticism. "Falls in love" only when it's a hopeless case or becomes completely withdrawn because of fear of being rejected or deserted in any case. Relationships with a large age difference. Extreme outer hardening as a result of difficult, unmastered inner wounds. Lacking in imagination, blunt, and inhibited when it comes to eroticism. Can't really pamper oneself. Bad taste.

♀
♄

♀-♅   **Venus-Uranus:** *Love of Freedom*

ARCHETYPE: The Beauty and the Liberator

SHADOW: The Seductress and the Traitor

COMPARISON:

♀ — ♅

Attachment	Freedom
Love of the partner	Love of self
Dependence	Independence
Flowing	Abrupt
Willing to adapt	Eccentric
Harmony	Individuality

GENERAL: Free (♅) love (♀), the unusual (♅) relationship (♀) with the greatest possible, mutual free space (♅). Original (♅) taste (♀). Modern (♅) art (♀).

HARMONY: *The Individualistic Relationship.* Original, humorous, but often noncommittal manner of making contacts. Lives and loves in an open, tolerant relationship based on the principle of liberty and equality. Great enjoyment of experimentation. Searches for the unique, unusual "modern" relationship that actually exists only in Utopia. Feelings of love can only grow on the soil of freedom. Only remains where one knows that one can also leave. Can separate from relationships fairly easily, particularly if they threaten freedom.

DISCORD: *The Person Who Can't Be Held.* The fireworks of love and flash-in-the-pan relationships without commitment and a future. Enters into relationships only halfheartedly and can't be held when things should be close and committed. Extreme mood vacillations and changing standpoints. Willful, gruff, and inconsiderate in a partnership. The unusual, the new, whatever hasn't been had in love and eroticism is always more tempting than what is familiar, matured, and steadfast. Unpredictable, unfaithful, unscrupulous. Recklessly destroys connections because one doesn't see their actual value. Deep disdain for all "normal" relationships.

♀-♆	**Venus-Neptune**: *The Dream of Love*

ARCHETYPE: The Beautiful Muse and the Wonderful One	SHADOW: The Weakling and the Drinker

COMPARISON:

♀ — ♆	
Art	Spirituality
Connecting	Merging
Loving	Adoring
Eroticism	Mysticism

GENERAL: Transcendental (♆) love (♀). Becoming flooded (♆) with music (♀). Experiencing boundless (♆) love (♀). Achieving highest spirituality (♆) through love (♀). Being touched in one's innermost heart (♆) by art (♀). Finding redemption (♆) through love (♀). Being inspired to artistic creativity (♀) by the divine (♆). The dream (♆) relationship (♀).

HARMONY: *Intuitive Love.* Deep feeling of being soul mates and a wordless understanding of each other that borders on perfection. Great willingness to be devoted and to sacrifice. Being upheld by the spirit of love. Delicacy of feeling. Mystic, romantic, idealized love that leads to experiences beyond the personal. Highly refined sense of taste and art, above all in the area of music.

DISCORD: *Intoxication of Love.* Insatiable, vast longing that makes a person extremely easy to seduce. "High-flying" love and intoxication of love with subsequent bitter disillusionment. Getting lost in deceptive, misleading ideals and confused, unclear relationships. Violently getting high with intoxicants as aphrodisiacs. Getting off the track erotically. Being deceived in love and/or deceiving others. Genuine encounters are avoided as a result of lasting disappointments or an instinctive fear of disappointments and only dwelt on in dreams. Or searching for fulfillment in transfigured, Platonic love. Corny lapses of taste.

♀
♆

♀-♇	**Venus-Pluto**: *The Magic of Love*

ARCHETYPE: The Enchantress and the Sorcerer	SHADOW: The Beauty and the Beast

COMPARISON:

♀ — ♇

Love	Power
Beauty	Shadows
Relationship	Dependence
Eroticism	Sadomasochism
Peace	Tyranny
Gentleness	(Subtle) violence
Grace	Irresistibility
Lover's bliss	Deepest transformation

GENERAL: Experiencing the power (♇) of love (♀). Being deeply transformed (♇) by love (♀). The extreme (♇) relationship (♀).

HARMONY: *The Extreme Relationship.* Loving completely or not at all. Comprehending the relationship as a challenge, an indissoluble pact, or a karmic connection. Being willing to live through the depths with decisiveness and fundamentally transforming oneself through the confrontation with the partner. Intensively passionate, sexual feelings. Irresistible aura and erotic magnetism.

DISCORD: *Passionate Entanglement.* Becoming entangled in an emotional, mostly unconscious power struggle. Inner compulsion to manipulate the partner, to make the partner emotionally, sexually, and/or financially dependent. Or to mercilessly humiliate the partner in order to ridicule and disdain the partner afterward. Craving for control. Malicious, sly, compulsive, jealous, insatiable. Fixed—sometimes perverse—ideas of relationships, eroticism, and sexuality.

♀-☊   Venus-North Node

HARMONY: Love, liking, grace, eroticism, affection, solidarity with another person, as well as a sense of beauty, appreciation of art, and good taste unite in harmony with the priority in life and are helpful on life's path. Feminine aura as valuable potential that should be recognized and developed.

DISCORD: Lasting difficulties in finding inner peace because love life has an inhibiting and disruptive effect on the actual direction in life. Feelings of being unfulfilled and great needs for affection that are difficult to satisfy.

♀-AC   Venus-Ascendant

HARMONY: *The Graceful One.* Natural, feminine, graceful appearance. Artistic and musical interests. Diplomatic skill, charming conduct, sociable manners, and pleasant nature.

DISCORD: *The Coquette.* Hollow beauty and silly, condescending conduct. Difficulties in expressing one's own feelings. Courts other people's sympathies. Vanity.

♀-MC   Venus-Medium Coeli

HARMONY: *The Popular Person.* The desire to be able to develop taste, a sense of beauty, an appreciation of art, or the joy of harmony within the scope of the profession. Using charm and sympathy in a skilled manner to achieve social and professional recognition.

DISCORD: *The Conflict between Love and Work.* Employing charm and eroticism in a questionable manner in order to advance professionally. Not being able to unite career and public activities with the ideas and demands of love and partnership.

♀
☊

Aspects of Mars

♂-♃	Mars-Jupiter: *Successfully Conquering*

ARCHETYPE: The Victorious Warrior and the High Priest

SHADOW: The Fanatic Destroyer and the Fundamentalist

COMPARISON:

♂	♃
Germinating	Ripening
Aggression	Kindness
Instinctive	Ethical
Primitive	Sublime
Pushing forwards	Striving upwards
Compelling	Convincing
Power of decision-making	Standard of value

GENERAL: Courage (♂) for convictions (♃). Fighting (♂) for the good (♃), for high aims (♃), or for a just cause (♃). Striving (♂) for distant shores (♃). Taking (♂) chances (♃). Developing (♃) pioneer spirit (♂). Fulfilled (♃) sexuality (♂). Acting (♂) with success (♃). Wealth (♃) of energy (♂).

HARMONY: *The Success.* Optimistically, courageously, and successfully fighting for high ideals and extensive goals. Representing one's own convictions with commitment, straightforwardness, and openness. The gift of bringing fighting spirit, nobility, optimism, and momentum into harmony. Great trust in masculine power. Rich and fulfilling sexual experiences.

DISCORD: *The Soldier of Fortune or the Crusader* Gambler or speculator who challenges fate and stakes everything on one card. Qualities such as being a daredevil, bold, aggressive, and touchy alternate in turn with insight and generosity. Tends toward excess and extravagance, and constantly wants more. Excessive in area of sexuality. Intolerant, dogmatic, and unteachably ridden by fanatic convictions. Fights with holy rage for a supposedly just cause. Plays the missionary with fire and the sword. Permits oneself to generously violate laws, in so far as the means justify the end.

| ♂-♄ | **Mars-Saturn**: *Controlled Energy* |

| ARCHETYPE: The Spartan Warrior and His Old Teacher | SHADOW: The Wicked Mercenary and the Grim Man Without Mercy |

COMPARISON:

♂	—	♄
Drive		Resistance
Spontaneity		Responsibility
Youth		Age
Hot		Cold
Rash		Experienced
Quick		Slow
Short		Long
Instinctual		Ascetic
Unrestrained		Controlled
Setting out		Departing
Beginning		End

GENERAL: Consistent (♄), unyielding (♄), or grim (♄) work (♂). Fighting (♂) to the (bitter) end (♄). Fighting (♂) against resistance (♄). Gritting (♂) one's teeth (♄). Cold (♄) war (♂). Controlled (♄) or suppressed (♄) urges (♂). Stiffened (♄) powers (♂). Driving (♂) with the brakes on (♄).

HARMONY: *The Untiring Individual.* Purposeful energy. Persistently and resolutely finishes what has been started. Enormous use of force that continues to increase when there is resistance. Reliably, decisively, resolutely, and conscientiously carries out assignments. Can pull oneself together and hold out whenever it's necessary to do so. In the area of sexuality, also untiring or—if required—ascetic.

DISCORD: *The Frustrated Person.* Great problems with aggression. Energy that is stimulated by constant resistance, making room for itself in a brutal and bone-breaking manner. Or lasting pent-up aggressions that turn inward as helpless anger. Fear of failure and inability. Sullenness, desire for revenge, cold-blooded rage, inner blocks and tensions. Problems with the sex drive and fear of impotence. Sexual inhibitions, guilt about sex, or forced, violent forms of sexuality.

♂
♄

♂-♅	**Mars-Uranus:** *The Fight for Freedom*

ARCHETYPE: The Rebel and the Revolutionary	SHADOW: The "Modern" Warrior and the Anonymous Spirit of Technology

COMPARISON:

♂	—	♅
Dynamic force		Spontaneity
Competition		Cooperation
Conquering		Liberating
Heated		Cool
Committed		Distanced

GENERAL: Abrupt (♅) discharge of energy (♂). Erratic (♅), surprising (♅), split-second (♅) actions (♂). Fighting (♂) for freedom (♅) and utopia (♅). Freedom (♅) of will (♂). Free (♅) sexuality (♂). Excited (♂) by high speeds (♅).

HARMONY: *The Lightning Flash.* Unusual reaction speed. Individual action with an enjoyment of decision-making, guided by superb intuition. Fighting for freedom. Pioneer in search for new paths and new goals in unknown regions. Likes to make use of the right moment. Values sexual freedom, is easy to get a response from, and quickly excited.

DISCORD: *The Uncontrolled Person.* Sudden, surprising energy and aggressive eruptions (runaway horses). Irritable, rebellious, defends oneself against every standard and any limitations, with violence if necessary. Overreactions, violent fits of temper, extremely nervous and impatient, in danger of having accidents. Loves the thrill of speeding and the titillation of everything dangerous.

♂-♅	**Mars-Neptune:** *Spiritual Energies*

ARCHETYPE: The Spiritual Warrior and His Guardian Angel	SHADOW: The Drunken Pirate and the Poisoner

COMPARISON:

♂	—	♆
Purposeful		Without a goal
Instinctive		Transfigured
Action		Dream
Sensual		Extrasensory
This world		Other worlds
Solid		Intangible
Strong		Weak
Violence		Non-violence
Perpetrator		Victim

GENERAL: Guided by higher power (♆) in all actions (♂). A fist (♂) in the water (♆). The shot (♂) of poison (♆). Fighting (♂) with spiritual (♆) weapons (♂) or non-violently in another way (♆). Conquers (♂) by yielding (♆). Dissolving (♆) aggressions (♂). Striving (♂) for what is boundless (♆).

HARMONY: *The Somnambulist.* Acting with uncanny certainty. Feels when the right moment has come or acts in the right way on the basis of unconscious inspiration (guardian angel aspect). Can work with spiritual energies as a healer and therapist, but also as an artist. May turn fantasies and visions into reality. Strong sexual fantasies and great deal of intuitive understanding. Interested in spiritual forms of sexuality (Tao, Tantra) or complete spiritual-ization of sexual energies.

DISCORD: *Mr. or Ms. Wishy-Washy.* Energies that are misguided or quickly fizzle out. Feelings of weakness and helplessness. Lets oneself drift without a goal and doesn't know what one really wants. In extreme cases, danger of neglect, deception, criminality, intoxication, and addiction. Aggressions are only expressed in an indirect manner. Fights by giving other people a guilty conscience as a victim or helpless person, or by provoking sympathy in oth-ers. Boundless sexual fantasies. Tends toward debauchery, as well as impo-tence or sexual encounters in a state of intoxication. Sometimes confused about one's own sexual identity. Can be seduced. May be unfaithful or vic-tim of partner's unfaithfulness.

♂
♆

♂-♀   **Mars-Pluto:** *Tremendous Power*

ARCHETYPE: The Invincible Warrior and His Invisible Power

SHADOW: The Possessed Torturer and the Black Magician

COMPARISON:

♂ — ♀

Strength	Power
Greed	Possession
Crude	Subtle
Muscle strength	Magical power
Fist	Curse
Destruction	Transformation
Operating	Healing magically

GENERAL: The courage (♂) for deep-reaching transformation (♀). Greed (♂) for power (♀) and power (♀) struggles (♂). Sexual (♂) possession (♀). Uncanny (♀), irresistible (♀), or dark (♀) forces (♂).

HARMONY: *Mack the Knife.* Development of immense, usually invisible strengths that originate in a deep energy of the soul. Strong, secretive, and irresistible aura. Being able to compel others without showing any recognizable outer signs of doing so. Spooky, invincible, decisive, courageous, and fascinating. Strong sexual energies and deep passion. Total intensity. All or nothing.

DISCORD: *The Sadist.* Inconsiderate, unconditional, fanatic assertion of one's own will. Rigorous, bestial desire for revenge when rejection has been suffered. Extremely instinctive and possessed by sexual obsessions. Seeks total lust. Sexuality as the venue for power struggles. Loves (violent) sexual humiliations. As a result of social ostracism of this topic, the aspect is frequently lived out on a completely unconscious level so that it is only expressed in unconscious acts of sadism while the conscious individual behaves in an emphatically reserved, practically harmless manner and is therefore all the more afraid of violence.

♂-☊　　　　　　　Mars-North Node

HARMONY: Bold, aggressive basic attitude that is confident of victory in mastering the true tasks in life. Works actively, hard, and successfully on one's goals. When it is important, one will fight for self and one's cause in a committed manner.

DISCORD: Great inner tensions and frustrations because the fighting strength, the will to conquer, as well as the driving force and the sexual desire distract from one's life priorities instead of striving toward them. Danger of creating artificial foe images and tendency toward disproportionate actions and overreactions as a result of suppressed aggressions.

♂-AC　　　　　　　Mars-Ascendant

HARMONY: *The Individual on the Offensive.* Knows how to clearly express will and assert oneself. Is very quick in matters of taking care of and asserting oneself.

DISCORD: *The Crafty Person.* Aggressive but inhibited character. Can't naturally and directly express one's energies. Either overheated behavior or depressed and cringing. Sometimes sly, underhanded behavior or constant heated confrontations with the surrounding world. Possibility of self-destructive tendencies.

♂-MC　　　　　　　Mars-Medium Coeli

HARMONY: *The Live Wire.* Knows how to purposefully apply one's energies in professional life. Is quite willing to accept challenges and prove powers of assertion and willingness to engage in conflicts.

DISCORD: *The Center of the Storm.* Creates many problems for oneself and others at work through senseless actions, impatience, or unnecessary quarreling. Erratic and lacking in conscious goals in one's professional life. Troublemaker.

Aspects of Jupiter

| ♃-♄ | **Jupiter-Saturn**: *Value of the Time-Tested* |

ARCHETYPE: The High Priest and the Patriarch or Hermit

SHADOW: The Pharisee and the Embittered Man

COMPARISON:

♃ — ♄

Expansion	Limitation
Opulence	Asceticism
Growth	Cutting back
Trust	Mistrust
Wealth	Poverty
Meaning	Form
Faith	Ritual
Success	Failure

GENERAL: Stable (♄), sustained (♄) growth (♃). Lasting (♄) values (♃). Strictness (♄) of belief (♃). Firmness (♄) of faith (♃). Boundaries (♄) of growth (♃). Lasting (♄) convictions (♃).

HARMONY: *The Tenacious Individual.* Good mixture of optimism and a sense of reality. Clear, steadfast convictions, stamina, patience, and endurance. Deep trust in the rhythmic alternation of growing and cutting back. Slow, but steady growth.

DISCORD: *The Unhappy Person.* Constantly torn back and forth between: optimism and pessimism, trust and mistrust, splendor and modesty, generosity and stinginess, joy of life and bitterness, fulfillment and renunciation, gain and loss, living faith and dead ritual. Strong emotional tensions as a result of many situations of change. Tends toward a more pessimistic attitude toward life.

♃-♅   Jupiter-Uranus: *The Ideal of Freedom*

ARCHETYPE: The High Priest and the Reformer

SHADOW: The Self-Righteous Man and the Anarchist

COMPARISON:

♃ — ♅

Ideals	Utopia
Growth	Mutation
Faith	Enlightenment
Religion	Philosophy
Virtue	Freedom
Trust	Betrayal
What is better	What is special
Evolution	Revolution

GENERAL: Sudden (♅) growth (♃). Good (♃), surprising realizations (♅). Trust (♃) in the future (♅). Strokes (♅) of luck (♃). Ideals (♃) of freedom (♅). The individual (♅) meaning of life (♃). The individual (♅) trip (♃). Religious (♃) freedom (♅).

HARMONY: *The Free Spirit.* Spontaneous, revolutionary insights. Optimistic farsightedness and good sense for future developments. Inventive. Advocate of freedom of religion and opinion. Seeks new values and the very personal meaning in life. Strives for free development of individuality. Courage to have one's own ideals.

DISCORD: *The Pigheaded, The Conviction-Changer.* Protest and "anti" attitude toward social values ("down with…" mentality). Problems with institutions, particularly the Church. Constantly changing. New goals and eccentric convictions. Exaggerated willfulness. Ultramodern theses. Very much concerned with an image of being "original."

♃ ♅

| ♃-♆ | **Jupiter-Neptune**: *Revealed Meaning* |

ARCHETYPE: The High Priest and the Mystic

SHADOW: The Self-Righteous Man and the Crackpot, Dreamer, or Fantasist

COMPARISON:

♃ — ♆

Development	Dissolution
Faith	Vision
Religion	Spirituality
Dogmatic	Mystic

GENERAL: Highest (♆) happiness (♃) or apparent (♆) luck (♆). Being guided (♆) on trips (♃). The hypocrite (♆-♃). Trusting (♃) one's guardian angel (♆).

HARMONY: *The Dancing Dervish.* Finding the meaning of life in a mystic experience or being found by meaning. Kindness and compassion. Genuine altruism, highest ideals, true spirituality, harmonious connection of faith and inspiration, good visionary gifts. Trance and illumination. Fine sense for happiness.

DISCORD: *The Religious Crackpot.* Feels oneself to be the chosen one, illuminated and wise. Seduces others or becomes the victim of peculiar sects, strange ideologies, and crackpot views of the world. Religious delusions. Victim of own dream images and yearnings. Intoxication.

♃-♇	**Jupiter-Pluto**: *Alchemical Black Gold*

ARCHETYPE: The High Priest and the Sorcerer	SHADOW: The Smug Man and the Power Person

COMPARISON:

♃	—	♇
Growth		Transformation
Olympia		Hades
Faith		Power
Good		Shadow
Conviction		Possession
Religion		Magic

GENERAL: Shamanistic (♇) view of the world (♃). Trust (♃) in the archaic elemental forces (♇) and the wealth (♃) of the depths (♇). The deep-reaching transformation (♇) for the better (♃).

HARMONY: *The Shaman.* Ability for psychological and spiritual transformation and renewal. Strong convictions and great powers of persuasion. Healing power. Confidence in powers that renew themselves. Having a sense of everything deep and profound.

DISCORD: *The Demagogue.* Glorification of power, misuse of power, ruling over others, and wanting to convince and seduce. Fanaticism and arrogance. Glorification of a fixed idea. Obsessive-compulsive neurotic.

♃ ♇

♃-☊	Jupiter-North Node

HARMONY: Trust in one's own abilities promotes success in the realization of the tasks in life, which are simultaneously connected with a deep experience of meaning. Magnanimity, optimism, happiness, and fulfillment on the path in life.

DISCORD: The search for meaning and priorities in life appear to be opposed to each other. Strong, inner dissatisfaction and exaggerated, unrealistic attitude of expectation. Often wants to wrest more from life than is possible. Is quick to ignore negative things in life.

♃-AC	Jupiter-Ascendant

HARMONY: *Trusting and Being Trusted.* Happiness aspect. Generous, optimistic, enthusiastic, open, vital, humane, freedom-loving, liberal. Radiates a natural type of dignity and authority. Strives for ideals.

DISCORD: *The Conceited Person, the Hypocrite.* Exaggerated behavior. Overestimates oneself and tends toward megalomania. Often tries to do more than can ever be accomplished. Likes to pretend. Doesn't tolerate criticism and is quickly insulted.

♃-MC	Jupiter-Medium Coeli

HARMONY: *Being Supported.* Good chances for advancement, frequently thanks to good contacts and helpful support. Success and luck in the realization of (professional) objectives. Possible popularity. Claim to leadership and leadership qualities.

DISCORD: *The High-Flier.* Taking steps that are too large on the way up or in the realization of life's goals. As a result, frequently stressed. Exaggerated striving for power, recognition, and influence.

Aspects of Saturn

ħ-♅   **Saturn-Uranus:** *Authority Conflicts*

ARCHETYPE: The Venerable Old Man and the Wise Fool

SHADOW: The Grouch and the Anarchist

COMPARISON:

ħ — ♅

Stability	Upheaval
Old	Young/New
Preserving	Reforming
Law	Freedom
Limiting the scope	Going beyond the scope
Rule	Exception
Traditional	Modern/Utopian
Normal	Abnormal
Chronological	Synchronous
Continuous	Suddenly
Guarantee	Betrayal

GENERAL: Breaking through (♅) and renewing (♅) old structures (ħ). Violating (♅) laws (ħ). The limits (ħ) of freedom (♅). Going beyond (♅) the scope (ħ). The sudden (♅) end (ħ). Restriction (ħ) of freedom (♅).

HARMONY: *The Framework of Freedom.* Balance between individual freedom and the laws governing public welfare. Knows how to develop and live out[6] an optimal measure of freedom within the set and lawful framework. Finds the right mixture between traditional values and structures and modern developments and forms.

DISCORD: *The Gagged Person or the Demolition Charge.* Bitter conflict between freedom and norms, between old and new. During certain phases, experiences oneself as unfairly gagged or limits oneself in order to outrageously kick over the traces in other phases. Then lives one's freedom in such a compulsive manner that it becomes a type of unfreedom as a result. *Must* free oneself from every type of limitation—even those that are just supposed—in order to prove independence at all times. Often filled with new ideas, but insecure, fearful, or fickle about actually translating them into action.

ħ♅

♄-♆	**Saturn-Neptune**: *Flowing Boundaries*

ARCHETYPE: The Graying Hermit and the Blind Seer	SHADOW: The Embittered Enemy of Life and Dread Personified

COMPARISON:

$$♄ — ♆$$

♄	♆
Boundaries	Without boundaries
Structure	Dissolution
Security	Insecurity
Rigid	Flowing
Clear	Nebulous
Factual knowledge	Inspiration
Sober	Intoxicated

GENERAL: Unclear (♆), flowing (♆), invisible (♆) boundaries (♄). Collecting (♄) spiritual (♆) experiences. Sensing (♆) or being drawn (♆) beyond one's own borders (♄). Dissolving (♆) old patterns (♄). Boundaries (♄) of longing (♆). Becoming sober (♄) after intoxication (♆).

HARMONY: *Flexibility, Liveliness.* Lives in the flow of life in harmony with the natural rhythms, which produce solid structures time and again, dissolve, and then connect to make new structures (water—ice). Can abandon oneself to spiritual, mystic, and intoxicating experiences without losing oneself.

DISCORD: *Weakness, Fear, Phobia.* Has great difficulties in setting boundaries and is easily deluged by other people's expectations or inexplicable phenomena. Can't get solid ground under one's feet. Everything that appears to promise security disappears sooner or later. Even the most solid of structures dissolve. In the reverse case (very strong ♄), excessive hardening occurs along with the appearance of having everything under control. The harder the facade, the more intensely it is undermined by inexplicable fears and phobias.

ħ-♇ **Saturn-Pluto**: *Limits of Power*

ARCHETYPE: The Wise Old Man and the Powerful Shaman

SHADOW: The Embittered Man and the Black Magician

COMPARISON:

ħ	—	♇
Form		Transformation
Control		Instinctive thirst for power
Steadfastness		Change
Death		Regeneration

GENERAL: Lasting (ħ), extensive transformation (♇) of solid structures (ħ). Experiences of departure (ħ) that lead to deep-reaching renewal (♇). The limits (ħ) of power (♇).

HARMONY: *Seeing the Light.*[5] Overcoming old structures in favor of a deeper truth. Knowledge about the times of departure and renewal. Willingness to steadily pass through crises and experiences of transformation.

DISCORD: *The Encrustation.* Fear of losing control (over oneself). Hardened and encrusted power structures. Compulsive insistence on what is old and aged or—to the contrary—virtually obsessive destruction of conventional, long-standing values. Massive problems with authority.

ħ ♇

♄-☊   Saturn-North Node

HARMONY: Concentrates on the independent mastering of one's tasks in life. Consistent, responsible, and untiring on life's path. Has high standards and places ambitious demands on oneself. Grows beyond one's own limitations.

DISCORD: Pessimistic to hopeless attitude in view of the tasks in life. Experiences oneself as completely blocked and afraid to pass over the threshold to becoming oneself. Often has the impression that duties and other burdens don't permit one to come to what's important. Easily falls into old patterns that one thought one had already overcome. Frequently places excessive demands on oneself.

♄-AC   Saturn-Ascendant

HARMONY: *The Disciplined Person.* Always behaves in a calm, polite, sometimes even formal manner. Tends to draw boundaries and respect other people's boundaries. Serious, reliable, disciplined, and tenacious.

DISCORD: *The Mistrusting Individual.* Reserved, inhibited, and fearful. Judges everything in a negative, pessimistic, or at least problematic manner. Stands in one's own way.

♄-MC   Saturn-Medium Coeli

HARMONY: *The Career Ladder.* Tends to climb the career ladder slowly but surely, step by step. Great stamina, even in phases of difficulties. Wants to achieve everything out of and with one's own power.

DISCORD: *The Occupational Block.* Inhibitions in the area of work, as well as inhibitions and obstacles when it comes to realizing one's objectives. Great doubts and feelings of inferiority in view of professional achievement. Negative attitude of expectancy. Can't let oneself be helped by others at all or has a hard time doing so. Fear of public appearances. Prefers to stay in the background.

Aspects of Uranus

The aspects Uranus enters into with the planets that move slowly usually exist for many years at a time. This is why they have less to say about the individual than the generation coming into the world during this period of time. However, there is always an individual meaning for these aspects when personal planets are included in the aspect or this generational aspect is part of a major configuration in the horoscope.

♅-♆   **Uranus-Neptune**: *The Inspiration*

ARCHETYPE: The Liberator and the Seer

SHADOW: The Lunatic and the Crackpot

COMPARISON:

♅	—	♆
Lucidity		Spirituality
Clarity		Haze
Intuition		Inspiration
Objectivity		Subjectivity
Against the current		With the current
Idea		Premonition
High-strung		Intoxicated
Individual		Boundless
Freedom		Addiction

GENERAL: Dissolution (♆) of individual limitations (♅). The vision (♆) that comes like a lightning flash (♅).

HARMONY: *Lucid Dreams.* Feeling oneself called to fulfill a special, very personal vision. Strong intuition. Dreaming of "unreal" experiences, visions, or mystic experiences of sudden, crystal-clear, lucid certainty. Illumination.

DISCORD: *Head in the Clouds.* Unclear concepts of individuality. Propagating unrealistic inventions or solutions to problems. Running after airy-fairy ideas. Losing oneself in the chaos of unconscious longings.

♅-♇	**Uranus-Pluto**: *The Metamorphosis*

ARCHETYPE: The Rebel and the Powerful Person

SHADOW: The Eccentric and the Power of Darkness

COMPARISON:

$$♅ — ♇$$

Freedom	Constraint
Conscious perception	Unconscious urge
Light	Shadow
Highest heights	Deepest depths

GENERAL: Sudden (♅) deep-reaching changes (♇). Rebellion (♅) against dependence (♇) and suppression (♇). Bursting (♅) the bonds (♇).

HARMONY: *Desire for Freedom.* Powerful urge for individual freedom. Sudden perceptions and insights into power structures or collective shadow areas. Rigorous upheavals. Liberation movements.

DISCORD: *The Despot.* Willful, irresponsible misuse of power for questionable, eccentric goals. Extreme inner tension and vacillations between highest heights and deepest depths, between total freedom and complete constraint.

♅-☊	**Uranus-North Node**

HARMONY: Can break with traditional systems without any difficulty in order to put ideas into practice in an original manner and master tasks in life. The development of one's own individuality combines with the priority in life.

DISCORD: Lives willfully, according to one's own laws. At the same time, always senses a painful gap between individual striving, the need for independence and freedom, and the actual tasks in life. Has intense problems with opening up in a committed way to what is truly essential.

♅-AC	**Uranus-Ascendant**

HARMONY: *The Alert Individual.* Very lively, open to everything new, crazy, and original. Always and quickly willing to adapt. Willful, independent character. Unusual aura and very individual behavior.

DISCORD: *The Mulish Person.* Unpredictable behavior. Subject to constant upheavals in life. Therefore often unreliable. Restless, not very cooperative, hopelessly headstrong, and not capable of adapting at all.

♅-MC	**Uranus-Medium Coeli**

HARMONY: *The Individualist.* Seeks, develops, and strives for individual goal in life. Needs a great deal of freedom, particularly on the professional path of life. Can be committed to humanistic ideals within the scope of working life.

DISCORD: *The Nonconformist.* Individual striving for freedom and the necessity of occupational life appear incompatible with each other, resulting in much rebellion, opposition, and conflict. Always searches for new goals. Isn't good at adapting and accepting universally valid rules.

Aspects of Neptune

The aspects that Neptune enters into with Pluto usually exist for many years at a time. This is why they have less to say about the individual than the generation coming into the world during this period of time. However, there is always an individual meaning for these aspects when personal planets are included in the aspect or this generational aspect is part of a major configuration in the horoscope.

Ψ-♇   Neptune-Pluto: *Spiritual Power*

ARCHETYPE: The Mystic and the Shaman

SHADOW: The Addict and the Devil

COMPARISON:

Ψ — ♇	
Dissolving	Changing radically
Secret	Uncanny
Powerlessness	Power
Mysticism	Magic

GENERAL: Dissolution (Ψ) of power structures (♇). Demagogically (♇) unleashed (Ψ) mass (♇) currents (Ψ). Spiritual (Ψ) power (♇).

HARMONY: *Powers of the Soul.* Sensitive and mediumistic gift in the development and application of original powers of healing. The ability to invisibly guide others. Being inspired from forces out of the depths.

DISCORD: *Possession.* Getting caught in the net of false, pseudo-spiritual teachings. The danger of not being able to resist the pull into the depths and become unstable, addicted, and dependent. Being helplessly flooded and possessed by archaic forces. Letting oneself be enticed into the misuse of power and/or becoming the victim of power oneself.

Ψ-☊   Neptune-North Node

HARMONY: Unerringly walks one's path in life and is guided by an invisible hand in the mastering of the life's tasks. Mature spirituality as part of the priority in life.

DISCORD: Nebulous concepts of life's priority or a numb feeling for the essential direction in life. Easy to distract from what is important. Easy to seduce. Also afraid of not being able to see it through or of all goals dissolving into nothingness.

Ψ-AC   Neptune-Ascendant

HARMONY: *The Compassionate Person.* Immediately senses outer impressions and moods. Extremely intuitive, empathizing, compassionate, sensitive, and vulnerable. Goes through life with uncanny certainty and knows that one is guided.

DISCORD: *The Blur.* Difficulty in defining boundaries and asserting oneself. Unable to strive for a specific goal in a concrete manner. Easy to manipulate and seduce. Tendency toward secrecy and deceit. Dubious personality. Frequent feelings of being lost without solid ground under one's feet. Often absent-minded and starry-eyed. Becomes easily dependent on things.

Ψ-MC   Neptune-Medium Coeli

HARMONY: *The Guided One.* Is guided by a guardian angel in choice of work and on professional path. Knows how to subtly lead other people as well. Gift for artistic and therapeutic professions, as well as assignments in the area of media.

DISCORD: *The Victim.* Has no clear goals in life, loses them time and again in the haze, or is continuously drawn away from goals and made the victim of seductions, intrigues, or other machinations on the path in life—and particularly at work.

Ψ☊

Aspects of Pluto

♇-☊	Pluto-North Node

HARMONY: Strong powers of fascination that draw one to the actual priority in life. Experiences of power and helplessness, deep-reaching experiences of purification, and sometimes painful transformations and encounters with one's shadow prove to be helpful and essential in completing tasks in life.

DISCORD: Vehement inner tensions and feelings of possession because strong forces pull or urge in another direction than the priority in life. The feeling of being enslaved to false conceptions.

♇-AC	Pluto-Ascendant

HARMONY: *The Hypnotist.* Capable of mobilizing enormous powers of the soul and thereby controlling, guiding, or influencing other people. Strong-willed, assertive, resolute. Charismatic aura. Able and willing to accompany other people through the crises and depths of life.

DISCORD: *The Shady Character.* Difficulty in dealing with one's own striving for power and sexual energies. Has an effect of being dark, mysterious, and sometimes subdued and in low spirits. Dominating, overbearing conduct. Craving for control and misuse of power.

♇-MC	Pluto-Medium Coeli

HARMONY: *The High-Powered Person.* Can activate remarkable energies of the soul—which have the effect of true magical forces in some cases—in order to achieve one's goal in life or a desired occupational position. Willingness to give up old positions and start something completely new. Leadership qualities.

DISCORD: *The Power Struggle.* The path in life—particularly the professional path—continuously leads to power struggles, which can result in loss of power and experiences of helplessness. But also a purely selfish, questionable use of power and the desire to want to defeat other people.

An ILLUSTRATED KEY
to the HOROSCOPE

An Illustrated Key to the Horoscope

In order to experience the many levels of the horoscope in a graphic manner, it can be very stimulating to have all the planets that are connected with each other become figures. The following table provides some pictorial classifications.

In keeping with this, the astrological constellation of Sun (☉) in Taurus (♉) in the 5th house in a square to Saturn (♄) in Leo (♌) in the 8th house would read as follows:

> *The King from the tribe of the Enjoyers stands in the spotlight. He isn't at all compatible with the Panicmonger from the tribe of the Greatest, who in turn stands in the underground.*

If there is also a sextile from Jupiter (♃) in Cancer (♋) in the 7th house:

> *He receives support through the Aristocrat from the tribe of the Helpers, who stands in the World of Partnership.*

If the Sun (☉) also forms a conjunction with Mercury (☿) in Gemini (♊) in the 5th house:

> *On his side of the stage stands the Local Guide from the tribe of the Smarties.*

This type of interpretation may help you better comprehend aspects that are complicated and difficult to understand.

These characters

SUN	MOON	MERCURY	VENUS	MARS
☉	☽	☿	♀	♂
King	Queen	Scout	Beauty	Warrior
Hero	Heroine	Local guide	Muse	Hothead
Father	Mother	Trader	Seductress	Suitor
Chief	Ruler	Explorer	Dove of peace	Conqueror
			Sweetheart	Fiend

From the tribe of

ARIES	TAURUS	GEMINI	CANCER	LEO	VIRGO
♈	♉	♊	♋	♌	♍
Nomads	Farmers	Writers	Helpers	Bosses	Practical
Amazons	Traditionalists	Curious	Daydreamers	Greatest	people
Berserks	Earthy	Scholars	Romanticists	Luxurious	Frugal
Conquerors	people	Butterflies	Spiritual	Pashas	School
Pioneers	Bankers		advisors	Stars	teachers
	Enjoyers				Masters

Are in or on the

1st	2nd	3rd	4th	5th	6th
Drawbridge	Financial	Library	Cradle	Glitter world	Workrooms
Outer world	world	Everyday	Inner world	Playground	Hospital
Entrance hall	Treasury	world	Homeland	Spotlight	Professional
Display		Marketplace	Fantasies	Stage	world
window		School	Child's room		Fitness park
			World of		
			childhood		

Conjunction = At his/her side stands ...

Sextile = He/She receives support through ...

Trine = He/She is friends with ...

These characters

JUPITER	SATURN	URANUS	NEPTUNE	PLUTO
♃	♄	♅	♆	♇
Priest	Old person	Eccentric	Prophet	Magician
Educated	Serious one	Fool	Dreamer	Healer
person	Nay-sayer	Free spirit	Crackpot	Devil
Philosopher	Panicmonger	Rebel	Drinker	Witch
Aristocrat		Inventor		

From the tribe of

LIBRA	SCORPIO	SAGITTARIUS	CAPRICORN	AQUARIUS	PISCES
♎	♏	♐	♑	♒	♓
Well-	Powerful	Nobility	Ascetics	Wise	Seers
groomed	Uncanny	Parsons	Doers	Utopians	Muses
artists	Wicked	Olympians	Conservatives	High-fliers	Dreamers
Diplomats	Healers	High-and-	Dependables	Individualists	Transfigured
Charmers	Sorcerers	mighty	Serious	Reformers	Samaritans
Indecisive		Missionaries			Martyrs
judges		Hypocrites			

Are in or on the

7th	8th	9th	10th	11th	12th
Marriage bed	Cellar	Pulpit	Tower	Guest room	Hermitage
Sacred	Cemetery	University	Hall of Fame	Group room	Remoteness
mountain	Red-light	Travel	Serious	World of	Isolation
World of	district	agency	world	community	Other
partnership	Shadow	Holy Land	Professional	World of	worlds
World of the	world	Wide world	Life	sisters and	Roof of the
intimate	Underground			brothers	world
other	Danger zone				
	Underworld				

Opposition	=	His/Her challenging opponent (counterbalance) is ...
Square	=	He/She doesn't get along at all with ...
Quincunx	=	He/She tends to have a difficult relationship with ...

The ASTROLOGICAL

PICTURE *of the* WORLD

The Astrological Picture of the World

The astrological picture of the world is geocentric, which means it places the Earth at the center and describes the movement of the stars as portrayed for our eyes and our emotional experience.

This is an anachronistic absurdity only for those who see in astrology a theory of planetary influences that can be more or less cleverly explained in a mechanical manner. If, instead, we see the movements of the heavens as an enormous and extremely differentiated cosmic clock that shows us what time it is on Earth, then the geocentric perspective is just as accurate as a heliocentric viewpoint.

The abundance of stars in the heavens that appear not to move at all are called the fixed stars (for example, the seven stars in the Big Dipper) in contrast to the few planets, of which seven are visible to the human eye (Sun, Moon, Mercury, Venus, Mars, Jupiter, and Saturn) and three additional planets that were first discovered in the age of technology (Uranus, Neptune, and Pluto). Apart from the comets, shooting stars, and today's satellites, these ten bodies are the only things that do not move zigzag within the picture of the heavens but systematically along an orbital path, the ecliptic. This circular path has fascinated humanity since time immemorial. It was once considered the celestial dam and the planets were seen as gods who traveled along this street. The Moon, the fastest moving, requires 28 days to wander

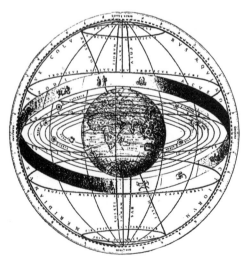

Figure 5. The world system according to Ptolemy from The Atlas of Cellarius, *published in 1708.*

through this circular path and thereby forms the foundation from the calculation of the months, while the Sun passes through the ecliptic in 365 days and, as a result, determines the length of a year even today.

There are a total of three different movements of the heavens that astrology records:

1. The daily rotation of all the stars of the heavens around the Earth, from which the Ascendant results, among other things.

Just as the Sun rises in the east every day, this is where the Big Dipper, Orion, and all the other constellations and planets also rise and wander across the sky to the western horizon. In the old way of conceiving things, it was said that: they travel with or through the rotation of the sky across the midheavens to set in the west.

2. The movement of the planets and luminaries in the heavens (for example, the annual journey of the Sun from the northern to the southern Tropic and back), which results in the sign of the zodiac, among other things.

The movement of the planets along the ecliptic becomes easier to visualize if we imagine that we are watching the sunset on the West Coast. At the same place where the Sun dips into the water, the Moon and the planets will also set sooner or later. This means they are on the same path. If we observe this process for a number of days in a row, we can determine that the sunset shifts a bit further every day: to the north up to the time of the summer solstice and then to the south until the time of the winter solstice. The north-south shift results from the slanted position of the planet path in comparison to the Equator.

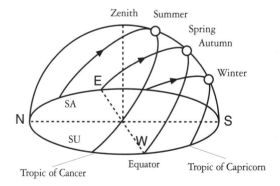

Figure 6. The seasons.

3. The very slow forward movement of the fixed-star heavens, whereby a new age begins every 2160 years. This movement cannot be perceived in the course of one human life without technical assistance. However, the Babylonians already knew about it more than 5,000 years ago.

The path through which the planets travel is the zodiac, the heart of astrology. The zodiac was divided into twelve equal sections by the Babylonians and named according to the constellations that formed the background of the respective section of the path along the Sun's orbit. The fixed-star formation that provides its name is called the constellation and the corresponding section of the path of the Sun's orbit is the sign of the zodiac. The background for the fixed-star heavens has moved forward in the

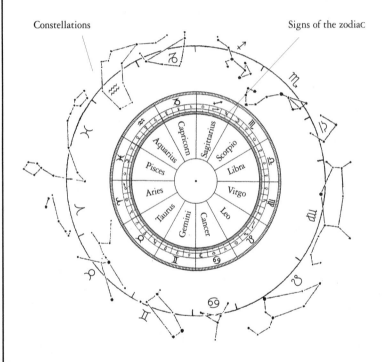

Constellations   Signs of the zodiac

Figure 7. Zodiac in the Age of Aries. Constellations and signs of the zodiac are identical.

meantime so that many people no longer understand why the section of the path was given its name. Yet, they have only lost their "name-giver" and not their significance for the earthly rhythms. The spring equinox continues to take place whenever the Sun enters the sign of Aries, no matter whether the fixed-star formation behind it is the constellation Pisces or Aquarius. Astrology observes the annual orbit of the Sun and not the fixed-star heavens!

The zodiac formed by this orbit of the Sun serves as the ground map in determining where which planets are at a certain time. A horoscope is the description of these planetary positions, seen at a certain point in time from a specific place.

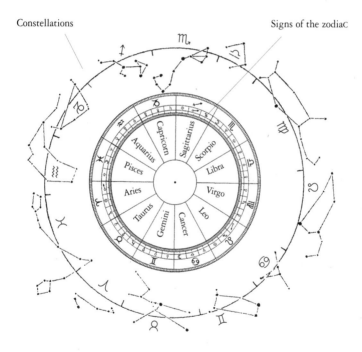

Figure 8. Zodiac at the end of the Age of Pisces. Constellations unchanged, but signs of the zodiac have moved forward.

Glossary of Astrological Terms

AIR SIGNS: The three signs that belong to the air *element*: Libra (cardinal), Aquarius (fixed), and Gemini (mutable).

ASCENDANT: The sign of the zodiac which rises on the eastern horizon at the time of birth. At the time of sunrise, the sign of the position of the Sun (the *sign of the zodiac*) is identical with the Ascendant. However, at sunset the Ascendant is the sign opposing that of the astrological sign.

ASPECTS: Significant distances between the individual planets themselves and with the *system of axes* points. The significant distances are those resulting from dividing the zodiac by the numbers 1 through 10 into sections). *Major aspects* are those divided by the numbers 1, 2, 3, 4 and 6. This creates the following aspects: *conjunction 0^0, opposition 180^0, trine 120^0, square* 90^0, and *sextile* 60^0. *Minor aspects* are calculated by dividing by 5, 7, 8, 9, and 10 (*quintile 72^0, septile 51^0, octile = semi-square 45^0, nonile 40^0, decile 36^0*), and dividing the major aspects in half (*semi-square 45^0, sesquisquare 135^0, semi-sextile 30^0*) as well as the distance of 150^0 = *quincunx*. The *harmonic theory*, which divides these aspects into harmonic and disharmonious, corresponds with that of music theory.

BASIC HOROSCOPE: Map of the heavens at the time a person is born, as seen from the place of birth. (Also: birth chart, radix, cosmogram).

CHARACTERISTICS: Hot, cold, dry, and wet are the four characteristics, in various combinations, traditionally assigned to the individual signs.

CONSTELLATIONS: The grouping of the fixed stars (Big Dipper, Orion, Taurus, etc.) of which twelve, in differing positions along the expanse of the Sun's annual orbit, gave their names to the twelve sections of this path. In astrology, it is not the constellations that are relevant, but rather the *signs of the zodiac* that were named after them.

CUSPS: The beginning of an astrological house, starting with the Ascendant and moving counterclockwise. Since houses are the strongest at their beginning and not their calculated center, astrology places great value on the beginning of a house.

DESCENDANT: The sign that lies opposite the *Ascendant* and on the western horizon at the time of birth.

DETRIMENT: See *Ruler*.

DIGNITY: See *Ruler*.

DOMICILE: *We use the word* DIGNITY *to indicate this position.*

DRAGON'S HEAD: See *Moon's Node*.

EARTH SIGNS: The three signs corresponding to the earth *element*: Capricorn (cardinal), Taurus (fixed), and Virgo (mutable).

ECLIPTIC: The apparent orbit of the Sun and all the planets around Earth: the celestial circle that the Sun, as seen from the Earth, seems to follow within the span of a year.

ELEMENT: The twelve signs of the zodiac reflect three *qualities* in each of the four elements in the form of *fire, air, earth,* and *water* signs.

EPHEMERIDES: Astronomically calculated tables with a geocentric perspective. Contain the orbits of the planets, from which the position of each planet can be seen (at any time).

EXALTED: See *Ruler*.

FALL: See *Ruler*.

FIELDS: Same meaning as *Houses*.

FIRE SIGNS: The three signs assigned to the fire *element*: Aries (cardinal), Leo (fixed), and Sagittarius (mutable).

FIXED STARS: Stars that seem to be fixed to the "vault of heaven." They form some ninety constellations, such as the Great Bear, or Orion, and, or course, those constellations that gave their name to the so-called "star signs." They move with the heavens, so as the vault turns they rise in the East and set in the West. Human beings cannot see the fixed stars or constellations move (while we can, for example, watch Venus).

Almost every star that we can see is a fixed star as there are only 10 wandering stars, the so-called "planets" (including the two luminaries) that move slowly through the sea of stars.

GENDER: The twelve signs of the zodiac are differentiated into six masculine (active, dominating) and six feminine (passive, receptive), which consistently alternate with each other: Aries = masculine, Taurus = feminine, Gemini = masculine, etc.

GEOCENTRIC: The most commonly held view in astrology, regarding the position of the observer on Earth as center of the cosmos, in contrast to the *heliocentric* view of the world.

HELIOCENTRIC: The view of the universe, according to modern knowledge, with the Sun as the center of our planetary system.

HOROSCOPE: Schematic representation of the map of the heavens at a particular time (at birth or another event). It contains the representation of the luminaries (Sun and Moon) and the eight planets viewed from the place of the event. The horoscope simultaneously records two movements of heavenly bodies:
1. the movement of the planets and luminaries through the zodiac
2. the movement of the zodiac around Earth

HOUSES: The four quadrants which result from the *system of axes* are each subdivided into three fields. The calculation of the system of axes is identical in almost all the various schools of astrology, but sometimes the method of subdividing differs (see *House Systems*). The resulting twelve houses correspond with the twelve signs of the zodiac, but they are not identical. This means that the 1st house corresponds with the sign Aries (the first sign of the zodiac), the 2nd house with the sign Taurus (the second sign of the zodiac), etc.

HOUSE SYSTEMS: The way of dividing the houses varies according to the method used. The best-known are the Koch (according to DR. WALTER KOCH), Placidean (according to PLACIDUS DE TITUS), Campanus (according to GIOVANNI CAMPANI), Regiomontanus (according to JOHANNES MÜLLER) and the Equal House method.

IMUM COELI: The Lowest Heavens (see *System of Axes*), 4th house.

LEVELS OF MEANING: Simply said, the various horoscope factors have the following correlations: the planets show which area of the personality is addressed, the astrological signs show how and the houses show where this theme is lived out, while the aspects express the tensions and harmonies among the various areas.

MEDIUM COELI: Midheaven (see *System of Axes*), the Midheaven.

MOON'S NODE: The astronomically determined intersection of the Moon's orbit with the Sun's orbit, which deviate from each other by 5.9^0. The two intersecting points located opposite each other in the zodiac are differentiated as Ascending (North) and Descending (South) Moon's Nodes. If the Sun and Moon are positioned together at one of these nodes, there is a solar eclipse. If they are simultaneously at the opposing point, there is an eclipse of the Moon. The Moon's Nodes are also called Dragon's Head and Dragon's Tail and are taken into special consideration in *Karmic Astrology*.

ORB: The permitted tolerance of deviation in the calculation of aspects. The orbs are between 1^0 and 10^0, according to the type of aspect and the school of astrology.

PLANETS: The eight planets and the Sun and Moon move along the *ecliptic*, in comparison to the immovable *fixed stars*, in the picture of the heavens. The seven visible to the naked eye are known as the classics (Sun, Moon, Mercury, Venus, Mars, Jupiter, Saturn). In addition, there are the planets discovered in the last 200 years: Uranus, Neptune, and Pluto.

PRECESSION: The slow advancement of the fixed-star heavens through the movement of Earth's axis. Therefore, the *constellations* which gave the *signs of the zodiac* their names move another 1^0 every 72 years. The result is the advancement of the firmament for the length of an astrological sign (30^0) every 2160 years, which astrology connects with the emergence of a new era. After the passing of the "Platonic Year"—which is 25,850 years—the fixed-star heavens have again advanced so far that the signs of the zodiac and the constellations are positioned "behind each other." Because astrology only concerns itself the with signs of the zodiac and sees the constellations as just the original donors of the names, precession is not important for the horoscope based on "Western Astrology."

QUALITIES: Within the four elements, astrology differentiates three qualities: cardinal (impulse-giving), fixed (impulse-receiving), and mutable (flexible).

REGENT: See *Ruler*.

RETROGRADE: Since the planets move along the path of the ecliptic, their speed, as seen from Earth, differs according to whether they are on the long side of the ecliptic or close to the tip. Since Earth also moves along such an ecliptic orbit, it is sometimes "faster" than another planet, which makes an impression of the planet moving backwards. Especially in *Karmic Astrology* this phenomenon is of considerable importance.

RULER: Each astrological sign and house is governed by at least one planet (or body). The planet is said to rule the sign or house. In the opposing sign and/or house, the planet is in its detriment. There are also *exaltations*, which are the signs/houses where the planet is dignified and very positively placed. In the opposing sign it is said to be in its *fall*. The neutral positions, those other than these four, are said to be in peregrine. This tells us the strengths and weaknesses of the individual planet positions. If the planet is in the sign/house in which it rules, it is dignified and is therefore very strongly positioned. This is also true for its *exaltation*. If the planet is in *detriment* or *fall*, its typical characteristics can only develop unconventionally and with difficulty. This perspective is primarily important for interpretation of the aspects when desiring to find out which planets are stronger or weaker according to the corresponding aspects.

SIGN OF THE ZODIAC: A) Astrological name for the twelve equal sections (each 30°) of the Sun's orbit through the zodiac, named after the *constellations* (which they were originally positioned behind, but are no longer identical with, because of precession). B) Customary, though not quite precise names for the signs in which the Sun is positioned at the time of birth.

SYSTEM OF AXES: The horoscope is divided into two main axes: the East-West horizon axis and the Imum Coeli-Medium Coeli axis (noon and midnight points of the Sun). The four intersections that the system of axes and zodiac form are: the Ascendant (AC) on the eastern horizon, the Descendant (DC) on the western horizon, the Medium Coeli (MC) at the noon point, and the *Imum Coeli* (IC) at the midnight point.

TEMPERAMENT: The classic Greek teaching of the four basic temperaments: choleric, sanguine, phlegmatic, and melancholic have their parallels in the four classic elements of fire, air, water, and earth, and the signs of the zodiac that correspond to them.

WATER SIGNS: The three signs belonging to the water *element*: Cancer (cardinal), Scorpio, (fixed), and Pisces (mutable).

ZODIAC: The path of 16° on each side of the *ecliptic* through which the Sun, Moon, and all the planets travel. The zodiac is divided into twelve signs, each having 30°.

Notes

1. In old pictures of the zodiac, Aries is portrayed as the leading ram with its head thrown back to look at the herd following him. Symbol of horn-wearing Moses, the leader of his tribe.

2. This famous observation comes from Arthur Schopenhauer, who had a Virgo Ascendant and stayed single all his life.

3. Demosthenes was a great Greek rhetorician who had a speech impediment during his childhood. He practiced incessantly by shouting at the surf with a pebble on his tongue until he taught himself to articulate clearly and understandably.

4. "Eureka" was Archimedes' joyful cry as he discovered a law of physics, with which he could track down coin counterfeiters, coincidentally while in the bathtub. In translation "Eureka" means: "I have (found) it" and has been an expression for surprising realization since that time.

5. The Bible reports that Saul, one of the biggest persecutors of Christians, was on the path to Damascus when he had a vision of Christ that caused him to become blind for three days and three nights. Afterward, he was transformed, named himself Paul from that time on, and became one of the greatest proclaimers of the religion that he had previously persecuted with hatred. Since then, the words *"Damascus experience"* or *"I see the light"* have come to represent all deep-reaching experiences and crises of transformation.

6. Johann Wolfgang von Goethe, in whose horoscope this aspect is distinctly in evidence, coined the famous sentence: "Only the law can give us freedom."

Bibliography

Adler, Oskar. *Das Testament der Astrologie.* 4 vols. Munich: Hugendubel, 1991-1993.

Akron. *Das Astrologie Handbuch* Munich: Hugendubel, 1995.

Arroyo, Stephen. *Astrology, Karma, and Transformation.* Sebastopol, CA: CRCS, 1978, 1992.

———. *Relationships & Life Cycles.* Sebastopol, CA: CRCS, 1993.

———. *Astrology, Psychology & the Four Elements.* Sebastopol, CA: CRCS, 1975.

———. *Chart Interpretation Handbook.* Sebastopol, CA: CRCS, 1989.

Arroyo, Stephen, and Liz Greene. *The Jupiter/Saturn Conference Lectures.* Sebastopol, CA: CRCS; now published as *New Insights into Modern Astrology.* Sebastopol, CA: CRCS, 1991.

Banzhaf, Hajo. *Der Mensch in seinen Elementen.* Munich: Hugendubel, 1993.

Boot, Martin. *Das Horoskop.* Munich: Droemer Knaur, 1988.

Ebertin. Reinhold. *The Combination of Stellar Influences.* Tempe, AZ: American Federation of Astrologers, 1972.

Green, Jeff. *Pluto: The Evolutionary Journey of the Soul.* St. Paul, MN: Llewellyn, 1985.

Greene, Liz. *The Astrology of Fate.* York Beach, ME: Samuel Weiser, 1985.

———. *Outer Planets & Their Cycles.* Sebastopol, CA: CRCS, 1983.

———. *Relating.* York Beach, ME: Samuel Weiser, 1978.

———. *Saturn.* York Beach, ME: Samuel Weiser, 1976.

Greene, Liz, and Howard Sasportas. *The Development of the Personality.* York Beach, ME: Samuel Weiser, 1987.

———. *Dynamics of the Unconscious..* York Beach, ME: Samuel Weiser, 1988.

Hand, Robert. *Horoscope Symbols.* Atglen, PA: Whitford, 1980.

Paul, Haydn. *Visionary Dreamer: Exploring the Astrological Neptune.* Shaftsbury, England: Element, 1989.

———. *Phoenix Rising: Exploring the Astrological Pluto.* Shaftsbury, England: Element, 1989.

Kühr, Erich Karl. *Psychologische Horoskopdeutung,* 2 vols. Vienna: Cerny, 1948, 1951.

Löhlein, Herbert. *Handbuch der Astrologie.* Munich: Goldman, 1980.

Lundsted, Betty. *Astrological Insights into Personality.* San Diego: ACS, 1980.

Marks, Tracy. *The Astrology of Self-Discovery.* Sebastopol, CA: CRCS, 1986.

Oken, Alan. *Alan Oken's Complete Astrology.* New York: Bantam, 1980, 1988.

Orban, Peter, Ingrid Zinnel, Thea Weller. *Symbolon.* Munich: Hugendubel, 1993.

Reimann, Fritz. *Lebenshilfe Astrologie.* Munich: Pfeiffer, 1976.

Ring, Thomas. *Astrologische Menschenkunde.* Freiburg, Germany: Bauer Verlag, 1969.

Rudhyar, Dane. *The Astrological Houses.* Sebastopol, CA: CRCS, 1986.

———. *The Rhythm of Wholeness.* Wheaton, IL: Theosophical Publishing House, 1983.

———. *Astrology and Personality.* Santa Fe: Aurora Press, 1981.

Sasportas, Howard. *The Twelve Houses.* London: Aquarian Press, 1989.

Schult, Arthur. *Astrosophie.* 2 vols. Bietigheim, Germany: Turm, 1971.

Sakoian, Frances, and Louis S. Acker. *The Astrologer's Handbook.* New York: HarperCollins, 1989.

Weiss, Claude. *Der Mondknoten in Häuser und Zeichen.* Zurich: *Astrologie Heute* 5-7, 1987.